A Story to Save Your Life

A Story to Save Your Life

Communication and Culture in Migrants' Search for Asylum

SARAH C. BISHOP

COLUMBIA UNIVERSITY PRESS
New York

Columbia University Press
Publishers Since 1893
New York   Chichester, West Sussex
cup.columbia.edu
Copyright © 2022 Columbia University Press
All rights reserved

Library of Congress Cataloging-in-Publication Data
Names: Bishop, Sarah C., 1984– author.
Title: A story to save your life : communication and culture
in migrants' search for asylum / Sarah C. Bishop.
Description: New York : Columbia University Press, [2022] |
Includes bibliographical references and index.
Identifiers: LCCN 2021057920 (print) | LCCN 2021057921 (ebook) |
ISBN 9780231204088 (hardback) | ISBN 9780231204095 (trade
paperback) | ISBN 9780231555364 (ebook) Subjects: LCSH: United
States—Emigration and immigration— Government policy. | Political
refugees—United States—Case studies. | Political refugees—Legal
status, laws, etc.—United States. Classification: LCC JV6483 .B574
2022 (print) | LCC JV6483 (ebook) | DDC 325.73—dc23/eng/20220206
LC record available at https://lccn.loc.gov/2021057920
LC ebook record available at https://lccn.loc.gov/2021057921

Cover design: Noah Arlow
Cover image: Helen Zughaib, "Syrian Migration Series #4,"
gouache on board, © 2017

Contents

Contents

Acknowledgments

This project was conceived during a fellowship at the Institute for the Study of Human Rights at Columbia University and came of age during a Fulbright in Central America. Along the way, funding from the Waterhouse Family Institute at Villanova University, the Centre for Media, Communication and Information Research (ZeMKI) at the University of Bremen, the Professional Staff Congress at the City University of New York, and the Office of the Dean of Arts and Sciences at Baruch provided integral support. I was able to focus my attention on writing because of time away from teaching generously provided by a distinguished fellowship at the Advanced Research Collaborative at the CUNY Graduate Center and a long-awaited year of sabbatical.

I owe a debt of gratitude to those who listened patiently, asked good questions, and were forthcoming with advice, including Elazar Barkan, Korab Krasniqi, Tika Pratiwi, Linda Mann, Bayar Mustafa Sevdeen, Joanna Talewicz-Kwiatkowska, Latife Uluçınar, Samantha Mandiveyi, Sandra Paunksniene, Phillip Polefrone, Jordan and Coco Van Horn, Cecilia Santos, Cynthia Wang, Katrina

Day, Don Robotham, Wilfredo Marroquín Jiménez, Tanya Goldsmith, and Rosa Anaya. The most longsuffering and generous of all critics was Bo, whose unwavering support, boundless intuition, and expert navigation through the backroads of El Salvador made everything possible.

I am thrilled to be able to feature on the cover a piece of art by Lebanese American artist Helen Zughaib, whose tender and profound *Syrian Migration Series* offers perspective that asks the viewer to walk alongside forced migrants, visually joining them in their journey.

Earlier versions of some pieces of this project appeared in the *Journal of International and Intercultural Communication*, the *Journal of Ethnic and Cultural Studies*, and the *International Journal of Communication*. The work benefited from feedback by attendees of the International Association for the Study of Forced Migration Conference, the International Communication Association Conference, and the Memory Studies Association Conference.

Many, many thanks to my invaluable research assistants, Roger Hernandez, Valentina Floegel, and, as always, Nora Lambrecht, without whom I would crawl along at a snail's pace. I'm grateful for the expert recommendations of the blind reviewers and to Stephen Wesley at Columbia University Press for shepherding this project through to its publication. Thanks also to my colleagues at Baruch and Mixteca and to the staff at African Communities Together, New Sanctuary Coalition, First Friends of NJ & NY, the Bellevue Program for Survivors of Torture, and the Center for Family Life for helping to facilitate fieldwork and, more importantly, for working tirelessly to advance the rights of asylum seekers.

Note on the Cover Art

The artwork on the cover is a painting by Lebanese American artist Helen Zughaib. Her *Syrian Migration Series* is a collection of forty-two paintings inspired by Jacob Lawrence's *Migration Series*, painted between 1940 and 1941 and depicting Black Americans traveling from the rural south to the urban north of the United States. With insights drawn from her own evacuation from Beirut, Lebanon, during the civil war in 1975 and time spent in Syria, Lebanon, and Jordan just before the Arab Spring in 2010, Zughaib invites viewers to see from the perspective of Syrian migrants who have been forced to flee their homes in search of safety. Her paintings emphasize the dignity, beauty, and perseverance of these individuals with the goal of promoting healing and reflection in our shared humanity. Zughaib's art has been widely exhibited in galleries and museums in the United States, Europe, and Lebanon and included in many private and public collections, including the White House; the World Bank; the Library of Congress; the U.S. Consulate General in Vancouver, Canada; the American Embassy in Baghdad, Iraq; the Arab American National Museum in Detroit, Michigan; and the Minneapolis Institute of Art.

A Story to Save Your Life

1

Halted Expectations

WHEN VALERIA'S SON, ALEJANDRO, was a year old, the Cuban government cut off access to his Zika treatment in retaliation for the family's ongoing participation in antigovernment protests. Valeria and her husband were committed to the resistance work they were doing, but they had seen harrowing informational pamphlets about what could happen to Alejandro without essential services like physiotherapy and ultrasounds; they knew their priority had to be to protect him. The family fled to Nicaragua, then began a 3,500-kilometer journey to the U.S. border via car, boat, and bus—all with baby Alejandro in their arms.

The beacon lighting Valeria's family's way to the U.S. border appears in Article 14 of the United Nations' Universal Declaration of Human Rights: "Everyone has the right to seek and to enjoy in other countries asylum from persecution." Valeria understood the limitations of that right. For their asylum case to be successful, the persecution her family endured must have been the result of their race, religion, nationality, membership in a particular social group, or political opinion. These five grounds, established by the United

Nations' 1951 Refugee Convention and reaffirmed in the 1967 Refugee Protocol, are the only grounds on which the U.S. offers asylum.

Valeria and her husband believed they had a strong case; along with their child, the young couple carried hundreds of pages of evidence cataloging the ways the Cuban government had mistreated them for their political views, and their bodies bore physical scars from the persecution they had endured. The day I met her, Valeria explained their position calmly in Spanish: "I am seeking asylum for my political opinion. And I am showing evidence that I have been tortured and threatened. That I have been hit. That they took my son out of his treatment for Zika. . . . He needs treatment like physiotherapy and ultrasounds on his head and tummy to know that everything is okay."

After many days, Valeria's family finally arrived at the Pharr-Reynosa International Bridge, which spans the Rio Grande at the border between Mexico and the United States. The bridge is known locally as *el puente con las mariposas* (the bridge with the butterflies) because of a metal and glass sculpture that appears on the arched, south-facing facade of the bridge's U.S. Customs and Border Protection (CBP) inspection station. When the sculpture was commissioned in 1997, its New York–based artist, Alison Sky, envisioned it as a playful and welcoming sight, intended to lift people's spirits, offering travelers a bit of comfort as they approached the intimidating inspection process. As the sun moves from the east side of the facade to the west, the traveling shadows of suspended monumental butterflies with human eyes incorporated into the patterns of their colorful wings are meant to reflect and celebrate the annual migration of monarchs and the movement of people and other living things across the international border.

I reached out to artist Alison Sky after seeing the sculpture and shared with her some of Valeria's memories from the bridge. Sky was dismayed to learn that rather than offering the welcome she had envisioned, the bridge has become a key site for the implementation of some of the United States' most inhumane immigration policies, including family separation and mandatory detention in the infamous centers that one physician who was granted access compared to torture facilities.[1] "In my life and in my art, I have created public works that humanize, inspire, animate, enliven and enrich people's experiences," Sky told me. "This is heartbreaking and horrific to me. It is a violation of the intention of my artwork, and a violation of the beliefs and guiding principles of my life."

Today, the uplifting image of the butterflies in midflight stands in ironic contrast to its bleak surroundings. The border station is equipped with gamma ray inspection equipment for searching vehicle cargo; a blue line that migrants are prohibited from crossing demarcates where U.S. territory begins. In 2020 a Mexican man cut his throat on the bridge and fell to his death after his application for asylum was denied.[2] To have come so far and gotten so close to safety only to be turned away was too much to bear.

For Valeria, the memory of her family's arrival at the bridge with the butterflies is still fresh. It was the culmination of months of careful planning, dangerous travel, and sheer determination. She told me, "When we arrived that day to the international bridge, we only got halfway because they wouldn't let you go any further. The CBP officers asked, 'What do you want?' and we said, 'We are a family, we are Cuban, and we came to seek asylum.'" She remembers that just saying the words came as a relief—the United States was visible on the other side of the river and the possibility of safety and treatment for little Alejandro was finally within reach.

The agents escorted them to the U.S. side of the border, but Valeria's initial elation began to unravel during her first moments in the country. She was alarmed to find that, despite her son's immediate medical needs and the fact that they did not attempt to enter without permission, the CBP agents treated them roughly, as though they posed some kind of threat. They loaded the family with some other migrants onto a bus that had metal bars on the door and windows and drove them an hour and a half east to one of the agency's holding centers in Brownsville, Texas. As they pulled up to the building, Valeria could see that paper had been taped over the windows of the center so that no one could see in or out. The families on the bus tried to find out from each other what might be going on, but they were quickly reprimanded. "The officials didn't let us talk to each other, and if we did, they'd say 'Be quiet!'" Valeria remembers.

The scene inside the center was chaotic: "They didn't give us any information, they just said, 'Sign here.' . . . And we said, 'These documents are in English—how can we sign them?' and they said, 'That's the law.' . . . And if you don't want to sign, they intimidate you and tell you it'll be worse for you." They signed the papers they could not read, and in exchange the guards provided them an aluminum sheet as a blanket and told them to sleep on the floor. "The air conditioning was so cold," Valeria remembers. "Around one o'clock in the morning they turn up the air conditioning to make us even colder. And if you ask them to please turn it down—that there are children—they tell us, 'No.' That we have to deal with it because nobody forced us to come seek asylum in the United States. That we should tell that to our colleagues coming after us . . . that they shouldn't come to seek asylum in the United States." The temperature in the holding centers at the border has earned them the nickname *hieleras*, or freezers. Asylum seekers have reported that guards in the centers claim the cold temperature helps to prevent the spread of sickness between detainees or, as in Valeria's experience, use it as a scare tactic to deter other potential migrants. In any case, it is a cruel and unnecessary physical misery for migrants who are often already malnourished, lacking warm clothing, and exhausted from their journeys. "Those guards that are put there," Valeria told me, "they aren't human beings. And if they are human beings, they don't have hearts."

In the *hielera*, each member of Valeria's family received three tacos a day: one in the morning, one in the afternoon, and a third in the evening. It was not enough to curb their hunger. The holding centers have no beds, showers, or private toilets. She cannot forget the two days she spent there, especially knowing that many asylum seekers are forced to stay much longer. The American Immigration Council recently reported that nearly half of surveyed families in CBP custody had been detained for more than seventy-two hours and that some single adults had been held for over a month, despite the fact that National Standards on Transport, Escort, Detention, and Search explicitly state that migrants "should generally not be held for more than 72 hours."[3]

At the end of the family's two-day detainment, officials handed Valeria and her husband a notice to appear in court a month later, and—to Valeria's shock—told them to walk across a nearby international bridge back into Mexico to wait. Valeria had researched asylum carefully before leaving Cuba, but this development was something she was not prepared for—she had never heard of anyone having to wait in Mexico. "I didn't know that applying for asylum would be like this—that I would have to be in a different country," she told me. "I knew that the process was long because I have seen that, I mean, I have seen on the internet that the process is long. But I didn't know that it would be waiting in a different country. . . . I had no idea it was like this."

The shock Valeria experienced was not a result of poor preparation or a lack of research; asylum practice changes frequently and without public warning, and complex, intersecting variables mean even applicants arriving around the same time from the same nation of origin can experience different outcomes. Factors including the kind of persecution an applicant faced, where they entered the United States, the personal whims of the Border Patrol agents they encountered, and the political landscape at the time of their entry all impact what comes next.

To understand the bewilderment Valeria felt at being asked to return to Mexico, we must trace back in time to consider what information was available to her before she left Cuba and began the migration that would render her an asylum seeker. Valeria sought out messages on the internet about life in the United States that shaped her decision to pursue it as a destination; that research helped form in her mind a picture of the asylum process she would need to navigate to achieve the promise of safety. We only need to hear Valeria's experience of being sent back to Mexico to understand that secondhand messages about the asylum process may offer knowledge that is at once useful and partial in nature—just "strips of reality," as communication scholar Arjun Appadurai writes, rather than an exhaustive view.[4] Valeria's predeparture knowledge was useful but incomplete: "I have always known that in the United States you can request asylum. I did not know that the process was so sad, that it took years . . . that it was so difficult and almost impossible to obtain," she shared.

Despite the fact that Valeria and her husband willingly sought out CBP officials to present themselves rather than trying to enter the country without being detected, the U.S. government considers them "defensive" rather than "affirmative" applicants for asylum. This designation is critical. Affirmative applications are submitted by individuals who arrived in the United States with temporary permission, such as a tourist or student visa. Defensive applications are made by those in removal proceedings because they were apprehended when crossing the border or found to be living without documentation in the United States.[5] If Valeria and her husband could have afforded to purchase plane tickets and managed to be approved for $160 tourist visas to vacation in the United States, they could have chosen their U.S. destination, flown there, and submitted an affirmative application for asylum. As affirmative applicants, they likely would have received permission to live in their own home, temporary relief from deportation while their case processed, and work permits so they could earn a living during the wait.[6] Herein lies the great class bias of the U.S. asylum system. For those who cannot afford to begin their asylum process this way, the only option is a defensive application, which, for many migrants, means awaiting their cases in Mexico.

Had Valeria's family arrived at the border just a few months earlier, their situation might look much different. But they arrived in July 2019, after the Trump administration instituted the unprecedented "Remain in Mexico" policy, formally known as the Migrant Protection Protocols (MPP). The irony of this name is not lost on Valeria: "It's duplicitous, the MPP. It says that the MPP is 'Migrant Protection Protocols' and that's a lie. . . . We don't have any security here, nor protection." Before MPP, asylum seekers who passed a basic interview designed to determine if they had a credible fear of persecution were allowed to stay in the United States to wait for their court date. Many received work permits and had access to some other basic social services. During Trump's last two years in office, many migrants arriving at the southern U.S. border abruptly found that they were barred from these provisions and would be forced to wait in Mexico.

Defensive applicants living under MPP are seven times less likely to be able to access legal representation than those applying for asylum from within the United States.[7] This reality puts Valeria's family and others like them at a pronounced disadvantage because, unlike affirmative applications, defensive cases are adversarial, meaning they proceed more like criminal cases in a courtroom setting with cross examination, evidence exhibits, and witnesses. Without a nuanced understanding of courtroom logic and processes, asylum seekers navigating these adversarial cases without representation stand little chance. Preliminary data suggests migrants applying for asylum while under MPP are drastically less likely to have their cases granted.[8]

Although President Biden denounced MPP as inhumane and suspended it his first day in office, his administration reinstated the program in December 2021. Thousands of vulnerable forced migrants will continue to reside in tents, temporary apartments, and shelters in cities along the border as they wait to be allowed into the United States. In a Pulitzer Prize–winning episode of the podcast *This American Life*, reporters from National Public Radio found there were just five toilets for 2,500 migrants waiting at a camp in Matamoros, Mexico—the city where Valeria and her family have had to make a temporary home.[9]

MPP is just one of the ways the U.S. political climate has normalized the criminalization and separation of families who have been forced to flee their homes due to life-threatening persecution. The Trump administration's asylum policy focused on narrowing the grounds on which a person can claim asylum to exclude victims of domestic and gang violence, severely limiting the refugee admission cap, and rhetorically undercutting the sincerity of asylum seekers' claims of persecution.[10] Trump called the asylum system "a big fat con job" and suggested that the migrants arriving at the U.S. border with Mexico in need of protection were fraudulent and dangerous gangsters who threated the lives of Americans.[11] "We have lived a nightmare here," Valeria confirmed somberly during our first conversation, when Trump was still president. "But we remain firm and have hope that God has the power, not President Donald Trump. God has the power."

Despite the horrors that marked the beginning of their asylum process and the disadvantages imposed by MPP, Valeria was confident in her case. Back in Mexico, she reorganized her paperwork, and she and her husband practiced telling their story to each other to make sure they remembered all the important dates and details, hoping that that once their family's court date arrived, they would be able to explain methodically what had happened to them in Cuba and would be treated with understanding and granted a favorable outcome.

Life after that favorable outcome would be very different. An applicant granted asylum becomes an "asylee"—a designation akin to refugee status. Asylees are eligible to apply for legal permanent residence after one year and may apply to become naturalized U.S.

citizens after five more years. But most asylum claims are denied. Of the 307,704 people who sought asylum in the United States in fiscal year 2019 (the most recent year for which data is available), only 46,508 were granted asylum—a rate of just over 15 percent.[12] Valeria's family is from Cuba, which increases their odds—at least hypothetically. Cubans and migrants from other communist countries have historically fared best in the asylum process; in fiscal year 2020, for example, 25 percent of Cuban applicants, 40 percent of Venezuelan applicants, and 59 percent of Chinese applicants were granted asylum.[13] While these odds may still seem bleak, they are much more promising than those for people who flee from countries the United States has deemed "safe." Fewer than 1 percent of Mexican asylum seekers' claims are granted, for example.[14] The stakes are high, and the grave danger asylum seekers face after being denied is well documented: Jeremy Slack's 2019 book *Deported to Death* found that migrants are frequently subjected to extreme violence including systematic massacres after being deported to Mexico; a report from Human Rights Watch offers evidence that, since 2013, 138 people have been killed in El Salvador alone after being deported from the United States.[15]

Considering that the majority face being returned to the very circumstances from which they fled, much hinges on asylum seekers' ability to effectively narrate their pasts to immigration officials. Both affirmative and defensive applicants must repeatedly recount the experiences that forced them to flee their homes. Applicants first present their narratives on paper as part of the I-589 Application for Asylum and then must retell parts of this story out loud when requested by the asylum officer who conducts the interview that marks the beginning of the legal asylum process. When officers refer applicants to an asylum hearing before a judge, both the written and verbal narrative appear again.

At each of these steps in the process, governmental authorities evaluate the ways an asylum seeker narrates the details of their persecution and compares the story to any available documentary or physical evidence in an attempt to determine two things: first, whether the person's story is credible; then, if so, how closely their experiences fit one or more of the five established grounds of race, religion, nationality, membership in a particular social group, or political opinion. A person's narrative is the lynchpin of an asylum case. The outcome, as immigration scholar Agnes Woolley points out, "depends almost entirely on the story of the claimant."[16] For asylum seekers, the ability to harness the power of storytelling may be the difference between life and death.

The research Valeria did about U.S. asylum law before leaving Cuba led her to believe that her family's case was airtight. She could hardly wait for the opportunity to tell her story. "My asylum case is a perfect case," she told me confidently. "It [is within] the five kinds of persecution—the five that they require. I can show evidence to win asylum because of my story. It's what happened to us. It's what we lived. When they ask us, we will tell them our story." While this logic is sound and clearly reflects the supposed tenets of immigration law, Valeria's optimism does not account for what immigration advocates call the "pervasive climate of disbelief" that engulfs the legal process.[17] *Having* a viable story is not enough, nor is being able to write it down—one must also be able to tell it.

Asylum officers and judges are trained to listen for any inconsistencies or irregularities in applicants' narratives that suggest fabrication. An applicant's slightest verbal or nonverbal misstep—whether the result of embellishment, nerves, or just the fallibility of memory—can disqualify their case. Many variables influence an applicant's ability to tell the truth about the past and be perceived as credible. Trauma may trigger blockages in memory. Cultural norms about displays of emotion and eye contact may unknowingly signal dishonesty in a new context. Fraudulent legal advice may lead an applicant to produce falsified documentary evidence, disqualifying them from protection even if their true experiences would have constituted a strong case. Actions as benign as leaving one space blank on the I-589 Application for Asylum have been used as sufficient grounds to deny a claim.[18]

These peculiarities—none of which Valeria's predeparture research prepared her for—reveal that the asylum process hinges on a person's ability to communicate why they need protection in standardized and highly nuanced ways. Within the context of this current reality, this book sets out to interrogate the power and limitation of narrative, explore from a communication-centric perspective the intercultural transfer of culturally bound storytelling conventions, and foreground the firsthand insights of asylum seekers. I argue that culturally bound storytelling norms negatively and unevenly affect case outcomes. I advance this argument by talking with migrants who have navigated the muddy waters of asylum in the United States both successfully and unsuccessfully, tracing their experiences through the life cycle of the asylum system—from expectations to result—to see how communication and culture bear down on and define each part of the endeavor.

Taking a communication perspective on the asylum process means paying close attention to intercultural differences in interactions, nonverbal communication, and the construction of the self through narrative. Without this view, one risks the implicit assumption that the outcome of an asylum case depends only on whether the applicant has a credible history of persecution. Instead, as the narrators throughout these pages will clearly show, the asylum process hinges on the nature and form of all kinds of verbal and nonverbal communicative exchanges between asylum seekers and government personnel in the interviews and court hearings that make up the legal asylum process.

Because asylum cases invariably involve the interaction of a foreigner with a U.S. resident officer or judge, they are inherently contexts of intercultural communication, and many communication behaviors are rooted in cultural norms that differ from one location to the next. Especially in cases without extensive written evidence of the persecution a migrant has faced, differences in cultural norms and communication styles are likely to have an outsized effect on the outcome of a case. Unfortunately, this project reveals that applicants, officers, and judges are often not aware of or adept at negotiating these differences.[19]

My research focuses specifically on asylum in the United States, but the U.S. asylum system does not have a monopoly on intercultural communicative challenges. In response to an influx of migrants from the Middle East and South Asia, international research has clearly documented the hurdles that narrative norms and cultural differences present in the asylum process in Australia and Europe.[20] These useful existing international studies notwithstanding, asylum seekers are regularly underrepresented in research about migration more generally, in part because they are too often conflated with refugees—who receive approval for governmental protection *before* their arrival in a country of resettlement—rather than regarded as a distinct group that faces the unique communicative challenges of the post-arrival legal asylum process.

Communication makes up the core of the asylum-seeking process, operating, as Gillian McFadyen writes, as "both a key, and a barrier, to refuge."[21] The power and pitfalls of narrative may assist or threaten an asylum seeker in the quest for protection. In this book, I set out to better understand what kinds of messages asylum seekers receive about the possibility of protection from the United States before their arrival, and to learn what kind of specific, culturally bound narrative conventions the asylum process requires. Rather than focusing on one stage of the asylum process, I take a holistic approach, tracing the roles communication and culture play in the life cycle of asylum seekers' journeys to the United States and, sometimes, back to where they began. To show how culturally bound communicative norms negatively and unevenly affect some asylum applicants, I share insights from hundreds of hours of oral history interviews with migrants who fled persecution, asylum officers, immigration judges, former CPB agents, attorneys, and doctors who conduct psychological evaluations of asylum seekers. I challenge the opacity of the asylum-seeking process by putting these individuals in dialogue with each other on the page. In the chapters ahead, their perspectives intertwine to reveal the remarkable influence of memory, narrative, and culture in the contested site of forced migration. Throughout this book, I include reflections from my own experiences serving as an expert witness in asylum cases, observing court hearings in New York City, and volunteering with a legal asylum clinic to assist forced migrants in navigating their asylum applications. Because it is important in work like this to be clear and explicit about one's method and process, I write in depth about my research design, methodological approach, and the hurdles I faced in the postscript and the methodological appendix available at the end of this book.

Hope Deferred

The day of her court hearing, Valeria and her family woke up at five o'clock in the morning and took a bus back to the bridge that separates Matamoros, Mexico, from Brownsville, Texas. "I went with so many expectations. . . . I thought it was going to be decided on that date." They had to wait in line outside for two hours, and the CBP agents in charge of the line treated them poorly. "They yell, 'Move over here!' 'Move over there!' like you're a dog," she remembers. "They only let me bring a diaper and a bottle of milk for my son, but they checked everything and took everything—rings, earrings, shoelaces, whatever you're wearing in your hair . . . and being in line, on the bridge, you can't ask them anything. You approach them to ask a question and they tell you, 'Move back!' in a really loud voice, and very annoyed, as if we were diseased."

Finally, they reached the front of the line and were led by armed guards into what they were surprised to find was just a makeshift courtroom with no judge present.[22] Valeria wondered if there may have been a misunderstanding, but after a few minutes a judge appeared via video conference on a small screen at the front of the room. Valeria gathered up her courage to tell this remote stranger about the worst things that had ever happened in her life. But instead the judge just asked them to confirm their date of arrival, told them when they should return for their next court date, and concluded the hearing. The whole thing took just a few minutes. Valeria felt like the wind had been knocked out of her. "All the judge does is let you know when your second court date is!" She told me with exasperation while recounting the memory. "They don't tell you *any*thing . . . and then you have to go all the way back." Valeria's careful planning had not readied her for one massive bureaucratic inefficiency in the system: the master calendar hearing.

A master calendar hearing is the first hearing in an asylum case. They exist so that the immigration judge can schedule the date by which an asylum seeker must submit their written documents, and can determine when the next hearing—an individual merits hearing—will take place. No testimony is accepted at the master calendar hearing, and the judge does not ask the applicant any questions about their reasons for applying for asylum. As a volunteer with a nonprofit in New York that pairs asylum seekers with citizens who accompany them to immigration court, I, too was shocked after attending my first master calendar hearing. "That's . . . it?" I asked one of the other volunteers. I assumed the fact that the hearing had begun more than two hours after it was scheduled and lasted all of three minutes meant that something had gone wrong, and I was surprised to learn that this was status quo. Since then I have come to loathe master calendar hearings. The stress they cause asylum seekers is palpable and is clearly exacerbated by the several hours of wait that regularly precede the hearing. At the immigration courts in downtown Manhattan, it is typical to sit in the waiting room for three hours or more after the scheduled time of the hearing—hours in which the distraught faces of other forced migrants leaving their own hearings amplify the dispiriting absurdity of this procedure.

Valeria and her family returned, frustrated, to the Mexican side of the border to await their individual merits hearing, which would take place the following month. Day by day, she watched as more families arrived at the border with chilling stories of the violence they had faced. CBP began limiting the number of people allowed onto the bridge to present themselves. "Every morning, they asked for ten women, ten men, and two or three families to pass," Valeria recalls. The pastor of a local Matamoros church would accompany the lucky few to the halfway point on the bridge in a show of solidarity. From that point, they were on their own.

Valeria remembers, "It was like that every day, with a lot of emotions, you could see how each person, when their turn arrived to pass, they would cry from emotion, and we would all clap." But the sound of the clapping started to feel inappropriate. One by one, families she had gotten to know over their months living in makeshift neighborhoods at the border started to receive the news that their cases had been denied. Over time it began to feel like no one was being approved. Watching this tragic scene play out every day of the week, Valeria became convinced: "There are injustices occurring in the courts. They go in, and of fifty people, *no one* wins. Or one person wins." Valeria had heard many of these families' stories herself—she knew many of them had cases as strong or even stronger than her own, and she became afraid of what that might mean.

By the time her family's individual merits hearing date arrived, Valeria's sense of eager anticipation had been subdued by all she had seen. The day began much like the first, with hours of waiting on the bridge. But this time when they were ushered into the courtroom and the judge appeared on the screen, they were finally able to tell their story. The chance to recount the narrative she knew would place them squarely within the legal boundaries for asylum and to corroborate it with the documentary evidence she had carried so far felt liberating—like she could finally let go of something she had been clinging to tightly for months. But as they concluded their story and finished answering the judge's questions, her relief began to wane. Valeria had expected some confirmation in the judge's disposition that they had satisfied the requirements for asylum and that the evidence they had presented had been definitive. Instead, not only did the judge seem unmoved, he seemed disinterested—tired even. Had he understood what they had told him? Did he care about the horrors they had faced? Valeria could hardly believe their story had this anticlimactic impact: "You say it in court, and they don't care. Nothing. The judges are just . . . there." Valeria and her husband stared back silently as the judge told them to return to Matamoros to await his decision.

Making her way back across the bridge and thinking about all the makeshift homes filled with other asylum seekers, Valeria told me she felt numb. This was the third time she had been made to cross back over the border into a country she knew was unable to protect her young family. Before long, news arrived that their case had been denied. Certain that they would face imminent danger if they returned to Cuba, and knowing they could not stay in Mexico, the family decided to appeal their asylum case—just before the Trump administration invoked Title 42 of U.S. health law on account of the COVID-19 pandemic to shut down the border courts indefinitely.

When I last spoke with Valeria in January 2021, she and her family were still living in the room they cobbled together into a temporary home on the Mexican side of the border, more than a year and a half after their arrival. They had not been able to access any medical treatment for Alejandro's Zika, and as they prepared to pass their second spring in Matamoros, a new crisis seemed to present itself each day. "Thousands of Cubans have died here, and not to mention those from Honduras, El Salvador, Guatemala, Venezuela. Thousands of people are dying here at the hands of organized crime. They show up floating in the river. They wake up with gunshots in their heads. We are living a catastrophe, and that's not even considering COVID. And on top of that, we don't have to possibility of going to a hospital. We don't have access to medicine. We don't have the possibility of anything," she told me.

The problem is not that the U.S. government does not know about these horrific conditions: Human Rights First reported in early 2020 at least 819 publicly recorded cases of torture, rape, assault, kidnapping, and other violent attacks against asylum seekers and other migrants returned to Mexico.[23] At a hearing of the House Homeland Security Committee's Subcommittee on Border Security, Facilitation, and Operations, representatives from Amnesty International stated that MPP "has made a mockery of the right to seek asylum as enshrined in domestic and international law"; they presented evidence showing that 50 to 70 percent of asylum seekers waiting in Mexico for their cases to be processed have encountered severe direct harm including kidnapping and rape.[24]

When twenty-five-year-old Óscar Alberto Martínez Ramírez, who was fleeing gang violence in El Salvador with his two-year-old daughter, drowned in the Rio Grande, the story appeared in every major news outlet alongside a photo of their bodies washed up in Matamoros. Like Valeria's family, Óscar was trying to get his daughter across the border to Brownsville, Texas. He attempted to swim the Rio Grande after finding out the asylum office at the border crossing was closed. "Many cross illegally because they can't take the unemployment and the desperation of not knowing when the courts will open," Valeria explained. For all the talk she has heard about Americans' commitment to doing what is right, Valeria has been surprised to find that even with the visibility of such horrific news stories, no one at all seems to be paying attention. I asked her, "What do you wish that people from the United States understood about what's going on with MPP?" After thinking for a moment, she replied gravely, "That there are children here, there are people who are sick, there are *people*. We are human beings. . . . And right now, it's us, but tomorrow it could be them. It could be them who are in a similar situation. They need to realize that it's time to stop this. . . . And, they should understand that we can't take it anymore." The endless days of life in the holding pattern have left her homesick but deadlocked: "I miss my country, my land, my flag, but I will not return while the government is still in power." Until the courts reopen and her appeal moves forward, Valeria feels she has no choice but to wait on the edge of the United States for the possibility of protection.

Envisioning a Future

To understand the implications of migrants like Valeria living for extended lengths of time under circumstances they never could have imagined, it is important to remember that the process of forced migration does not begin when a person leaves their country behind or end when they arrive at their destination. Lev Golinkin, who arrived in the United States as a refugee from Ukraine when he was a child, writes,

> The drastic images which make the newsreels create the impression that people turn into refugees overnight. In my family's experience, that isn't true. Becoming a refugee is a gradual process, a bleaching out, a transition into a ghostly existence. . . . A thousand little anchors once moored you to the world. Becoming a refugee means watching as those anchors are severed, one by one, until at last you're floating outside of society, an untethered phantom in need of a new life.[25]

A potential asylum seeker may spend years envisioning what life could be like elsewhere before being forced out of their home, or they may have no time at all for envisaging before their life is unexpectedly uprooted and they have no choice but to be on their way. No matter the circumstances or the timeline, no one who moves from one place to another does so in an informational vacuum. A person's expectations—about the asylum process, the choices it demands, and the life it could make possible—have a direct impact on their ability to successfully navigate the narrative terrain of the process and be perceived as deserving of asylum.

When the United States began accepting refugees in the wake of World War II, the country boasted of its humanitarian ability to welcome persecuted migrants. Submitting the 1967 Protocol on the Status of Refugees to Congress in an effort to expand the scope of the 1951 Refugee Convention, President Lyndon Johnson extolled "the American heritage of concern for the homeless and persecuted, and our traditional role of leadership in promoting assistance for refugees."[26] More recently, however, the country has become less forthcoming about its signed commitment to offer refuge to those who need it, even to the point of producing public radio ads and posters for dissemination in Central America suggesting that the possibility of asylum in the United States does not exist (see chapter 5). As the United States becomes less and less explicit about the asylum relief it has committed to offering, migrants considering applying for U.S. asylum may have to rely on less official sources of information about the process, including conversations with friends or family who previously made the journey.[27] Migrants from the most privileged expats to the most marginalized refugees may encounter American film and television that influences perceptions of what life is like on the other side of the United States border. These mediated and interpersonal messages intertwine and serve to create cognitive links about U.S. life in an asylum seeker's mind long before they arrive.[28]

The first time I met Valeria, she walked me through a nuanced historical overview of the "wet foot, dry foot" policy, which allowed Cubans who reached U.S. soil from the mid-1990s to 2017 to remain in the United States and qualify for residency. Beyond her historical knowledge of U.S. immigration policy, Valeria explained she also had conversations with people who lived in the United

States whose experiences influenced her decision to seek asylum there. She shared:

> I have friends who—thank God—are in the United States, and when they would come to Cuba, they would tell me that the United States of America was a country where they didn't violate the laws, and where they respected human rights. Which is different from us [in Cuba] where we can't talk or have opinions. Where they want to beat us to death. I mean, being born in a Communist country, and living the injustices that my country commits . . . and then having every friend who would visit Cuba tell us that the United States was a lawful place where they treated you well, where women and kids were untouchable? *That* was the moment I knew that there was no country other than the United States of America where I would feel that me and my family were safe.

Valeria's recollection reveals the power of interpersonal communication to shape a person's picture of a place they have never been, and in turn to influence their migration plans. Such conversations can encourage a future asylum seeker to superimpose others' experiences onto their own future in their mind's eye and to entertain the possibility of future safety while in the midst of danger.

In conversations with successful and unsuccessful asylum seekers from Asia, Latin America, Europe, and Africa, I listened as many described what they knew about the asylum process before leaving home, and the messages and conversations that contributed to this knowledge: the American blockbusters they watched as children, the neighbor that applied for asylum decades ago and now seems to live the American Dream on full Facebook display, the aunt who calls home less and less but still sends back amounts of money that seem unthinkable in her home country. It was clear from their memories that information about the United States is not available in equal quantity or quality to all potential migrants. The lack of transparency about the asylum process and the rate at which U.S. migration policy changes leaves many applicants without the knowledge and resources they would need to advance a successful case. And two asylum seekers arriving even just months apart may have sharply different experiences, as the acting presidential administration, the ebb and flow of public opinion and attention, health crises like COVID-19, changes in international relations, and the state of the U.S. economy all affect the reality at the border.

Valeria's meticulousness in gathering before she left Cuba the detailed documentary evidence she knew she would need to advance her family's case appeared in sharp contrast to other asylum seekers I have talked to and worked with, who sometimes did not even know that the asylum system existed before they arrived in the United States. A young woman named Anna told me she had ample documentation of the persecution she faced in her hometown but did not realize she would be asked to provide it in order to request protection. As a result, she explained, "When I left El Salvador, I didn't know anything about the asylum process, so I left my country in an emergency, I left without anything." Likewise, Mary, who fled domestic violence at the hands of her husband in Nigeria, told me, "I didn't know there was anything such [as asylum]. I didn't, because if I had known, I would have run away a long time ago." This unfamiliarity is not unique; migration scholar Bridget Haas interviewed twenty-six asylum seekers from seven different countries now living in the American Midwest and found that not a single one of them knew of a concept called "asylum" before arriving in the United States.[29]

Individuals who leave their homes without even knowing what asylum is or bringing along the evidence that would be helpful in proving eligibility for protection have a harder time aligning their narratives to fit the process's conventions. In Haas's work, the majority of the asylum claimants she interviewed—once they came to terms with the disappointment that they could not immediately begin to pursue their new livelihoods upon their arrival in the

United States—expected the asylum process to last a few days or weeks, not the several years it often takes to receive a result. "Ultimately," Haas writes, "the disjuncture between expectations of treatment in the United States and the reality they faced was a source of confusion and distress for asylum seekers."[30] Coming to understand how unlikely favorable asylum outcomes are only after their arrival compounds the difficulty of advancing a convincing case. Life-changing events that might have seemed almost inconceivable when they occurred must appear both probable and credible when communicated to governmental personnel.

Because the discrepancy between expectation and reality about U.S. life is so profound, the U.S. government invests in predeparture orientations for refugees who will be relocated to the United States. "The purpose of overseas CO [cultural orientation] is to help refugees develop realistic expectations about life in the United States," the orientation curriculum states.[31] But unlike refugees, asylum seekers ask for protection *after* their arrival in the United States, rather than before, so they do not have access to tools like overseas orientation to help them negotiate the differences between their expectations and the experiences they are likely to have in the United States.

Reflecting on the time she spent in Eloy Detention Center, separated from her son and in constant cold, asylee author Rosayra Pablo Cruz describes the destabilizing power of unmet expectations and the uncertainty that the asylum process produces. Beyond the physical discomfort of detainment, Cruz explains, exists a challenge more substantial and ever present. "More difficult than anything else is not knowing what is happening, what will happen next. It is more difficult than being hungry, more difficult than being cold," she writes.[32] Cruz's perspective offers a grim reminder that asylum seekers' trauma does not necessarily end when they arrive at the U.S. border. Any one of the hallmarks of the current U.S. legal process—family separation, prolonged detention, the several years of waiting sometimes required before a determination is reached—can heap additional trauma onto an individual already compromised by an experience of persecution. Asylum hearings have been found to reactivate the symptoms of posttraumatic stress disorder, and psychiatric pre- and posttest evaluations of asylum seekers before and after their asylum interviews clearly demonstrate that the interview results in a worsening of clinical symptoms.[33] In this sense, asylum seekers' trauma is twofold—"The trauma that propels us to this land, and the traumatic experiences that await us," Mexican American author Reyna Grande writes.[34] Despite the tendency of the legal asylum process to reactivate and exacerbate hardship, applicants must maintain enough emotional and psychological clarity when repeatedly asked to offer a cohesive narrative to secure a chance at protection.

Behind closed doors and paper-covered windows, asylum cases are decided in the United States every day. Out of view of the American public, governmental personnel determine the fate of men, women, and children who are fighting for their lives. This project places the reader in conversation with those in the room when decisions are made. These key informants reveal what happens when the quest for asylum in the United States goes wrong, and their intertwining stories illuminate how one of the most pressing issues of our time hinges on the power of narrative.

During my most recent phone call with Valeria, she told me, "I had this grand idea, that I still have, that the United States was a country where people were treated well if they were seeking asylum, and that they gave it to you." Expectations often collide and crumple as asylum seekers become mired in a legal immigration process that both passively neglects and actively threatens their well-being throughout an unpredictable period of legal stagnation. But Valeria has not set aside her "grand" expectations of the United States. She told me: "Every night we go to bed with the hope that tomorrow is another day and that something good will happen. Because the truth is, we don't know where this will lead us. We just don't know."

In Their Own Words

Josh Childress, Former U.S. Customs and Border Protection Agent

SO, AS FAR AS MY BORDER PATROL peers went, I felt pretty at home. I felt like I was just one of the guys. For the most part, I was like "Oh yeah these are my kind of people," which is to say, fairly capable but not necessarily . . . you know, like, they haven't really done anything else with their life so they're taking a shot at this, you know?

But at the same time, I was like, man, it seems like there's a lot of ways to get yourself in trouble just by doing your job. I'm a veteran of Iraq and Afghanistan. I'm like, I don't want to have gone to Iraq and Afghanistan and survived those, and then to end up going to jail because I made a bad decision as a Border Patrol agent. But you learn down the road that all of that stuff is just kind of window-dressing. Like, it doesn't really *apply* to anybody, they just have to teach you that. But at the time, I didn't know any of that. Once I got back to my station and started the field training, I was like "Oh yeah this is great." You know? Cause, you realize that there's a lot of protections in place for all of that stuff.

I mean, it's kind of what we see with all of the police brutality cases. You could watch a video of somebody just being completely demoralized or, you know, brutalized or killed, and then the cops just get off, cause they're like, "Well, the officer felt threatened." And, well, that's essentially what you learn—as long as your reason for being in the situation was lawful in the first place, and you're doing everything as right as you think you can, and you feel threatened, it doesn't matter if you screw up. Just don't lie about it and you'll be fine. I mean, that was essentially what we were told— "Hey don't worry about that, you know, there's a union that'll back you up, there's lawyers." Basically, they just give you the comfort that even if you do screw up, it's okay. Just be forthright about it, and, you know, you'll be fine. You've been certified by the government, and you carry credentials saying you have the authority to make arrests, to use force. And so, that's kind of your ticket to, you know, do what you see fit in any given situation.

It turns out I loved the job. For my day-to-day I would show up to my briefing, learn about what happened the last twenty-four hours, go check out the truck, go check out my gun. I mean, I always had my sidearm, but I would always check out an M4 rifle as well. I would get my truck, get my gun, and then go out to my section of the border. And so, you know, I'm in a truck, by myself, and there's usually a supervisor somewhere, within a few miles of you, but you rarely ever see them. They're there only if you need them. I'm by myself, with all of the equipment that I need in my truck, and I get to work my area however I want to. And, you know, there's methods that they taught you but especially once you get a little bit of time under your belt, you can—as long as you can explain why you're doing something, nobody is going to give you a hard time about why you're doing it. So the autonomy of just being able to go out there and do my job however I want to is something I've never experienced before. Cause I've always just had somebody over my shoulder, you know, looking down at me, critiquing what I'm doing. So the autonomy was great.

And when I wasn't working—we were fairly slow most of the time—I was listening to podcasts, I was listening to books, audiobooks. So I was getting paid very well, to learn stuff, and, at least in the beginning. It was exciting and fun, like, you know, I got to chase down people that I thought were bad guys, and track them, which, I mean, that's an interesting thing in itself, it's like, learning how to track a person, essentially like an animal. I mean, I know it sounds awful to say it that way but that's kind of how you're doing it, doing the same thing as the caveman would to track down their prey.

No good agent really relies on cameras and sensors, they rely on their flashlight and their eyes to track down these people that cross the border. So that was fun. You get to be very analytical, which I enjoyed. You get to try to figure out like, "Is this guy trying to trick me somehow?" There's different things that they can try like walking backward to make it look like they're returning to Mexico instead of furthering their entry, or running around and hopping on hard spots that they know won't leave a print to try to throw you off the track. There's tons of stuff to learn and it's really an art when you take it seriously and try to get good at it. I was outside most of the time. I like being outside. It was just, it was a really cool job, I really enjoyed it.

You have to write a report after every apprehension. And it's almost to the point where you don't really need to write a new report every time because everybody's got the same story. "Oh I came here to work"; "I came here for a better life"; It turns into kind of a Groundhog Day.

One of the questions we're supposed to ask during the processing portion is, "Do you have any tattoos or scars?" And this one guy, when I asked him the question, he said, "Yeah, I have some scars." And so I said, "Show me." And he lifts up his shirt, and his back was just like, covered in these huge scars. Obviously from lashings he'd received. And I was like, "What happened?" In my not-very-good-Spanish, like, "What the hell happened?" and he essentially was told by some drug traffickers to carry a load in order to cross, which is not uncommon. And he refused, so he said they tied him to a tree and whipped him for it. For refusing to carry drugs with him. And, I mean, I was still pretty into the job, and still pretty excited about everything, but that was the first time where I was just like, I knew the guy was going to get deported, but I was like, I do not feel good about sending this guy back.

Of course, when I told this to other people, in the Border Patrol, they're like "Oh, he's lying." You know, "He probably crossed the cartel, and that's why they did that to him." So there's been a couple of those instances where I've relayed stories from people that I've apprehended or interacted with somehow, and everybody else that I told the story to are like, "Oh, they're full of it, they're lying to you, man. That's not what happened." There's a very cynical behavior that runs through the Border Patrol. It's easier to dehumanize someone if you think they're lying to you.

I think the cynicism is a defense mechanism that, well, if you've convinced yourself that everybody that you're dealing with is a liar, and just trying to get over on the system, and get one over on you, then it's a lot easier to keep shutting them out. But I don't think, I don't remember processing anybody's claim that I didn't believe. Essentially, these people have done nothing. Most of them, have done nothing more than walk across a piece of geography. Not to say that there aren't people that were trying to cross that had criminal records, but I mean, we're supposed to be a Christian nation, like, there's not a lot of forgiveness going on for criminal records these days.

I believe human beings, not just Americans, should be free to make their own destiny. And so I had to come to the conclusion that I either believed in human freedom or American freedom, and I realized that by denying people the right to live wherever they choose, work wherever they choose, I was not treating them as human beings.

There were constantly changes with determining how we would process the asylum seekers. But there were never any clear guidelines. In fact, there was a lot of misinformation going around. So one of the problems that I ran into with processing the asylum seekers was, we were given the guidelines for what qualifies as credible fear, and essentially it boils down to—it has to come from a government actor. They have to be afraid of some sort of persecution originating from police or government persecution. If they were just like, "Oh, well I'm poor and hungry and I'm afraid to go back or I'm afraid of the gangs," well, gangs aren't government actors so, that's not a credible fear of persecution, cause it didn't fit the definition we were given. We weren't asylum officers, but we had to refer them for an asylum interview. So if we didn't hear something that fell within the criteria of, what we were taught, met that standard, then we wouldn't . . . it's essentially just checking a box. So if we didn't hear something that met that standard, we would just not check the box. Well, I had never been trained or taught that domestic violence was a reason for asylum. I didn't know that domestic violence was an acceptable reason until I heard Jeff Sessions say it wouldn't be accepted anymore. Or that he didn't want it to be accepted anymore. Now, I can't speak for anybody but myself, but, you know, each individual agent was making those decisions on a daily basis, of, when they were doing their questioning, whether that box for the asylum interview got checked. So yeah, it's a lot of apathy and poor training.

I think you leave the academy not really knowing how to do your job. But I mean, the whole thing is so, it's such an automated process almost, that I don't think anybody really understands what's going on when it's happening to them. I mean, it's not unreasonable to think that hundreds of people are slipping through the cracks because they're not saying the right words, or they don't understand what's really going on. A lot of times, especially with the Guatemalans, the adults wouldn't even speak Spanish. They would speak some Mayan dialect. If they had a kid with them, the kid often spoke Spanish and the dialect so they could kind of translate. But even our translation services usually didn't have anybody that spoke the Mayan dialects available, so that was always a source of confusion and frustration for those that cared to get the case-work right.

And probably around the beginning of 2016 or the end of 2015, I'd hit a point where the work wasn't as fun anymore. In the beginning, I had enjoyed everything. I loved the waiting around, I loved the setting up, I loved the chase, the apprehension, everything. But after a while, the chase was still fun, but then I'd apprehend the people and then I would just be like, these people aren't as scary as everybody makes them out to be. You know? There's not a difference between, you know, because one person has a piece of paper and the other doesn't, like, they're essentially the same. They're the same kind of person. And so I'd started getting this kind of, like, unease. And on the converse, it was really exciting when I would catch somebody and they'd like put up a little bit of a fight, or I'd catch them and I'd get excited when they had a criminal record cause then I'd get to feel good about myself. Like "Oh, I got a bad one off the streets." I was dealing with this kind of contradiction where I was not feeling good about everybody that I was catching, but in my mind I was rationalizing it, that, "Oh well, you know, you're just being soft. You're just being weak." You know. "You're letting your emotions get involved here." But I guess I realized that maybe not all of my conclusions were correct. I started paying more attention to that gut feeling that like, "Hey, this isn't right, you know, putting your hands on people and taking their freedom from them, treating them like number and treating them like a bad guy, or criminal." I essentially started to explore that, and the deeper I dove in, the more disgusted I got.

And even then, I mean, even when I was looking at the full thing and was not happy with it. I'm like, you know, well what do I do? You know I'm not going to give up this career, cause at this point, I'm about halfway to retirement. And, you know, it's great paying job, great benefits, very secure. It's like, am I going to give this up because I'm a little uneasy about some of the people that I'm apprehending?

I went and downloaded a bunch of podcasts about history and immigration and borders and found some YouTube videos and read some essays. And I remember vividly. I can remember exactly where I was sitting in my truck while on patrol. I knew exactly where I was assigned that day. And I was listening to a podcast where a guy explains his moral justification, his economic justification for open borders, and that was the moment I knew, "I can't do this anymore." But I didn't know what the hell else I was going to do. In the time since I had taken the job, I had bought a house, had kids, got married. So it wasn't just like I can just drop everything and ride off into the sunset. I have to figure out. Cause I, you know, I didn't have a job lined up. I mean, I had a prospect, and I ended up getting that job, but I didn't have a job lined up. So, I mean, I still ended up working for probably another year after I came to the conclusion that I couldn't do it anymore.

I finally pulled my supervisor and said I was leaving, I had to do a bunch of meetings and interviews with the management staff. One of my old watch commanders heard that I was leaving, and he stayed after his shift to come in and sit on my meeting cause he was like, "Childress, I've worked with you. You're like one of our hard chargers. What the hell happened?" And I basically, I said something to the effect of, "Well, um, you better not let your guys listen to podcasts anymore if you want them to stick around," or something like that. And I didn't get into it. I really didn't get into a ton of detail with management about why I was leaving, it's just that, "Hey, I've changed my mind. I can't participate in this anymore. I gotta go."

Probably the hardest thing I have to deal when I look back on my time with CBP is realizing that, I mean, I still participated in all of that stuff. It's just . . . it's hard to look back. It's like watching a movie, except it's you. I feel like I should have known better. Knowing what I know now, or believing what I believe now, I look back and I'm like, "Why did it take you so long to figure that out, or to come to those conclusions?" But I'm glad that I did, and I guess that's all you can do. I mean, you can't . . . it's hard to not regret when you look back and realize that you've done things that you, now, think are awful. I try not to beat myself up too much, but there's definitely a . . . I don't know. I'm just kind of an emotional guy anyway so I think there's that level of emotion tied to it that, oh my God, I can't believe I used to do these things.

2

Long Stories Short

FOR SEVERAL YEARS, MARY endured almost daily physical and sexual abuse from her husband in Nigeria. Recounting her experiences to me, she shrugged and explained, "I got married and I was told that the man has a higher hand. Whatever he says is final." Because of her community's normalization of male dominance and abuse, Mary had a hard time finding support. Even the local police, to whom on several occasions she reported injuries including broken bones and disfiguration, told Mary that her struggle was a "family matter" and that they would not interfere in a dispute between husband and wife.

For years, she hid small amounts of money until she had finally saved enough to sneak to the airport with her children while her husband was away and fly to the United States. After they arrived and presented themselves as candidates for asylum, a U.S. immigration officer asked her why she hadn't left her husband earlier. "I told him that I didn't know any better—I didn't know what to do. First of all, I didn't even know I was being molested. I didn't even know I was going through it back then. I thought it was a normal thing because of what we're told." Mary's experience points to a serious challenge facing asylum applicants: local cultural norms may affect how asylum seekers both understand and narrate their experiences in ways that can negatively affect the outcomes of their legal cases.

A person's sense of what is normal changes the way they speak about the past. This becomes a problem for asylum seekers when it means they describe their traumatic experiences in unexpected ways—ways other than how governmental personnel expect credible asylum seekers to talk. Because government agents have specific stylistic and rhetorical expectations for the interactions that stand between an applicant and protection from violence, many applicants are at a disadvantage from the start. The current legal system exacerbates these communicative challenges rather than mitigating them. It requires asylum seekers to conform to precise persuasive narrative conventions as well as to the expectations of each individual interviewer; the goalposts are likely to shift every time they communicate with a new governmental representative.

The narrative burden placed on asylum seekers is formidable and repetitive—they must recount multiple times, to multiple people, in writing and orally, the experiences that forced them to flee their homes. In the government's quest to use a person's autobiographical narrative to determine their credibility, little is out of bounds. Asylum officers and immigration judges regularly ask applicants to produce physical evidence of bodily harm, describe the graphic details of violent sexual encounters and torture, and account for any and all delays in their decisions to flee their homes.

The challenges of telling a stranger about the worst things a person has ever experienced are compounded by the common practice of judges comparing the narrative an applicant tells in court to a recorded iteration from earlier in the asylum process—sometimes *years* earlier. Despite decades of research showing that traumatic experiences can lead to memory distortion, an officer or judge noticing even a small discrepancy from one retelling to the next can set off an adverse credibility determination.[1] In this context, mitigating the potential for misunderstanding in a setting marked by trauma and competing cultural norms takes on a new and menacing urgency.

Making the Familiar Strange

In some cases, human rights violations and other persecutorial practices become so normalized and naturalized in a person's life that they may not mention them at all when they apply for asylum, even if these parts of their experience would be the most likely details to lead them to an approved case. After the successful outcome of her own asylum case, Aisha, who was born in Gambia and speaks six languages fluently, began working as an interpreter for asylum cases involving other African women in New York City, many of whom had experienced female genital mutilation, or FGM. Aisha told me, "Depending on some stories, like the FGM, you see [women] remorseful to bring it out, because some of them feel like the FGM sometimes—they preach that it's sacred, you don't have to tell other people about it, [especially] people that did not go through the process. So, sometimes people, they still have that [idea] in them, so they kind of hold back a little bit."

While talking to a stranger about enduring gruesome physical violence is a daunting hurdle on the way to protection, it is imperative to the asylum process that survivors of FGM overcome the belief in the practice's cultural sacrality and describe it instead as a form of torture. But existing research has shown that the internalization and minimization of traumatic experiences is common in cases of abuse, even when the abused party would not tolerate the same behavior directed toward a hypothetical other.[2] As Aisha emphasized, this is especially true of applicants whose persecution was long-standing: "Because this is what you survived all your life, you tend to even think it's normal." When persecution begins to feel natural rather than unusual, it can take a good bit of work for an individual to defamiliarize what happened to them so that they can talk about it plainly.

Amelia Wilson, a staff attorney at the Immigrants' Rights Clinic at Columbia University, told me she has encountered several cases of persecution that had come to seem so normal to her clients that it was difficult for her to convince them of the necessity of talking about these events during their asylum process. In one recent case, Amelia represented a young woman who was raped by her father at a young age and later physically and sexually abused by her husband. But when Amelia quizzed the client with some questions likely to be asked during her asylum hearing—"What's the worst thing that ever happened to you?" and "Have you ever suffered harm in the past?"—her client did not even mention this abuse. Instead, she would answer by talking about the hardship that a miscarriage had caused her.

"It was so heartbreaking," Amelia told me. "She would identify other things that weren't that she was beaten mercilessly by her husband on a daily basis, or that her father had raped her." Although Amelia did eventually convince her client of the necessity of communicating these experiences during her asylum hearing, it pains her to think about the many survivors who keep such experiences quiet. "I think a lot of the women who have suffered DV [domestic violence] at the hands of their husbands, they haven't seen it themselves as persecution," she shared. "It's so normalized in certain cultures that men would beat their wives. . . . They've internalized their own subjugation."

The internalization of persecution is not limited to survivors of domestic violence, although it is perhaps most well documented in this population.[3] Amelia has also represented several applicants who applied for asylum on the basis of persecution they experienced as a result of social attitudes toward their sexuality. In one case that was ongoing when I interviewed her, she explained, the client "talks about their own sexuality in a way that is shameful, [which] has acted adversely to their credibility because they use terminology that we don't use . . . that makes it sound like *they're* even homophobic." Amelia remembers another client who always referred to himself as "a gay." "He won't say, 'I'm gay.' He's like, 'I'm *a* gay,' or say, 'Well, I am a faggot.' He'll use derogatory terminology, not in an empowering way like he's reclaiming the word, but in a way like he's just a person who is not worthy of fair treatment. He'll justify things that have happened to him because of his sexual orientation." Having internalized prejudiced thoughts toward particular groups may lead asylum applicants to unintentionally undermine their own cases in the way they communicate about their identity.

This presents a peculiar problem for asylum applicants when their practices of secrecy or internalized homophobia mean that they present themselves in ways that are not perceived by representatives of the government as legibly LGBTQ+. Some applicants react to this pressure by behaving in artificial ways based on stereotypes of sexual minorities.[4] In a process so contingent on determinations of credibility, this can be dangerous conduct. Some cases revolve less around whether an LGBTQ+ applicant might have a credible fear of persecution than around whether they are in fact part of a sexual minority; even if they are believed, applicants who do not read as obviously LGBTQ+ to the asylum officer or immigration judge may be encouraged to simply continue hiding their sexuality in their nation of origin to avoid persecution.[5]

Further, as Héctor Carrillo has shown, beginning in the early 1990s, "the need to legally establish the immutability of homosexuality"—that is, to have it be recognized by U.S. immigration officials as a fixed characteristic rather than a practice that applicants could be expected to change in order to remain safely in their nations of origin—recommended the adoption of an essentialist, biological understanding of sexuality that obscures any cultural influences over an LGBTQ+ applicant's actions and presentation.[6] This approach risks failing to draw sufficient attention to the ways individuals were persecuted within a unique cultural context based on their membership in a particular social group. While a savvy attorney may be able to overcome this hurdle with clients by practicing with them ways of talking about their specific, culturally rooted experiences of sexuality and persecution, clients without representation may never get the chance.

Existing trauma research complicates explanations about why an asylum seeker may verbally downplay the harms they experienced by showing how memory changes over time in response to both the context in which one is asked to recall an event and the status of one's recovery from trauma. This work shows that rather than existing in individuals as static realities, as psychologists Sharon Dekel and George A. Bonanno describe, "memories are continually reconstructed in accord with previous knowledge and experiences, attitudes, belief systems, and the conditions and context at the time of recall."[7] Individuals experiencing symptoms of posttraumatic stress disorder when they recount a memory tend to recall more trauma than when they are not experiencing symptoms.[8] Likewise, individuals whose experience of trauma leads to worse mental health outcomes become more accurate narrators of a traumatic event over time, while individuals who recover more readily modify their original narratives to be more benign, matching their progressive recovery.[9] In the context of asylum, it is easy to see how these cognitive realities may work against applicants—if an asylum seeker's mental recovery from traumatic events is inversely correlated with their ability to describe the severity of the persecution they faced, their resilience may ironically imperil their chances of a positive determination of credibility.

Even when applicants are able and willing to describe the hardships they face, cross-cultural differences in the conceptions and descriptions of those hardships may inhibit their case. Former immigration judge Jeff Chase described this phenomenon to me clearly:

It's really important for the asylum seeker to realize that things that are commonly understood by them—that they might not feel they need to explain when talking to a member of their own family or a neighbor—when they talk to the credible fear asylum officer or immigration judge, [they] have to act like this person doesn't know *anything* about where I come from and how things operate there. So, if they're going to say that, for example, their domestic partner was abusive to them or the gang was extorting money from them, they should really make sure to paint the full picture of how things operate there.

Uprooting the normalcy of some culturally bound terms, Chase suggests, can bolster one's case; however, for the reasons the narrators in this project have already described, painting a "full picture" is difficult. The significance of Chase's advice is emphasized by Walter Kälin's work showing that asylum authorities "tend to substantiate negative decisions [by showing] that due to contradictory and implausible statements or apparent lies the applicant has not been able to prove his or her claim."[10] Lived experiences that seem implausible within an immigration judge's cultural framework may be particularly difficult for asylum seekers to prove even if those experiences are commonplace and unremarkable in the asylum seeker's former cultural context.

Moreover, an asylum seeker and an agent of the government may employ differing definitions for words that describe social realities. The burden to ensure clear interpretation of such words falls to the asylum seeker, who may be unaware that a discrepancy even exists. Judge Chase offered an illustrative example: "Someone coming from a small-town American viewpoint hears the word 'gang,' and they might think of some teenagers that hang out on a corner that bother people walking by." Many cases Chase heard during his time on the bench involved highly organized and dangerous groups such as MS-13 and the 18th Street gang that act, he explained, "as de facto governments in the areas that they live. They're controlling basically armies where they're having billions of dollars in cash flow from drug sales and extortion, where their reach is international, where they're carrying out functions that would normally be associated with governments." In the case of attempting to find relief from persecution of a gang that matches this description, an asylum seeker would need not only to recognize a likely difference in the way gangs are defined in these contexts but also to clearly and convincingly demonstrate the gang's scope and threat overall.

As much as government recommendations for dealing with asylum seekers from different backgrounds may seek to standardize interactions between officers or judges and asylum seekers, it is left to the individual governmental representative to reach their own conclusions about credibility and deservingness. One metric for the dissimilarity between the ways these assessments are made is the wide disparity in outcomes from one immigration court—or one immigration judge—to another. From fiscal years 2014 to 2019, of the five immigration courts that handled almost 50 percent of asylum cases, denial rates ranged from 26 percent (New York) to almost 92 percent (Houston). Over that same period, two immigration judges denied 100 percent of the cases they ruled on, while ten others denied fewer than 10 percent.[11]

Because every case hinges on immigration officials' interpretation of applicants' autobiographical narratives and the relationship of those narratives to the conditions in their home countries, the U.S. State Department used to provide frequently updated country-specific profiles that would be submitted into evidence in all asylum claims. These reports are no longer published. As a result, Judge Chase explains,

> the judges are thus left to rely on the State Department's Country Reports on Human Rights Practices, which are issued once a year (and therefore might be out of date within months). The Country Reports are not prepared specifically for use in asylum claims. They may be brief, and address a country's major issues in generalized terms, while failing to address lesser or more localized issues at all.[12]

Moreover, while the State Department assures users that the remaining Country Reports on Human Rights Practices are diligently researched and their contents approved by a number of area experts, their contents are subject to political manipulation.[13] For example, Amnesty International charged in 2018 that the most recent reports had been altered by an "unprecedented and alarming level of politicized editing by the Trump administration that undermines the credibility of the reports."[14] Likewise, Human Rights Watch claims the 2017 reports had "massive omissions" that threatened to undermine the perceived credibility of asylum applicants.[15] Of course, even the most well-intentioned and thoroughly researched country condition reports cannot account for the experiences of every citizen; applicants whose experiences of persecution fall outside the norm for a given country may have an even more difficult time proving their credibility.[16]

The likely possibly of "politicized editing" and omissions in the State Departments' reports make the testimony of individual expert witnesses highly important for filling in the narrative gaps between the asylum applicant's testimony and the generic country reports. "I can think of many cases in which a country expert's testimony resulted in a grant of asylum," Judge Chase reflected.[17] But asylum seekers may not know how to involve an expert in their case, and even if they do, expert witnesses are at times unavailable or prohibitively expensive, so asylum seekers without the means to afford them may have no way of bridging this narrative gap.

Sometimes even mundane and barely perceptible differences in culturally bound ways of describing a memory directly affect asylum cases. These differences are supported by intercultural research in social psychology; everything from the emphasis a memory puts on the self or the community to the level of detail included when recounting autobiographical memories have been shown to vary from culture to culture.[18]

Elizabeta Markuci, an attorney at a nonprofit organization that offers pro bono immigration-related legal services, pointed out to me that even something as banal as differences in the way distances are measured from one culture to the next can cause misunderstandings in an asylum case. She remembers that in the first asylum case she ever represented, there was a "misunderstanding of distance based on the fact that that individual was from a country that uses the metric system," she explained. Although such a matter seems trivial, Elizabeta pointed out that because officers and judges are trained to look for even minor discrepancies in narratives as signals of the possibility of fraud, even a small culturally rooted misunderstanding might have a big impact. "There are so many little things that could be a critical fact . . . if you don't have [an] advocate next to you, [who is] taking notes, monitoring, making sure, going through the testimony, going through the facts, aligning all those things," she emphasized.

Cultural norms big and small permeate asylum cases in ways both visible and invisible. Both immigration personnel and asylum seekers exist in several overlapping cultures at once; intersecting and dynamic attributes such as age, religion, political beliefs, socioeconomic status, and geographic location influence one's sense of what is or is not normal and may affect the style in which one communicates. Acknowledging the effect of culture on both behavior and the interpretation of behavior in the asylum process, U.S. Citizenship and Immigration Services' Asylum Officer Training curriculum includes a module titled "Cross-Cultural Communication and Other Factors That May Impede Communication at an Interview."[19] The materials contain several communication-centric directions for officers, including "Focus on the interviewee and listen to what he or she is saying," and "be aware of the potential for miscommunication when a second language is used."[20] Much of the content is cursory; the section on eye contact, for example, is composed of only two sentences: "Eye contact varies from culture to culture. What may be considered a normal length of time for eye contact in one culture, may, in another culture, be termed 'staring' and considered rude, causing the other person to feel uncomfortable."[21] No mention is made of which cultures this statement applies to or of how trauma impacts the ability to make eye contact.

The reflections of individuals who have endured the asylum process describe a nexus of dissimilar communication styles rooted in disparate cultural norms. These differences in some cases threaten to make applicants seem less credible and thereby jeopardize their ability to prove a "well-founded fear of persecution." The officers and judges I interviewed made clear that this is a common and pivotal obstacle.

Judge Charles Honeyman told me that over the course of his career he heard testimony from "some truthful [applicants that] were so ineffective and stumbling as to be unbelievable," while in other cases there was "the potential for some proportion of people who have fraudulent or exaggerated claims to get through and get granted asylum and all the benefits because they're going to tell a story well—what I'm saying is that there is not a perfect science." These cases hinged not on the severity of the persecution a person faced but their ability to recount it. Former immigration officer Martha Parmalee explained, "There have been cases where I thought, this person has a real case, but they're just afraid. They won't tell me. No matter *what* I did, I couldn't get it out of them. Those really bothered me, those cases." A person who cannot communicate what they have endured has virtually no chance at a successful case, and the chances of success very much depend on the nuances of a person's communicative ability. Because this is the case, a closer look at how this underexamined facet of the asylum process impacts applicants and influences outcomes is vital.

From Chaos to Order

Abe was born in Nigeria and had to flee when others' knowledge of his sexual orientation began to threaten his life. Entering his asylum interview expecting to be able to share at length about the hardships this experience had caused him, he was flummoxed when the officer interviewing him seemed to grow frustrated by the amount of detail Abe was providing. "He just wanted 'yes' or 'no' kind of answers, so, I guess I was overdoing it, maybe that was the problem," Abe told me. "I was trying to buttress my points, making him understand more. Maybe that was what pissed him off. I don't know. He was [saying], 'No, I just want this, I just want this!' I [replied], 'Yes, I understand, but I'm trying to—if you ask me an open-ended question, you don't just expect me to just say yes or no, I have to be able to *explain* to you.'" The differences between the asylum officer's and Abe's communication styles created what Abe described to me as a "friction" throughout the course of the interview.

Abe knew enough about asylum law to understand that if the immigration officer conducting his interview did not find him credible, his only remaining choices would be to pursue a difficult appeals process or accept the prospect of deportation. A feeling of frantic desperation accompanied his narrative as he realized, "if I'm not able to pass this stage, then that's the end." Being rushed through the interview only flustered him further. "The way [the officer] was [verbally] hitting back at me, says probably I'm taking too much of his time. I guess he has other guys to attend to," he remembers. He left his interview disappointed that he had not been allowed to share the complexity of his experiences and was scared to learn the result.

During the "credible fear" interview that determines whether one's case will be heard before a judge, the U.S. Citizenship and Immigration Services (USCIS) instructs applicants to "tell the Asylum Officer your experiences *in as much detail as possible* so that the Asylum Officer can determine whether you qualify as a refugee."[22] The ability to relay sufficient detail is paramount, but not all details are welcome. USCIS has no use for memories that do not involve the five particular classes of persecution detailed in the 1951 Refugee Convention: race, religion, nationality, membership in a particular social group, or political opinion. The entirety of the process is designed to see if an individual meets this definition; wrangling the complex and chaotic details of their lives into such narrow narrative parameters presents a communicative challenge that sometimes proves insurmountable.

Certainly much of the difficulty of narrating one's experiences of persecution in a way that aligns with the legal parameters of the asylum system stems from the reality that many individuals who arrive in the United States in need of protection have no understanding of asylum or the five grounds on which to prove one's need for it.[23] Still, the narrators in this project emphasize that knowledge of the conventions does not guarantee success. Attorney Elizabeta Markuci explained that even when applicants understand what the legal standards are, the nuances of the law are so complex that it's unlikely their stories will just "naturally" fit the parameters. "It took me a *while* in law school [to learn] those concepts, right? So how do you distill that for someone?" she wonders. "There's the statute, the law that you have to prove, but how do you interpret the law?" Successful interpretation requires applicants to organize the chaotic events preceding their forced migration into a linear narrative that offers an unobstructed understanding of who caused an individual's persecution and why.

USCIS's Asylum Officer Training Materials address this problem explicitly in a section called "The Interviewee May Not Know What Is Important to Disclose."[24] It reads, "The interviewee is not likely to be familiar with U.S. immigration laws and regulations and what is necessary to establish eligibility. . . . He or she will not be familiar with the interview process. You [the officer in training], however, are the authority on relevant law, what is necessary to establish eligibility, and the interview process."[25] This section rhetorically removes the relevance of asylum seekers as experts in their own life experiences—the experiences that establish eligibility under the Refugee Convention—and endows the officer alone with the power to know and extract what is relevant from the interview.

Former officer Martha Parmalee believes that "the most difficult" task confronting asylum seekers is to fit their sometimes confusing and chaotic histories into the tidy parameters required by the five available categories. "If it's not clearly political opinion, race, or religion," Martha shared, it proves especially difficult to "try and figure out what kind of 'particular social group' you might fit into." This difficulty is compounded, as immigration scholars Marco Jacquemet and Massimiliano Spotti describe, by the fact that the asylum process is a trans-idiomatic environment in which applicant and official may use incompatible words to name the same concepts or experiences even when both parties speak the same language.[26] Of course, this incongruence is amplified significantly when an interpreter is required.[27]

One of the variables that immigration attorneys encounter often is the difficulty of knowing and being able to prove the motive for a story's "villain"—the person or party responsible for the persecution that an asylum seeker faced or fears they will face in the future. Elizabeta explained,

> One of the jokes that people repeat in the practice of immigration law is like, no persecutor is going to give you a note [that says,] "I tortured you because you are part of this political party or because of your race or because of your religion." So showing that connection is sometimes really challenging, and that's why you submit so much documentation to make those puzzle links that [show] you're not just someone who's at the wrong place at the wrong time.

The ability to point to a motivated persecutor is imperative for establishing a clear villain against whom the asylum-seeking protagonist can attempt to prevail.

In this context, documentary proof is often called upon to substantiate oral explanations. Former immigration judge Sue Roy explained, "For instance, maybe you can't prove that 'Joe the

MS-13 member' was targeting you specifically, because you don't really know who he was, right? But you know that he was extorting you for money." In this case, Judge Roy would tell an applicant, "Get your bank records that show that you were taking out [funds] every month. Those kinds of things can still help support your claim and shouldn't be that hard for people to get."

In Judge Roy's hypothetical scenario, documentary records support narrative arguments to the benefit of the applicant. But her suggestion that these records shouldn't be difficult to procure does not fully account for contexts where systems that, at least in theory, exist to protect citizens sometimes work against them. For example, Mary told me she went through "a lot of problems to get the police report" in Nigeria that would offer evidence of the physical harm she suffered at the hands of her husband. "They said they don't want to give it because they needed money, they needed a bribe before they could give out a report. . . . The system is corrupt. If it was not corrupt, nobody would want to leave in the first place." The problem is not simply a lack of records, Abe corroborated; visiting some police stations in Nigeria can be dangerous. He told me people pray that they will never need to go.

These circumstances put some migrants at a disadvantage since documentary evidence may be viewed as more credible than oral testimony. Without evidence, Abe knew his claim would be less viable. "A police report . . . they believe that is like more presentable, compared to having a testimony." Feeling the pressure of having little other choice, and lacking confidence that his complicated narrative would be enough without documentation to corroborate it, Abe acquired a forged document before he left Nigeria that stated he had been invited to participate in a conference in the United States. He hoped to use the document just to pass U.S. Customs at John F. Kennedy International Airport in New York City, but the officers detained him; he would spend the next six months in jail before receiving pro bono representation that helped him to prepare a more accurate case that was ultimately successful.

These accounts illuminate some reasons credible applicants for asylum may be unable to produce asylum narratives that would lead to a successful outcome. As the narrators have shown, even applicants with claims that should make them eligible for asylum may find that complication, confusion, or chaos in their experience prohibits them from communicating their story in accordance with the strict and uniformly applied boundaries of current immigration policy. That is, not only must applicants have faced persecution that was a direct result of their race, religion, nationality, membership in a particular social group, or political opinion, but they must also prove that this is the case through oral testimony that is remarkably efficient and evidentiary, stylistically conforming to the boundaries of what officers and judges believe to be plausible, and in a national context where the decision makers' beliefs, expertise, and grant rates vary dramatically.

Chronology and Coherence

In a January 2020 presentation to prospective asylum applicants titled "How to Write Your Asylum Story," attorney Amir Rasoulpour told participants, "In reality, your story is complicated, not necessarily chronological or in order, and things are not black and white. [But] your *asylum story* is not your full story. It is a story that focuses on the elements of asylum and presents them chronologically and clearly."[28] Rasoulpour's instructions make visible the inevitably dichotomous nature of narrative in asylum proceedings—the requirement for a partial but still precisely chronological narrative. Reflecting on her own experience of recounting traumatic experiences for a chance at protection, Ethiopian American refugee author Maaza Mengiste remembers that "sometimes, there was no language capable of adding coherence to what felt impossible to comprehend."[29] An applicant cannot provide an unedited and comprehensive view of their experience to support their case and must instead curate a selective distillation, strategically choosing to reveal and conceal some lived experiences, maintaining linear clarity even while omitting major segments of life not relevant to the asylum process. The challenge of making order out of chaos is exacerbated by culturally bound ways of chronicling time, the impact of trauma on memory, and the uncertainty of understanding which details to communicate and which to exclude.

When Jeff Chase began providing legal representation to asylum seekers in the 1980s, most of his clients were from Afghanistan. "One of the most difficult parts of preparing their asylum applications was determining dates," Chase wrote on the blog he keeps about immigration law; "not only the dates relating to events critical to their claim (i.e. when they were arrested; when they fled), but even the most basic info: the dates of their birth."[30] Chase's struggle resulted from the fact that the official identity cards issued by the Afghan government would record someone's birthday by stating, for example, that the person "was approximately eight years old in 1982." Chase's attempt to pin down an exact date to record on the I-589 Application for Asylum, he explained, was "further complicated by the fact that Afghanistan uses a completely different calendar from the west." Since sometimes neither Chase nor his clients could reasonably determine their exact birth date, Chase started to record his Afghan clients' birthdays as January first. "When I once attended a master calendar hearing on January second, the [government] attorney joked that I must have been extremely busy the previous day, celebrating all of my clients' birthdays," Chase remembers.

The application's requirement of relevant dates does not account for cultural differences like the ones Chase describes. The twelve-page I-589 Application for Asylum provides applicants with forty-eight spaces to "provide specific dates" about "each event or action described," such as the dates when they faced persecution, when they sought help, and when they arrived in the United States. In

October 2019 USCIS changed the language on its website to read that it would not accept any applications "if you leave any fields blank."[31] The following month the American Immigration Lawyers Association reported that rejections "due to claimed incompleteness" of the I-589 form were growing more frequent.[32] The *Guardian* reported on several such examples, like one in which an application was refused because it did not include a passport expiration date; like many asylum seekers, this particular applicant did not *have* a passport and thus no expiration date to report.[33] In 2021 USCIS relented, announcing they were "reverting to the intake process we applied before October 2019. . . . We will not automatically reject your form if you leave a space blank. However, we may reject your form or your case might take more time if you leave required spaces blank."[34] The fact that rejecting a case because of a black space is now a menacing possibility rather than an automatic process offers little relief.

Bureaucratic insistence on dates that some applicants are unable to provide threatens the chances of protection for some viable candidates. Their applications must be complete when submitted, but recording any date that is later found not to be exact carries the real danger of jeopardizing their credibility and threatening the outcome of their case. Compounded by the idea that traumatized individuals may have an even more difficult time remembering dates than others, the static application leaves asylum seekers with few choices.

The potential impact of highly personalized trauma is an especially intractable problem in this regard. The varied and unpredictable effects of traumatic experience on autobiographical memory are well documented and may include memory disorganization that can lead to difficulty encoding and organizing a narrative and an emphasis on emotional rather than more tangible details in recounting an event.[35] Steph Hellawell and Chris Brewin's salient work shows that memories of traumatic events may be available only as perceptual snapshots—flashes of partial but poignant sensory recollection—that are involuntarily triggered rather than remembered via the kind of voluntary recall that one must attempt during the asylum process.[36] Likewise, Belinda Graham, Jane Herlihy, and Chris Brewin observe that asylum seekers' memories are "overgeneral," that is, less specific when compared to those of someone without posttraumatic stress symptoms.[37]

Trauma can also lead to memory distortion, affecting the accuracy of an individual's memory. Both the effort of intentionally remembering traumatic events—an effort required throughout a sometimes years-long legal asylum process—and the incursion of unintentional, intrusive traumatic memories can lead people to "inadvertently generate additional imagery relating to those traces that fits with the experienced event," adding content from memories of other events or even of media representations of similar events as though they were real memories.[38]

In March 2019 I arrived at Bellevue Hospital to meet Dr. Hawthorne "Hawk" Smith, the director of the Program for Survivors of Torture (PSOT). PSOT is renowned for providing what Hawk calls a "resilience-based, strengths-based approach" to comprehensive mental health care for people who have been forcibly displaced from their homes and offering clients psychological evaluations that are regularly used as evidence in immigration court. The traumas that PSOT's asylum-seeking clients report having experienced are broad and bleak: many have been physically beaten, made to witness the murder or torture of others, sexually assaulted, deprived of food or water, suspended in painful positions, or made to withstand mock executions and death threats.[39]

Hawk used a poignant simile to describe how such experiences can affect a person's ability to accurately recall their past during their asylum process: "If we look at our brain as a library and our memories as books, under normal circumstances, the books are organized, codified, placed in a structured way, an organized way . . . but when someone is in a situation of extreme stress, extreme trauma . . . those books sort of get placed haphazardly—by the time someone is asked, 'So what happened on that day in September?' and they go to look for that book, the book is not there." Hawk's experience working with severely traumatized migrants corroborates what trauma research has long reported: traumatic experiences inhibit individuals' abilities to recall and narrate with chronological specificity the details of their lives.[40]

Although asylum officers are trained to look for inconsistencies in applicants' testimony, Hawk pointed out that gaps in memory and "a little bit of inconsistency—it actually is not something that signals that the person . . . loses their credibility. In some ways, that is *more* consistent to someone who's actually been traumatized and trying to hold it together." In other words, traumatic experiences may cause the exact kind of lapses in memory and contradictions that signal dishonesty to the officer or judge evaluating an asylum case, illuminating a crucial challenge for traumatized applicants.

Aisha remembers from her own asylum process just how unpredictable memory is. She told me, "Sometimes, you go through certain things, you are traumatized, you forget when they ask you. You can remember something, but somebody else comes and starts asking you, you can forget. It happens because of trauma." The reality Aisha describes is further complicated by the unpredictability of the duration of any asylum process. Whereas some recent asylum seekers have been rushed into credible fear interviews only hours after they arrive in the United States, giving them too little time to prepare, others I spoke with have been made to wait years for their interviews, during which time they must cling to painful memories so they will be able to recall them in exacting detail when their time finally comes.

To be clear, the issue in some cases is not that asylum seekers simply cannot remember what happened in their past but rather that they cannot recall and recount the memory with flawless specificity in the exact moment that they must in order to have a chance at a successful case. Aisha emphasized that the ability to remember traumatic experiences is quite likely to fluctuate depending on the context: "Sometimes it happens . . . maybe if I talk to you today, you might not remember something but if I reach you, maybe, another time, you can remember." Existing work in the psychology of memory and its relation to trauma substantiates Aisha's experience.[41] Unfortunately, because each asylum seeker receives just one credible fear interview, the asylum system cannot account for the variability of memory's accessibility in any given moment.

Amadeo was one of Hawk's clients at PSOT. He remembers painfully the difficulty of trying to remember and write down the details of experiences he had hoped to forget after he fled Peru. The process took a toll. He told me, "Emotionally, I was a wreck back then, I guess. But the process itself was long. It wasn't easy. I think that the hardest part was [when] they asked me to write my story of how my life was back in Peru. It took me, like, a month to remember everything. Because I think back then, I [tried] to erase many memories, many bad memories that I had, and when I brought them back, I wasn't feeling well." PSOT worked with Amadeo to help him understand how to select and tell the parts of his story that would most clearly align with the eligibility requirements for asylum. Amadeo's experiences of persecution were on account of his belonging to a "particular social group"—one of the five protected grounds—and the pain he experienced when reconstructing his memories in narrative form lifted when he was granted asylum and finally felt that he could leave his past behind.

Former officer Parmalee explained to me how applicants' uncertainty about which aspects of their experience to engage and which to avoid threatens their ability to construct a chronological narrative: "Part of the problem is, if people don't know what the requirements are, they're frightened. They know what they went through [but] they don't know what's important and what's not," sometimes causing the applicants to jump forward and backward in time as they narrate their lives. "Depending on their culture," Parmalee told me, asylum seekers may not realize that "I don't need your grand-father's history. I don't need to know what they're doing to your people. I need to know what they did to *you*, and who did it, and why." For applicants who see themselves less as individuals and more as members of a collective community group, explaining the full extent of their experience in a chronological fashion would require contextualization that the asylum process simply does not have the capacity to permit.

The problems that result from the presence of differing cultural norms in the asylum process have no easy solution. But amid all the challenges, there are many attorneys, psychologists, immigration officers, and judges who believe in the universal human right to seek asylum and have demonstrated creative adaptability and compassion toward asylum seekers.

In her experiences accompanying clients to court to provide testimony about their psychological evaluations, Dr. Adeyinka Akinsulure-Smith recalls instances where judges recognized how difficult verbal testimony would likely be in a particular case and mercifully chose not to require the applicant to recount the graphic details in the courtroom. She told me, "I've been with people who've had really empathetic judges who've said, 'You know what? I've read the affidavit. I read this woman's statement, she went through all these rapes. We don't need to go through the details, let's just move along.'" Sparing the asylum seeker from retelling the painful details of her story after she had already recounted it multiple times for her attorney, an asylum officer, and the psychologist attending her case, this judge chose to prioritize the applicant's written testimony instead, demonstrating one way judges may sometimes be able to make use of different modes of communication to mitigate rather than exacerbate the trauma of the asylum process.

The fluctuating U.S. political climate weighs heavily on those working in support of the human rights of asylum seekers. Martha

Parmalee retired from her post as an asylum officer one year after Donald Trump became president. "I'd still be there if we had a different administration," she told me. "It just got too much. I can't deal with him, separating families and throwing children in the cages. . . . I just felt beaten down by it. I think what the [Trump] administration is doing to these people is criminal." Judge Chase retired in May 2017 and regularly speaks with other judges who are still on the bench. During Trump's last year in office, Chase shared that some judges told him, "You have no idea how bad things are. You can't even imagine. Whatever you can imagine, it's 100 times worse." The year he retired, Chase founded the Roundtable of Former Immigration Judges, a group that has been outspoken about the harmful effects of the unprecedented attacks against the right to seek asylum that the Trump administration enacted, including limiting the types of claims eligible for asylum and requiring judges to process cases in less time than is necessary to give each fair consideration. More recently, the group denounced the Biden administration's reinstatement of MPP the "Remain in Mexico" asylum policy.

In an article reporting on the unusual number of immigration judges who retired early under Trump, Hamed Aleaziz details the policy changes that undermined judges' prior sense of authority to fairly judge asylum cases; many felt like "cogs in a deportation machine, as opposed to neutral arbiters given time to thoughtfully analyze the merits of each case," Aleaziz reports.[42] Newly retired judges regularly reach out to Chase's group wanting to join. "The second they retire, I get to hear from them, and so many of them just come out so angry," he explained. When the individuals who are determined to uphold the universal right to asylum are driven from the job by policies that they feel they cannot ethically defend, more room opens up for lifetime appointments of personnel who do not question the threat to human rights the current system invites.

The United States' responsibility to treat asylum seekers ethically and fairly requires greater attention to the role that communication and culture play in the search for legal protection. It is clear that the parameters required by the asylum process do not account for culturally specific ways of remembering and storytelling, for the effect of cultural differences in autobiographical memory, or for the impacts of trauma on the construction of a coherent narrative.

In Their Own Words

Alina Das, Immigration Attorney

WALKING INTO 26 FEDERAL PLAZA, you're immediately struck even outside of the building by how imposing it is. It is a very large, tall federal building in the middle of downtown Manhattan. Depending on the day and depending on the number of entrances that are open, you can often see a line of people around the block. And that's immediately jarring, as one can imagine, for those who are seeking relief.

When people enter the building as you come out of this long line, the first thing you do is go through security. For some of my clients who've had very harrowing interactions with security and police, even walking through that security line can be a traumatizing event, because you are struck with the fact that this is a federal building, and that people are searching you and treating you as a potential suspect as you even enter that space. Which is something that those of us who have not had negative interactions with law enforcement or government officials take as kind of routine security, but it's a different experience for people who have been either physically harmed or were detained and otherwise have traumatic experiences with law enforcement.

I tend to meet with clients outside the building so I can walk in with them. Sometimes it's not possible, and you are left a bit lost trying to find your way to each other. The building has many floors, and the immigration courts are currently on two of them. It's incredibly confusing for anyone who hasn't been in the building. There's no clear signage or sense of where the immigration courts are. If you speak a language other than English, or, to some extent, Spanish, it's very unlikely that you will necessarily know or have any printed instructions about where to go.

The twelfth floor is the main floor that has a kind of clerk's office. But the courtrooms are scattered everywhere, and there's a series of printed paper that gets posted under courtroom numbers, and you're supposed to figure out which courtroom you're supposed to go to from that. And then you might find out that your courtroom is not on the twelfth floor, that it's on the fourteenth floor. Not all of the elevator banks go to those floors, and you see many people, families included, walking through the hallways trying to figure out where to go and whether they're in the right place.

There is no right to government-appointed counsel if you're facing deportation, and so people may or may not have lawyers in that space. Those who do have lawyers may or may not have met them before the day of that court hearing. And that only adds to the feeling of chaos and lack of control and order in those spaces. Because you'll see people who are lawyers calling out the names of their clients trying to search for them as well as people who appear to be immigrants waiting for their court hearing trying to find their attorneys, and it just contributes to the confusion.

Once you've identified where you're supposed to be, it's still unclear what a person is supposed to do at that point. The courtroom is a room like any other office building room. They tend to be these windowless rooms that have a seal for the Department of Justice and the Executive Office for Immigration Review at the front, and that gives it a little bit of a sense of being a courtroom, but otherwise it's just tables and chairs and a divider in front of a few rows where people can sit and watch what's happening.

We try to speak to the people we represent very carefully about what to expect in immigration court and try to meet with them outside so we can be there with them to help the process. To walk into court with them, to wait with them until their case is called. That experience, even under circumstances where we all try to be as prepared as possible, is incredibly harrowing because you're sitting in these cold, bureaucratic rooms, barely able to hear or understand what the judge is saying and seeing the fate of people who, also like you, may have long-standing ties to the United States or may fear persecution and death if deported. Seeing these people's fates be decided in a matter of minutes, and watching that as you're waiting for your turn, sometimes seeing people weep and cry in front of you because they just lost their case, or being told that they have to move forward even though they haven't been able to find an attorney.

Seeing people be berated—whether it's immigrants themselves or their lawyers—by the immigration judge, maybe the people did make some sort of mistake in their filing, maybe they didn't, but that level of hostility can arise pretty quickly in the setting. And immigration judges are certainly overworked and overtasked, not given sufficient resources to do the jobs that they believe that they've set out to do. So, all of that pain and the trauma and the tension of those moments is on full display. All they see is that pain and that anxiety. And then it becomes their turn to stand up and present their case. There's so much about this process—from the moment you look at the federal building and try to enter it, and then find your courtroom, and see this judge and wait in that room—that happens before you even begin your own case that is painful and traumatic and confusing and leads to a lot of harm in and of itself.

I don't think I've represented anyone in an individual hearing who has not been traumatized by having to go through that hearing process.

3

Emotional Labor

WHEN HE RETURNED HOME FROM a day at the beach to find that his home in Venezuela had been burglarized and vandalized, Marcus knew he had to leave to save his life. Having been targeted on two prior occasions because of his membership in a particular social group, Marcus understood this attack was a message: They knew where he lived, they were tracking his movements, and they would return. He arranged for a tourist visa and booked travel to New York. As he boarded the plane, the weight of everything he was leaving behind hit him: "I was crying on the flight," he remembers.

In New York Marcus submitted an affirmative application for asylum, participated in a credible fear interview, and was instructed to go to the USCIS field office in Long Island to learn the outcome of his case, which would be delivered by an officer behind a glass window. He remembers:

> My appointment was at two o'clock. I came there and I had to wait one hour, and while I was waiting, I saw families, I saw a

lot of people there waiting. In the waiting room, you can see other people get the answer [determining the outcome of their case]. I could hear the conversation that they had with the officer. The chairs were close to the window, so you could hear everything. There were people crying. There were families crying because they denied their asylum. Actually, I think that *all* the people that I saw, they were denied. It was very sad. While I was watching that, I was feeling sad, like whoa, this is happening. This is *happening*.

Marcus thought his case was strong, but the emotions of the other families shook him: "Because that hour that I had to wait, I saw people crying, I could hear how the officer said [to the others], 'Your asylum has been denied' . . . I don't know, the officer was saying a lot of things about it, how the process will go when you get denied asylum. I got scared." By the time his turn came, he was almost certain he would be denied.

When the officer called him to the window, Marcus found he had beaten the odds: "She said, 'Congratulations, your asylum has been approved,' and it was like, whoa—I was in shock. I was like whoa. Wow. I was just watching her, but I wasn't smiling. I didn't say a word because I was in shock. After I signed a lot of papers, she was telling me a lot of things . . . and I was just thinking. I wasn't there. I wasn't there. I took my documents, and I went out, and I called my mom. When I called her, I started crying. I couldn't believe— like, wow."

Marcus's hour-long wait in the field office before receiving the positive news about his case outcome was brief compared to other asylum seekers I interviewed who had to return on multiple occasions to supply additional documentation and sometimes wait more than half a day for a chance at the window. Still, even his abbreviated account offers a good deal of information about the kinds of communicative messages that pervade the physical spaces where asylum decisions are rendered.

61

Marcus describes not only the emotions he experienced over the course of the afternoon when his case was decided—confidence, sadness, fear, shock, and disbelief—but also the substantial effects that the nonverbal emotional displays of the other asylum-seeking families had on him that day. Given the long odds and immense consequences of being denied asylum, applicants are likely to feel and express a range of emotions as they progress through the legal process. But emotions are not merely a side effect of the asylum process; they play an integral role.

As a volunteer with a nonprofit legal clinic in New York City, I work with asylum seekers to prepare their I-589 Applications for Asylum. The application requires a written summary of the persecution an asylum seeker has faced. I have seen how excruciating the first passes through their narrative can be. Although all of the volunteers are trained in trauma-informed interviewing and go about the work as gently as possible, it is not atypical for an applicant to be emotionally overcome by the experiences and memories they must dredge up during the process of working to explain or write down their experiences on the I-589.

That this is only one of the many times during the asylum process they will be asked to recount to strangers the worst things that ever happened to them adds an oppressive weight to such moments. Applicants have to repeat their narrative and revisit the emotion of it when they participate in an interview with an immigration officer and when they appear in front of a judge during a hearing—not to mention the additional retellings involved if the applicant has access to an attorney, a doctor who will provide a physical or psychological evaluation, or an expert witness on their case.

The nonverbal communication of emotion, sometimes called "affect," can be read in a person's hands, voice, face, movement, and posture. Since the passage of the REAL ID Act in 2005, affect holds some legal power to influence the outcome of a case: the act, in an attempt to outline a "uniform standard for credibility," determined that immigration judges may base a credibility determination on "the demeanor, candor, or responsiveness of the applicant."[1] Demeanor includes a wide range of expression; one judge defined it as "carriage, behavior, bearing, manner, and appearance."[2]

When an immigration judge reaches an asylum decision by determining that an applicant's demeanor has indicated a lack of credibility, the judge is required to note on which particular aspect or aspects of the asylum seeker's demeanor the decision is based. These may include observations about an applicant's hand-wringing, rapid speech, or pausing before answering questions, for example. However, while the judge has to record the nonverbal behavior in question, the REAL ID Act does not require a judge to explain *why* a specific behavior has been interpreted as indicating a lack of credibility, let alone offer proof that a particular nonverbal action signifies untruthfulness.[3]

Trauma's effects on an individual's ability to process emotion and display affect often works against asylum seekers, creating new problems in an already difficult evaluative process. Many have sustained long-term, serious trauma, including death threats, domestic violence, torture, and being made to watch family members be tortured or murdered. The mere mention of these experiences can trigger a trauma response, and that response can result in affectual extremes; a person may completely decompensate, losing the ability to control their emotional display, or may present a flat and detached demeanor, as though they are talking of something that happened to a stranger or in a film.

Attorneys who work with asylum seekers know that either end of the spectrum of visible emotional demeanor is dangerous. Many, including Marcus's attorney, role-play asylum interviews and hearings with their clients ahead of these events in an attempt to emotionally prepare them. "My lawyer told me, 'I need you to come and we should practice. I'm going to ask you a few things,'" Marcus remembers. "She was very confident. She was very confident, and I wasn't." The attorney prompted Marcus to recount his story by asking him questions she believed were likely to come up in his interview with the immigration officer. When he would become too emotional, they would pause, regroup, and try again.

The legal asylum process presents a dilemma. Applicants' testimonies must be emotionally effusive enough to suggest to an asylum officer or judge that they are narrating real events but sufficiently calm and composed to communicate a clear chronology of hardship. This leaves some applicants in a double bind: the emotional distress caused by and displayed in an interview or hearing may prevent an asylum seeker from presenting a clear narrative, frustrating asylum officers and judges and provoking suspicion, but the absence of emotional affect may also cause officers and judges to find testimony implausible. Either response can negatively impact the chance of a successful case, even if the applicant's past experiences qualify them for asylum.

Marcus was fortunate to be able to apply affirmatively and to afford a dedicated attorney with the foresight and experience to carefully prepare him to navigate the emotional obstacle course that would be his asylum interview. "She did a great job," Marcus told me. But many asylum seekers first meet their attorneys on the day of their asylum interview or must endure the process alone. In these cases, the moment in which the interviewing asylum officer requests a person's backstory may be the first exhaustive verbal retelling that applicant has ever attempted.

If an officer interprets an affirmative applicant's demeanor as demonstrating untruthfulness, they may decline to approve the case and instead refer the applicant to a judge. If that judge likewise denies their case after a hearing, the asylum seeker may appeal. However, because most nonverbal demeanor is not recordable in the transcript of the hearing, the appellate court often cannot review this aspect of the credibility determination and, as a result, the judge's determination typically stands. The case *Mendoza Manimbao v. Ashcroft* illustrates this clearly:

Weight is given [to] the administrative law judge's determinations of credibility for the obvious reason that he or she sees the witnesses and hears them testify, while the Board and the reviewing court look only at cold records. All aspects of the witness's demeanor—including the expression of his countenance, how he sits or stands, whether he is inordinately nervous, his coloration during critical examination, the modulation or pace of his speech and other non-verbal communication—may convince the observing trial judge that the witness is testifying truthfully or falsely. These same very important factors, however, are entirely unavailable to a reader of the transcript, such as the Board or the Court of Appeals.[4]

The weight given to a judge's interpretation of demeanor and the reluctance to reconsider this determination on appeal presumes that judges have a unique talent for measuring credibility using nonverbal cues.

As detailed in *Sarvia-Quintanilla v. United States I.N.S.*, the idea is that "an immigration judge alone . . . is, by virtue of his acquired skill, uniquely qualified to decide whether an alien's testimony has about it the ring of truth."[5] This view is echoed in a 2009 decision from the Ninth Circuit Court of Appeals that determined that "IJs [immigration judges] are in the best position to assess demeanor and other credibility cues that we cannot readily access on review."[6]

But the idea that judges' expertise makes them "uniquely qualified" to read credibility from demeanor observations is dubitable. It is challenged, for instance, by immigration judge Bruce Einhorn, who concludes from his seventeen years on the bench that "credibility is the single most inconsistently assessed variable in asylum adjudication."[7] Likewise, law professor Michael Kagan charges that, rather than resulting from expert skill, credibility determinations are "frequently based on personal judgment that is inconsistent from one adjudicator to the next, unreviewable on appeal, and potentially influenced by cultural misunderstandings."[8] Writing in the *Columbia Human Rights Law Review*, Nicolas Narbutas contends that "consideration of demeanor gives the implicit biases held by immigration judges the opportunity to rationalize and manifest themselves into inaccurate negative credibility determinations . . . resulting in confusion, inconsistency, and the total inability to constrain immigration judges' discretion."[9] Demeanor during a hearing does not offer unmistakable insight into an applicant's psyche. Allowing demeanor observations to sway case determinations provides a way for some officers' and judges' implicit bias and inexact cultural assumptions to masquerade as reliable discernment.

The inconsistency of credibility determinations based on demeanor is no surprise—communication scholarship shows no consistent correlation between a person's nonverbal demeanor and the truthfulness of their verbal communication, even under everyday conditions.[10] The difficulty of both modulating and interpreting emotional demeanor is exacerbated under high-stakes conditions like the asylum process where the mix of past persecution, the trauma of having to leave one's home, and the difficulty of the asylum process itself intertwine in ways that may cause applicants to become overwhelmed by emotion or, like Marcus described, to be in such a state of shock that they feel completely emotionally absent and disconnected from what is transpiring.

Emotional Distress: Narrating Through Tears

Conversations with the attorneys who represent asylum seekers in court suggest it would be difficult to overstate the degree to which the display of emotional distress can affect the outcome of a case. Attorney Amelia Wilson told me about one New York judge in particular—"I'm not going to use their name because I don't want to immortalize my criticism," Wilson said—who refuses to even hear cases when the applicant is recounting their story through tears.

Wilson believes that, considering all they have endured, her clients should be allowed to express themselves in whatever way makes it possible for them to get through telling their stories, but she has repeatedly seen this particular judge refuse this affordance to asylum seekers. Wilson explained, "She thinks everyone is faking it. I remember a gentleman was talking about how his daughter's death had impacted him, and he started crying, as one would do, and she right away raised her voice, started yelling, kicked him out of the courtroom." Wilson tried to reason with the judge by pointing out that crying can be a natural human response to so much hardship. But the judge was firm, refusing the applicant reentry into her courtroom until he could recite his testimony without crying. When it comes to intolerance for tears in asylum hearings, Wilson revealed, "I'm telling you that she's not even the worst judge in the U.S. Not even close."

Former judge Charles Honeyman pointed me to instances of public record in which judges have been admonished "for making demeanor observations that are inappropriate." New York City judge Noel Ferris was reprimanded by the Second Circuit Court of Appeals for calling an applicant's emotional display "way out of proportion" when the applicant cried while describing how his wife had been beaten and forced to have an abortion. In an interview with the *New York Times* after his case had been appealed, the applicant shared, "I felt very painful talking about the abortion. I was very upset and my tears were coming down my face, and the judge was very impatient. She told me to go out."[11] The idea that credible emotional displays can be substantiated by their proportionality to the severity of a past trauma—and that shedding tears is "out of proportion" to recalling gruesome physical violence against one's spouse—suggests that this judge made a determination about demeanor that was personal rather than empirical.

Blocking out traumatic memories is a coping mechanism commonly used to avoid the emotional pain of the past. Vietnamese refugee author Việt Thanh Nguyễn writes, "I do not remember many things, and for all those things I do not remember, I am grateful, because the things I do remember hurt me enough."[12] Having received refugee status, Nguyễn no longer needs his painful memories to ensure access to protection. But until asylum seekers receive formal immigration status, they do not have the luxury of forgetting or avoiding the emotional retraumatization that the asylum process often demands.

Some applicants find that narrating the past to an immigration officer or judge brings up more and more memories they may have suppressed, causing them to experience and display fresh emotional hardship. Mary remembers that as she was preparing for her case with her lawyer, "The more I talked about it, the memory came." She found, "The more I kept talking, the more I cried." Mary's verbal recounting brought more traumatic memories to the surface; if this resurfacing had happened during a hearing, depending on the presiding judge, Mary's emotional reaction to those memories could have gotten her kicked out of the courtroom. When traumatized individuals are not allowed to express their stories with the emotion that naturally accompanies them, they may become unable to share their testimony comprehensively—a turn of events likely to doom their case.

Dr. Adeyinka Akinsulure-Smith, who is sometimes called on to testify about the psychological evaluations she writes on behalf of her clients, told me she has experienced hearings where "I'm sitting next to my client [and] their anxiety, their fear is palpable. You can feel it coming off of them." Asylum seekers become emotionally overwhelmed due not only to the pain of past hardships but also the fear that the asylum process itself incites. Anna, who fled El Salvador, remembers her credible fear interview vividly even though it was almost three years ago:

It was terrifying . . . emotionally, I wasn't prepared to talk about my experience. For me, it was very hard to open up to somebody and having to tell them why was I coming to the United States. But I knew I had to open up and talk to them about my experience, because my goal was to stay in the United States so I don't have to go back to my country. But overall, it was a terrifying experience because I had a lot of things going on in my head.

Being required to talk about her experience despite not being emotionally prepared for it resulted in an asylum interview that Anna remembers as a terrifying experience. She had little choice but to comply; applicants must risk their psychological safety for the chance at political protection. As has become the norm, Anna's case has been drawn out for several years. She is still waiting to receive notice of the hearing that will determine whether she will be allowed to remain in the United States or denied and deported back to El Salvador.

The feeling of terror that the asylum interview incites can intensify when an interviewing officer does not verbally or nonverbally demonstrate empathy. Mary told me she had the distinct feeling that the person interviewing her did not care about her, and the weight of that impression was almost too much to bear. She explained, "The person that's asking you questions doesn't know who you are. He doesn't care who you are. He's doing his job. He's been given a job to do, he had questions to ask. He's doing the job based on what they ask him to do. But on the other hand, that also affects the asylee. It affects you. Because the questions he asks you? They pierce you." Likewise, Aisha emphasized, "It's very, very hard. You panic, you get scared, and all that." She still thinks back often to her own interview and remembers, "I didn't want to say so much because the more I mentioned, the more I was haunted."

These applicants' reflections of being emotionally pierced, terrified, and haunted by the regular, everyday workings and requirements of the asylum process offer poignant illustration of existing research that suggests the tenets of the contemporary legal asylum process may retraumatize applicants.[13] They also exemplify refugee author Hannah Arendt's notion of the "banality of evil" in which horrendous acts with dire consequences can be committed by ordinary or even well-meaning individuals through processes that are not obviously or purposefully violent but rather "terrifyingly normal."[14]

Arendt suggests that a simple "inability . . . to think from the standpoint of somebody else" may facilitate and perpetuate all kinds of horrors through seemingly mundane and commonly accepted practices.[15] When applied to the context of asylum, Arendt's perspective offers a reminder that immigration officers and judges certainly need not be inherently evil nor bear any hostility toward asylum seekers to still inflict egregious emotional harm.

While some officers and judges exhibit calloused responses to traumatized and sometimes visibly emotional asylum seekers, the empathy of other governmental personnel I interviewed was palpable. Neil Hernandez, whose dissertation research on twentieth-century immigration bureaucracy inspired him to become an asylum officer, told me that he "look[s] at the applicant as enjoying the freedom to express their story any way they deem fit. And, and I fully understand them, because we're talking about difficult circumstances that they may have experienced that might run a range of emotions. And I'm completely prepared for that and accepting of whatever any emotion they might express."

Likewise, some asylum seekers report sensing kindness from their interviewing officers that caused them to feel less afraid about sharing difficult experiences and hopeful about their cases. Wang told me that during her asylum interview she began to struggle with words when talking about not being able to return to China when her grandfather died. She remembers, "I got really emotional talking about my grandpa, and I almost cried. And then the officer was like, 'Yeah, take a breath, and no, don't get too emotional' and she let me cool down before starting to talk to me again." I asked Wang why she thought the officer stopped her when her demeanor began to show she was becoming emotional. She replied, "I feel they are very well trained about handling our emotions. . . . The officers are very nice. They are really nice. They—well, my officer. I have also heard other officers might not be nice. So, she was really easy to talk to. She was very accommodating." The stark differences between the kinds of demeanor exhibited by asylum officers points to the variability of possible experiences in a system that depends on interpersonal communication between those who need protection and those with the power to grant or withhold it.

There is enormous variance in U.S. immigration judges' asylum grant rates that transcends any single explanation. TRAC Immigration, a nonpartisan research center at Syracuse University, maintains decision records for all U.S. immigration judges showing that some have an average of granting 95 percent of cases they hear, while others grant an average of 1 percent. One Louisiana judge has denied every single one of the more than two hundred cases she has heard over the last five years.

This massive divergence in case outcomes has led immigration scholars Philip G. Schrag, Andrew I. Schoenholtz, and Jaya Ramji-Nogales to conclude that some immigration judges' unwillingness to acknowledge the ways individual psychology and other personal and cultural variables influence a case has "created an atmosphere in asylum proceedings that often resembles the crap shoot of a casino more than the judicious proceedings of a court of law."[16]

While the discrepancy in judges' grant rates often confounds those learning about it for the first time, it comes as no surprise to the immigration attorneys who see firsthand the variance in the ways judges treat and respond to some asylum seekers' disposition in court. Attorney Elizabeta Markuci shrugged when I asked her if she could offer an explanation for the difference between judges' grant rates: "The law is not applied fairly to all individuals," she answered unambiguously.

Granted, there are many variables in any asylum case that are beyond a judge's control—whether the applicant has an attorney, the amount of evidence presented, and the accuracy of interpretation, for example—but none of these variables can fully account for the magnitude of the variance across grate rates, signifying that judges interpret deservingness differently, and the nature and form of applicants' narratives and demeanor are central to that interpretation.

Considering that everything from a judge's mood to their implicit bias might influence the outcome of a case, immigration attorneys and advocates work to mitigate any circumstances that might trigger a judge's ire, including unpredictable emotional displays. One common strategy when asylum seekers' emotion seems likely to overwhelm them while telling the narrative of the persecution in their past is to provide the applicant with multiple low-stakes opportunities to narrate their story over weeks or even months in a safe space to mentally prepare for the higher stakes and less gentle prodding that will occur in a hearing.

In *No Justice in the Shadows*, attorney Alina Das describes the process of trying to prepare Luisa, a survivor of domestic violence, for immigration court. Das writes, "We knew that every time we forced her to go through her testimony, we were retraumatizing her."[17] Still, Das knew there was no better alternative. Without any documentary evidence of the abuse she had endured, Luisa's case would hinge on her ability to overcome her emotion enough to describe her violent encounters with her husband in explicit detail on the day of her hearing.

Aisha has served as a translator during several of these preparatory sessions between attorneys and their asylum-seeking clients, and she sometimes struggles to produce an accurate interpretation when clients are too emotionally overwhelmed to speak clearly:

The clients will be crying, crying, crying. Sometimes [the attorneys] have to stop and come back again another time because some stories are so hard that if the people start talking about what they were doing, they cry. It's so emotional. At that point, the lawyers don't want to stress them out. They understand that we can't [finish] today, we'll meet another day. So it takes time to get all the information together. It's not [just] two weeks. It takes months sometimes to even get all the information that they need to be able to file.

In situations where attorneys have ample time and clients are not facing immediate hearing dates, this back and forth can be a productive way of managing the unpredictability of emotion in the asylum process. But for the many applicants who face the process without legal representation or whose cases are scheduled more quickly than expected, the first time they recite their testimony may be in front of the government official who has the authority to determine their fate, leaving them no leeway.

The Calm in the Storm: Emotional Suppression

Several asylum applicants I have talked with remember feeling during their asylum interviews and hearings that they were physically overcome in ways they could not control, unable to moderate their emotion. But others described how they deliberately and successfully suppressed their emotions and attempted to control their affect, sometimes maintaining calm to the extent of becoming altogether disassociated from their story. Abe, whose story appears in the previous chapter and who was forced to flee his home in Nigeria after receiving threats on his life because his sexuality, was shaken by the amount of self-disclosure required during his interview with the asylum officer assigned to his case.

Reflecting on the experience, Abe told me that having to tell so much intimate detail so quickly to a stranger was "like taking off my clothes in front of everybody, that was how I felt." But he was determined to not reveal his terror. "I was trying to suppress my fear, my anger, and all that. I was always trying to stay calm. . . . It was like the fight for my life at that point." Abe's impression that he was fighting for his life as he appealed for protection in the United States is not metaphorical; there are hundreds of confirmed reports of people being murdered after being denied asylum and returned to their countries of origin, and Abe was certain the threats he had received would continue if he was deported back to Nigeria.[18] He feared for himself and for his family. "Because my sexual orientation is known in my community and if I go back and I'm arrested, it must affect my family, you understand," he emphasized.

Beyond all the emotion of dredging up the violent details of his past and worrying about what could happen in the future, Abe faced a more immediate stressor—the officer's demeanor intimidated him. "I must say, he didn't look nice, actually, wasn't friendly," he admitted.

Abe had rehearsed what he was going to say and was trying to recount it in the methodical sequence he had practiced, but the officer kept cutting him off as though his answers were too long, initiating a quicker back and forth that left Abe scrambling for responses. He was still resolved not to let his facade of calm crack under the pressure. "I tried to be as calm as possible because I was scared, actually. I was scared, I must tell you. It was just, God, I don't know how I pulled through," he reflected, shaking his head. "But I was still not to flare up. You understand? Because, if you ask me a question and I'm an adult, I know I should be able to convince you. I was trying to convince him."

Abe's attempt to suppress his feelings of panic and to appear calm and convincing before the officer was echoed in several conversations I have had with other applicants for asylum. These efforts to maintain calm may keep an applicant from becoming overwhelmed by emotion—which, for reasons we have already seen, can be a valuable strategy. But it can also be dangerous. To some judges and asylum officers, an applicant's suppression of emotion suggests a lack of credibility. The expectation that an applicant will display some emotion, but not too much, leaves asylum seekers in a dilemma: both emotional displays and the suppression of emotion may work against them.

Wilson explained how frustrated she becomes when her asylum-seeking clients are expected to toe some invisible line of emotional display that changes from judge to judge. "There are judges who will accuse respondents of malingering or accuse them of fake crying, but then, if they don't cry, then they're not expressing *enough* emotion," she shared with exasperation.

The centrality of demeanor to the process results in what Judge Einhorn charges are "credibility determinations that are grossly unpredictable to asylum seekers and their lawyers (should they have any) and injurious to asylum seekers and to the reputation of immigration judges."[19] In other words, determining an applicant's credibility based on emotional demeanor is bound to result in failures of judgment. Wilson stressed, "People express grief differently, and they experience hardship differently. There are cultural ways of grieving, and cultural ways of talking about harm and torture. So how do you explain that to a judge?"

In fact, asylum officers and judges do receive training about cultural differences in emotional display and the effect of trauma on affect as part of their onboarding curriculum. USCIS warns its officers, "Different cultures view expressions of emotion differently. Though an asylum officer raised in the United States might question the credibility of a child who, without crying or expressing emotion, is able to retell how his or her parents were killed in front of him, it could be that the child was raised in a culture that deems improper any expression of emotion in front of an authority figure."[20]

Including such guidance in the officer training curriculum suggests an attempt to keep officers from incorrectly interpreting emotional displays and using this interpretation in deciding a case. That this training exists is a promising sign, except for the persistent evidence that "interviewers are less likely to believe the account if it is not accompanied by suitable emotional expression"—and what emotional expression is "suitable" remains inextricably culturally bound.[21] Moreover, existing scholarship on credibility determinations clearly demonstrates that implicit bias influences how judges assess the cases they preside over.[22] The intentional or unintentional meaning judges draw when an asylum seeker displays calm rather than distress introduces a unique challenge to the asylum process.

Dr. Renée Sicalides, a psychologist who works to prepare asylum seekers and their children for court, explained to me why some applicants may even appear to "make light" of their experiences during the asylum process. "The way they defend against it [is to act like] it's really not that big a deal." She recently worked with an asylum-seeking father who was likely to be deported without his young daughter, who had been born as an American citizen after the family's arrival in the United States. The father "presented as very laidback and stress free," she explained. "He'd often say, 'It's okay. We'll get through this. It'll be fine.' But he was obviously very worried and upset because he didn't want to leave his family."

Dr. Sicalides knew this father's lackadaisical demeanor was not genuine and that it was likely to work against him in court, so she would not let it slide. "I had to ask really pointed questions and to dig for information and his feelings," she explained. She would purposefully trigger his emotions to activate them, asking questions like, "Okay, so in other words, you're cool with not being here when your daughter graduates high school, or when she gets married—you're okay with that?"

This "dig" for his feelings was immediately successful; although it caused the father emotional pain as he admitted how difficult it would be for him to be separated from his daughter, Dr. Sicalides knew from experience that confronting and displaying this emotion could be integral to winning his case. The judge needed to be able to "see the depth of the emotional and psychological attachment

[to] the child," she explained, "and how traumatic it would be to break this bond." Considering the work of some attorneys to calm their clients' emotions before court in contrast to Dr. Sicalides's attempt to trigger some emotional affect reveals the delicate balance that must be struck in the face of the danger of emotional surplus or lack.

In cases where asylum seekers use calm to show their agency and tenacity, Dr. Sicalides explained, they nonverbally demonstrate that although they endured persecution, they are "good soldier[s]," capable of overcoming adversity. She told me about another client of hers who "kind of minimized her own experience . . . it's about covering it all up. It's about saying you're okay . . . but she was unable to say really how traumatic it was for her, she distanced herself from the trauma." This client's lack of affect was so convincing that "she appeared to be functioning fairly well," even though Dr. Sicalides knew her past still tormented her, leaving her to wonder, "How long will she be able to keep this going?" While an officer or judge may read calm as evidence of an individual's indifference or mendacity, calm demeanor may be but a thin veneer helping one to manage a tortuous reality.

Josh Childress, a former Customs and Border Protection officer, told me he sometimes encountered a kind of "machismo" from incoming migrants at the southern border of the United States. Childress was responsible for determining whether a person should be processed as an asylum seeker. He explained, "I'd say, you know, 'Are you afraid to go [back] to your country?' " In some cases, he remembers, individuals he sensed were in fact in danger "stood up straight and would be like, 'No.' " Officer Childress knew that he "could get [him]self in trouble by telling them, 'No, you need to tell me that you're afraid,' " but he felt conflicted—if the person maintained their resolve and would not admit to experiencing fear, he was supposed to leave the box on his intake form that read "Asylum Seeker" unchecked, and the person would be placed into deportation proceedings. "It's not unreasonable to think that hundreds of people are slipping through the cracks because they're not saying the right words," Childress revealed.

The absence of verbal or nonverbal displays of distress may result from voluntary suppression, as Abe and Officer Childress describe, or occur as a coping mechanism in response to trauma, like for the woman Dr. Sicalides describes. In these latter instances, as psychologist Stuart Turner writes, "Extreme trauma, memories, nightmares, or even vivid flashback experiences produce such marked psychological reactions, with overwhelming emotional distress, that the only viable response is to attempt to shut them out, an internal 'numbing.'"[23] This effort can produce an appearance of calm so profound that it seems the individual could not possibly have encountered the horrors that appear in their asylum claim.

Wilson remembers one of her clients having "such bad PTSD [posttraumatic stress disorder] that he's dissociative. So, when he talks about what happened to him, he becomes very flat. He goes out of his own body." Wilson was concerned for this client when it came time for his hearing, thinking, "He won't sound credible if he's not emoting." Her experience has taught her that displays of emotion "play a huge role" in applicants' perceived credibility. The problem is not calm itself—if every trauma resulted in a dissociative display, judges could come to expect it and use it as a tool for gauging credibility. The problem is rather the *variability* of the effects of trauma on affect. Psychologist Hawk Smith explained this to me most clearly:

> There are people who react to traumatic stressors in varying ways . . . when we sit down with people who might be emotionally laden, if you begin to talk about the trauma, they may cry, they may wail, they may decompensate in the room or whatever, it's just so emotionally laden for them. But at the same time, we might also meet with folks who manifest kind of like a dissociation between their cognitions and their emotions, so they can sit down and talk to you in almost a monotone.

This kind of calm, according to Hawk, may be as much the result of trauma as crying is and therefore should not be used as an indication that clients are not being truthful about their experiences.

A person's emotional affect when recalling traumatic memories is also certain to fluctuate over time, intensifying or diminishing as the period between the traumatic events and talking about them grows. As a result of case backlogs and changing policy, an asylum seeker might be rushed into a credible fear interview mere hours after arriving in the United States or made to wait several years, so that there's no sure way for asylum seekers to plan in advance for having to recount their narratives at a particular time.

Daniel arrived in the United States in 2013, and although he applied for asylum immediately, he has yet to learn when his interview will take place. Affirmative asylum applicants are able to check the status of their cases on the USCIS Case Status website. Each day Daniel hopes for news: "Every day now, I check my case. It says the same—'You have 2,229 days here in this country, and you are waiting for interview'—that's it." The anxiety this stasis causes Daniel has grown over the years; the wait has gotten more and more difficult as he has watched acquaintances and even family members who arrived after him be ushered into interviews and receive decisions.

"Maybe for three years, four years it was good, five years it was good . . . but the last three years, now—it's too many years, it's eight years! Now I feel, like, not safe. In any moment, maybe I cannot live more in this country," Daniel told me. "I feel nervous because I check every day, check in the mailbox if I have something, if I have any letter about the Immigration Office, and nothing. [I think to myself], 'Wow. When?—I need to make a life.'"

Until he knows what his future holds, Daniel feels like he is suspended between two lives. "I am not a resident or citizen. I have eight years in this country, so I feel like in the air, like I don't know what can I do now," he shared. "I don't know. It's too difficult right now what I feel, to explain what I feel."

Whereas Daniel has had to wait so long to tell his story to an asylum officer that it now causes him daily anxiety, others find themselves rushed into interviews before they have fully processed the trauma they experienced in their home countries, leaving them panicky and underprepared. Marcus told me that when it came time for his interview, "I knew that I had to explain everything, but sometimes I think I wasn't ready to tell her every detail. I knew that I had to write every detail, but it's different when you have to talk about it." Writing about and talking about the persecution that one has faced require distinct communicative functions. A person may be fully prepared for one and still at a loss when undertaking the other.

Many asylum seekers I have interviewed and worked with did not fully understand the asylum process upon their submission of an application and therefore did not know what to expect, making it naturally more difficult to remain calm during the wait for an interview. Abe shared, "I didn't know how long this was going to take . . . I didn't even understand what the law states about applying for asylum. I didn't even know what it entails. So, it was depressing and tough for me." Unfortunately, even if Abe had been more familiar with the law, it would have been impossible for him to predict how long his case would take and how his interviewing officer's demeanor would affect him.

Highly aware that the unpredictability of the system is one of the primary deterrents to an applicant's well-being and ability to begin healing from trauma, the psychologists who work with the few asylum seekers who are able to access psychological support during the asylum process spend a good deal of time on calming practices. Calming practices are designed to help an individual work through their trauma and develop more control over their thoughts and feelings in order to achieve a mental state that allows them to talk about their experiences in front a judge without becoming overwhelmed. But in some cases the calm these advocates work to cultivate is interrupted; all three psychologists I interviewed described to me the frustration they feel when their calming efforts are, in the words of Dr. Akinsulure-Smith, "taken hostage" by sudden movement in a case that clearly imperils the applicant's well-being and chances for success.

Dr. Akinsulure-Smith explained that her practice at Bellevue Hospital's Program for Survivors of Torture greatly depends on having ample time to build trust with a client before ever addressing the details of their asylum claim. But increasingly, she faces a problem:

> One of the things that I always find challenging is, so we're building all this trust and rapport and taking our time. And then there's [a] process that, just as it is out of our clients' control, many times it's also out of our control. I may be doing all of this rapport building, we're okay, we're not going to talk about— right now we're going to focus on helping you sleep better. We're going to do some relaxation; we're going to do some grounding stuff. Then, I get a call from the attorney saying, "Okay, [we're] going into court in a month!" And so then we go from having been stabilized to nightmares coming up, anxiety attacks. I always talk about it as our treatment being taken hostage by the asylum process. Then it becomes, okay we're going to stop what we're doing with our treatment. Focus on calming you down.

Whereas asylum seekers in the situation Dr. Akinsulure-Smith describes may feel they have too little time to prepare, in fact it's common for cases to be postponed even after they are scheduled or for case decisions to be deferred at the end of a hearing. Applicants are then held in limbo in the legal process for even longer. Dr. Akinsulure-Smith shrugged. "So you never know what's going to happen. You never know if your hearing is going to get postponed. People who've had all this angst, all this anxiety, get there [to the hearing] and then—Oh! It's been postponed. So go back and regroup. Yeah. There's a lot of variability in what might or might not happen that can be horrible." During this time, she stressed, "Your life is in limbo. If you can get employment authorization, okay. But otherwise, [not being authorized to work] adds to the distress and the symptoms, making things worse."

The importance afforded to emotional demeanor by asylum officers and judges creates an invisible, unrealistic, and constantly shifting benchmark for asylum applicants, who are expected to be calm enough to clearly and methodically recount their histories of persecution without becoming overwhelmed by emotion but who also must maintain enough of a connection to their emotions that they appear emotionally credible. As the narrators in this chapter reveal, striking a balance between being calm enough but not too calm is complicated by trauma and by the unpredictable scheduling of asylum interviews and hearings, which may occur suddenly or only after a wait that lasts several years, jeopardizing not only applicants' narrative ability in front of the governmental personnel who determine their fate but also asylum seekers' mental health, well-being, and ability to plan for the future.

In Their Own Words

Ethan Taubes, Asylum Officer Trainer

I WAS LOOKING FOR WORK. I heard through the grapevine that there was this gig called being an asylum officer, which I had never even heard about and I was intrigued. I kind of was blindsided by working for the government. It was a little bit like working in the belly of the beast. I really did not have an appetite for it. I was very contrarian and oppositional and kind of like a rebel. I'm from the '68 generation in a way and did a lot of protesting and demonstrating. We have to change life and we wanted world revolution. Things didn't turn out the way we hoped to say the least, but I overcame my initial reluctance. The government's the government, and I didn't quite trust its institutional prerogatives and honesty and all that or goodwill. But I was pleasantly surprised. I entered into a very special agency. It's unique—I think—it's kind of unprecedented in the government. It attracts highly qualified people. People that are really just dedicated to that mission.

Asylum is a unique type of engagement. There was a revolution in the asylum adjudication regime in this country in 1991, and part of what resulted from that critical moment was the creation of a professional Asylum Officer Corps so that there would be people who actually were subject-matter experts interviewing applicants seeking sanctuary and asylum protection in the United States. Because before, that had not existed and asylum had been completely politically driven and viewed through a Cold War lens, which distorted the entire process.

Even though we had signed and ratified the Refugee Convention and the Protocol, we were not really abiding by its spirit. A refugee was really defined through who the State Department decided to designate as a refugee and not because they met the refugee definition. This was all part and parcel of that Cold War perspective.

Prior to 1996, anybody who applied for asylum automatically got a work permit, right? There was no waiting period, so this created a huge backlog because there was a lot of filings of frivolous asylum claims. We're talking into the hundreds of thousands, and we were not staffed that way. You had to ramp up like crazy, and they didn't. The office space was just kind of—there was no real training syllabus or curriculum at that point. Everything had to be invented basically from scratch, and that was done and now it's perhaps one of the best training programs in the federal government.

[There] is a very sophisticated training syllabus. It's a five- to six-week period of going down to FLETC [Federal Law Enforcement Training Center] in Georgia. It combines a lot of different techniques of going over international law but also looking at all the doctrinal areas and includes also trying to mix it up with talking to doctors who deal with vicarious trauma, and trying to understand cultural differences and how that can distort perception, and the problem of unconscious bias. It's a very complex mosaic of all the different types of disciplines that you need to basically master.

You can break it down to really three very different disciplines that have to be synthesized and mastered in order for one to become a consummate and effective asylum officer: the first is the most obvious, which is to be able to conduct a fair and impartial interview. You can be a wonderful scholar, but if you don't have intuitive interpersonal skills, if you don't know how to develop a line of questioning, if you don't know how to be non-adversarial, if you don't have a good bedside manner that invites a person who might be particularly traumatized or who is an excellent prevaricator to show their hand, to expose themselves, to confide in you—you will not be very successful in developing a record in the requisite amount of time that you have because it's like a shotgun marriage. You don't have a lot of time to waste. That's number one.

The second thing that you have to really be able to do well is to conduct research because there are no regional experts. You don't have a certain group of officers who deal with gender-related claims or Latin American claims because that would create administrative chaos. If, say, all three Latin American experts were sick one day, we'd have to send every applicant from Latin America back who was set up for an interview that day and, administratively speaking, you can't run a bureaucracy that way. Basically, as an officer you have to be an expert in every particular orientation. The research is critical because, we don't have the luxury of cross-examination. The only way that we can really test and probe and vet an applicant's credibility is through how well-researched and prepared we are and by looking over all of the documents. Research involves going through the file very, very carefully and comparing different types of testimony, whether it's the written application or information contained in other documents or the country conditions.

You want to drill deep and granular into a lot of different things. If you know nothing, if you come with a veil of ignorance, then how are you going to determine credibility? You could be taken in by anybody and you wouldn't be able to distinguish the wheat from the chaff, the impostor from the genuine refugee.

So there's process issues, procedural issues, and third, there's also substantive law issues. That means you have to be able to interpret case law, look at statutory and regulatory law—it all works together. To show you how slippery or challenging that is, just take the example of the Supreme Court, where you're dealing with the same set of facts and yet different philosophical points of view can lead you to very different outcomes on how you interpret that record.

There are many challenges. I think there are different stressors in this job. Again, there's a subjective component to that. I think for me, I came from an advocacy background. I did not have a kind of impartial, tribunal type of sensibility. I needed to readjust my perspective and approach—it was a bit of a transition. I had to think very seriously and carefully about controlling my advocacy tendencies one way or the other and also not to make moral judgments.

There are sometimes applicants who come before you who you're not particularly thrilled by their kind of moral character, but they nevertheless meet the refugee definition. Or there can be people who seem extremely sympathetic but have insurmountable barriers because of legal bars or because there are serious inconsistencies or discrepancies that can't be overcome, where they have basically dug their own graves, their own credibility graves or hung themselves with their own rope. There's just nothing you can do to salvage the claim. You try.

You also have to have a very high tolerance for ambiguity. This is not a science. You're not dealing with mathematical proofs. You don't have a lie detector on your desk to say, "Well, this person is telling the truth." It really is an art, and it's kind of like you have certain indicia of reliability that you are looking for one way or the other.

None of us are experts in country conditions to the degree that we should be in being able to avoid serious error. . . . And that's just one layer of it. There can also be factual misunderstandings, or misjudgments. There can be so many different errors on the level of interpretation or of the wrong standard that you're applying or of misinterpreting somebody you mistakenly believe is inconsistent. It's a very fallible and fragile process, the work that we do. The chances of abuse of discretion in that process is so high simply because we're not gods, right? We're not infallible. We're not clairvoyant.

4

Nonverbal Communication
and Credibility

THE OFFICER WHO INTERVIEWED Maria at the culmination of her asylum case was friendly. "She was very kind, very humane, and made me feel very comfortable to speak with her," Maria remembers. Even the setup of the office helped to put her at ease. Maria had felt intimidated at the mandatory U.S. Immigration and Customs Enforcement check-ins she had previously attended at the imposing USCIS field office in downtown Manhattan, and she was grateful to find her interview was in a more intimate and less menacing location. "It was not very intense, like the office in Manhattan where you see a lot of security surrounding," Maria recalled. "It was more in a comfortable setting. . . . It was very hidden but not very terrifying as going to the office back in Manhattan."

The officer conducting the interview listened carefully to Maria's story, taking notes on the details from behind a computer screen while Maria and her attorney sat on the other side of the large desk. Maria answered the officer's questions dutifully, but she tensed when the officer asked if she had ever been detained by immigration officials at the U.S.–Mexico border. "No," Maria answered, just as she had practiced with her lawyer. The officer looked back at her computer screen, and asked again: "Were you *ever* detained?"

"No," Maria replied again.

Turning from her computer to face Maria more directly, the officer spoke softly. She told Maria that it was better for her to tell the truth and that a lie could affect her ability to have a successful case. "I decided to tell the truth, because I knew that she was already seeing the truth on the computer screen," Maria told me. The officer knew what Maria had hoped she could avoid altogether: her most recent journey had not been the only time she had entered the United States.

After fleeing her abusive husband with her two young children, Maria had gone to live with her mother in a nearby town but could not find work and knew it was just a matter of time before her husband came looking for them. She left for the United States in hopes of getting a job that would allow her to earn enough money to hire a lawyer and bring her children to New York, where they would be protected from abuse. But just a few months after her arrival, Maria's daughter became frighteningly ill. Without hesitation, Maria returned to Mexico and stayed until her daughter recovered. But when she tried to return to the United States without being detected at the border, Maria, along with the group she was traveling with, was detained by U.S. Immigration and Customs Enforcement and released back into Mexico, where they waited only a few days before entering again, this time without being detected. Within a few years, Maria had earned the money she needed to pay the guides that would lead her children across the border. Reunited in New York, they were at least temporarily safe from her abusive ex-husband, but their future was still anything but sure.

As soon as Maria admitted to the officer that she had been detained before, she felt ashamed. "I was feeling very guilty because I felt like it was all my fault," she told me. The guilt was not just about lying to the officer; she had also lied to her attorney, with whom she had grown close during the months leading up to her interview. Although Maria knew she was supposed to tell her attorney everything about her story, she feared that if she knew about Maria's former detainment, she would not agree to represent her. "I was very fearful that they would not take my case and they would shut it down. I knew that if I went back to Mexico . . . I was very scared to go back," Maria explained. She had recently learned that her ex-husband had raped their daughter; he had also threatened to kill Maria if they ever returned to Mexico. It was a risk that she was determined to avoid at all costs—"that's why I was fearful and not confessing the experience I went through," she emphasized.

The coyote who had guided Maria and others on their previous unauthorized journey to the United States had advised everyone in her group to use fake names if they were caught, and Maria had hoped that since she had followed that advice, no one would be able to affiliate her with that trip. She did not know exactly where she had been detained or remember what name she had given, but the asylum apparatus includes a fingerprint database of everyone who has been apprehended, and Maria's prints had produced a match.

"After the interview was over, I apologized to the person interviewing me and also to my lawyer for not mentioning the experience I went through," Maria explained. "I told them I didn't want to say anything because I didn't want to go back to Mexico, and I didn't want to lose. That my daughter was already in the United States, and for me to go back to Mexico was one of my fears, that's why I was neglecting [to reveal] the experience I went through."

When they left the asylum office, Maria's attorney asked to speak with her privately. "She was very angry at me because she had asked me this before, and she had asked because she wanted to know what to do in case this happened," Maria described. Her attorney was clearly frustrated and the way she spoke to Maria made her realize the potential consequence of her omission. Maria had been untruthful because she felt it was her only way forward, and now that the truth had come out and she had seen her attorney's response, she was certain that the government would shut down her case due to her lie. She told me, "If [the officer] had sent me back, I would not have been angry at her, but I would have felt guilty because it was my fault for not confessing it in the first place." Her reflection helps illustrate why some asylum seekers with defensibly credible claims that qualify them for asylum still lie when recounting the past. For Maria, the possibility of re-exposing her children to the physical and sexual violence her ex-husband was likely to inflict if they returned to Mexico overshadowed everything else.

Maria's experience also provides insight into the many kinds of nonverbal and paralinguistic communication and behaviors present in asylum interviews and hearings, and how immigration personnel, applicants, and attorneys observe and interpret these nonverbal cues, consciously or unconsciously, as they navigate a case from different perspectives. Maria's vivid memories of the officer's kindness and the calming physical configuration of her office show how such conditions can put a person more at ease. Her recollection of the moment she realized she had been caught in a lie, from the way the officer was looking at her after looking at her computer screen to the angry tone her attorney used after learning the truth, reveals how these nonverbal behaviors act as clues that impact asylum seekers' experiences of their interviews and expectations about what will follow.

This chapter addresses two questions: To what extent do immigration personnel use asylum seekers' nonverbal communication as they work to make sense of and determine the credibility of an asylum claim? And what do the firsthand reflections of asylum seekers reveal about their eye contact, movement, and body language during the asylum process and the relationship of these behaviors to culture and trauma? Because the audio recordings produced during asylum interviews and hearings leave out much of the nonverbal communication that takes place, obscuring the nature and scope of the role it plays, the perspectives of those directly involved in the asylum process are vital for answering these questions.[1]

Throughout this chapter I draw from conversations with judges, attorneys, asylum officers, and asylum seekers from Latin America, Africa, and Asia and from my own ethnographic observations of asylum hearings at the immigration courts in New York City to recover the visibility of nonverbal communication in the legal asylum process.[2]

Nonverbal communication, in its most capacious definition, "includes all communicative acts except speech."[3] This broad definition includes emotional affect and paralinguistic characteristics like speaking rate and volume as well as kinesthetic displays such as body movement, posture, and facial expression—all of which are used to interpret meaning.[4] As we have already attended thoroughly to emotional affect in the previous chapter, here I turn to these other paralinguistic behaviors and kinesthetic displays.

If nonverbal communication merely reinforced verbal communication in the asylum process, interrogating its effect would not be as imperative. But it is clear from existing communication research that nonverbal communication may either reinforce or contradict verbal communication.[5] Moreover, in cases where verbal and nonverbal communication are incongruent, nonverbal communication may "alter an accompanying incongruent verbal message in the direction of the nonverbal cues"—that is, nonverbal communication is more convincing than verbal communication, so when the two disagree, the receiver is likely to rely on the nonverbal message.[6]

Much work has been done to try to find a relationship between some nonverbal behaviors and truthfulness; the idea that a lie can be detected using the speaker's tone or eye contact is an appealing premise, but the results have demonstrated an uncertain and unpredictable relationship between such behaviors and veracity.[7] The meanings assigned to the nonverbal communication that accompanies the autobiographical storytelling required by the asylum process is complicated by the fact that nonverbals differ from culture to culture. Asylum hearings are by nature intercultural, and a wide body of existing work shows clearly and repeatedly that culture affects how nonverbals are both displayed and interpreted.[8]

In the context of the legal asylum process, a determination that an applicant is being untruthful does not need to be accurate in order to have serious consequences. Sizing up the impact of nonverbal communication requires a perspective that allows asylum applicants themselves to describe the experience of being required to autobiographically narrate their trauma.[9] This is especially true because inferences about nonverbal behaviors too easily privilege an observer's interpretation and can lead to mistaken assumptions about a narrator's intent.

Although work on the matter of nonverbal communication in the asylum process has been scant in the United States, some existing international work has taken up this matter. Toni Johnson's writing shows how "the asylum court must rely on more than just language" to interpret an applicant's testimony and how asylum seekers in the United Kingdom may assert their agency through silence during court hearings.[10] In a study from Belgium, Katrijn Maryns and Jan Blommaert demonstrate how paralinguistic factors like accent and phonetic fusions interact with grammar to serve as clues about asylum applicants' geographic and temporal experiences, even if applicants do not discuss these experiences directly.[11] Didier Fassin and Estelle d'Halluin write that the asylum seeker's body itself "has become the place of production of truth" in the asylum process in France as a body's scars may communicate nonverbal evidence of physical torture in asylum cases.[12] This chapter builds on these international studies by putting their findings in conversation with asylum seekers, judges, attorneys, and psychologists who reflect on the lived experience of sending and receiving nonverbal messages during asylum interviews and hearings in the United States.

Two theoretical principles offer guidance through this thorny territory. I draw throughout this chapter on communication scholar Stuart Hall's notions of *encoding* and *decoding*.[13] Hall describes the processes by which ideas and thoughts are translated (encoded) into communicative symbols for the sake of meaning making between two individuals or groups. The receiver of a message must then decode—or apply personal meaning to—these symbols so that they can be put to use. I also make use of James Carey's assertion that reality is "produced, maintained, repaired, and transformed" through communication to illuminate how nonverbal behaviors have tangible consequences in the context of asylum.[14]

Whereas Hall and Carey are primarily interested in how communicative meanings are packaged into and shared via language, we can easily apply the tenets of their arguments to nonverbal communication, as others have done.[15] We can deduce from Carey and Hall's work that, like speech, nonverbal communication acts as a series of symbols that a listener decodes and derives meaning from—meaning that creates, sustains, or disrupts some reality. Just as the meaning one derives from words depends highly on what Hall calls a listener's "structures of understanding"—that is, life experiences, assumptions, ideologies, and connotative definitions—so too does the meaning one derives from nonverbal communication.[16]

Carey and Hall push meaning to the forefront of any communicative process as both the impetus for and the result of communication. This approach follows from their shared disbelief that communication can convey the substance of any reality. For Carey, communication "has no essence" of its own.[17] Hall likewise insists that "events can only be signified" and any piece of communication "cannot, of course *be* the referent or concept it signifies."[18] This is critical to understanding why nonverbal communication functions in such problematic ways. Without the ability to communicate the substance of an experience, an asylum seeker must package the meaning they intend to deliver into a symbol: words or nonverbal messages.

When we apply Hall and Carey's assertions to the asylum process, two realities come into focus. First, it becomes clear that the autobiographical narrative an asylum seeker tells in a credible fear interview or a court hearing is not the experience of persecution itself but rather an interpretation of the experience, which will be interpreted again ("decoded," in Hall's language) by an asylum officer or immigration judge. Storytelling is a skill not equally mastered by all; in the asylum process, as we have already seen, all kinds of factors can affect one's ability to successfully narrate the past, including the effects of trauma, time constraints, varying levels of preparedness, the presence and quality of legal representation, and the nature of the governmental personnel's questions.

Second, Hall and Carey's work reveals that nonverbal communication tells a story of its own, in Carey's words, "render[ing] communication a far more problematic activity than it ordinarily seems."[19] If, as my interviews and observations suggest, nonverbal communication has the power to influence asylum decisions, it demands a much closer look.

"What does a torture survivor look like?"

When Edgar arrived in New York City in 2018, he was full of hope: "I got here with a lot of great expectations. The whole world knows that this country is considered a country of opportunities, and so my expectations were good." Edgar had sustained serious physical violence in Venezuela due to his political opposition to the government, and he felt confident that U.S. immigration officials would understand and accept his need for protection. But when he arrived at the building where his asylum interview was to take place, he started to feel a nagging doubt: "Because the feeling of uncertainty, the long faces that you see, the low attitudes, all of the things you feel in that moment, and considering that the security guard, the man in charge of security, speaks to you rudely, looks at you rudely. . . ." Shaken by the scene but resolved to do his best during the interview, Edgar waited patiently with his attorney for the officer to call them in.

"When we walked into the interview, the officer was very, very blunt, or rude," Edgar remembers. "I mean, she didn't look at me. She would, like, scold me when I wanted to speak—she wouldn't let me talk. Basically, she intimidated me. . . . She was on her computer, and she mostly looked at the lawyer, she didn't look at me much. Only when she didn't like my answers, she would tell the lawyer and then look at me." While explaining one of the violent encounters he had survived in Venezuela, Edgar got the feeling that the officer thought he was lying. The panic he felt about being seen as dishonest initiated a nonverbal response no one expected—he laughed.

At the sound of this nervous outburst of laughter, the room immediately stilled. Edgar remembers that the officer "put her hands on the desk, and she looked me directly in the eye; the lawyer looked at me like '[How could you] even think about laughing?'" Flustered, Edgar tried to explain his behavior: "I said, 'Well, I'm sorry. I made a mistake.' I said, 'Understand the pressure I'm under, I mean, it's normal for people to get nervous in front of you. I didn't come to say lies.'" The officer listened to his explanation, but Edgar suspected the damage had been done. "I felt like she was looking for a way to reject [me], like the more rejections, the better," he told me. He left feeling dejected. Having determined that she did not have sufficient grounds to grant asylum, the officer instead referred his case to a judge who is scheduled to hear it in 2022. Until then, there is little Edgar can do but wait.

Edgar's memory of his interview highlights the range of nonverbal communicative behaviors that impact even a single step of the asylum process. From the security guard's tone to the "long faces" and "low attitudes" of other applicants Edgar observed before his interview began, the unsettling effect of the lack of eye contact the officer displayed, and the surprise in his lawyer's face upon hearing unexpected laughter, nonverbal communication imbued Edgar's experience and affected his interpretation of the day's events. He was so discouraged by the experience that he has repeatedly considered trying to self-deport before his court date arrives, even though he knows that he would be almost certain to experience more violence at home in Venezuela.

Edgar is one of many narrators who has emphasized the central role nonverbal communication has played in their legal pursuit of asylum. Jorge, who was born in Colombia and, like Edgar, has had his interview but is still waiting for his court date, told me the way his interviewing officer moved and the look on her face during the interview made it seem as if she was bothered. He remembers: "I don't know, I felt like she was—like her gestures, her face expressions—I think she was annoyed when she was listening . . . she didn't treat me poorly but I could feel that vibe." What another young asylum seeker named Travis remembers about the demeanor of the officer who interviewed him was how little he could understand from it: "During the whole process, she [was] pretty, how do you say . . . emotionless? She was pretty behaving professionally, rigid. There's not much you could read from her face or her feelings." An interviewee named Marcus shared that, during his interview, the officer kept her gaze focused on the paperwork in front of her: "I was watching her eyes, and she was reading or writing . . . it felt like she wasn't paying attention. When you are telling something very important, you want the person to keep eyes on you." It is clear from these accounts that asylum seekers are not merely observing the nonverbal communication of their interviewing officers but also attempting to interpret what it *means*—such as Edgar reading the officer's facial expressions as annoyance or Marcus interpreting a lack of eye contact as inattention.

As participants in a legal process very likely to render them ineligible for continued residence in the United States, asylum seekers use whatever meager resources are available to them to navigate the byzantine legal process. Nonverbal communication may provide clues to indicate how the process is going, but Stuart Hall reminds us that decoding in unfamiliar and intercultural contexts is not an exact science; nonverbal messages are "transformable into more than one connotative configuration" rather than predictable deliveries of fixed meanings.[20]

This interpretive uncertainty is exacerbated by the circumstances under which asylum seekers give their testimonies. Former officer Martha Parmalee explained, "There's a limited amount of time you're allowed for the interview"; officers constantly face the pressure of extracting testimony in a short window. Martha told me, "That's too much, in my opinion, for real cases." The idea that "real cases" may require more time to process than the government allots is alarming and suggests that even individuals with credible claims are not being given enough of an opportunity to prove them. In 2018 the Department of Justice (DOJ) released a memo announcing that they would begin evaluating immigration judges on how many cases they close and how fast they hear cases, setting a standard of seven hundred complete cases a year.[21] To elicit the amount of testimony needed to make a decision in a restricted amount of time, officers and judges may feel pressure to intuit an individual's credibility as quickly as possible and, as a result, may depend more on nonverbal communication than they would otherwise.

When I asked former judge Charles Honeyman how important an applicant's nonverbal communication is in the determination of a case, he answered, "I think that more often than not, demeanor observations should not affect an outcome of a case. Unfortunately, I think for some judges, they're very important."

Immigration personnel drawing meaning from asylum seekers' nonverbal behavior has not always been legally allowed. Ethan Taubes, who has served as both an asylum officer and a supervisor and trainer of asylum officers, pointed out that before the Real ID Act was passed in 2005, "officers were basically prohibited from considering demeanor unless it was really an extraordinary circumstance because it's so unreliable." Demeanor likely implicitly influenced immigration personnel's credibility determinations before

2005, but the Real ID Act made such interpretations officially permissible. Despite swift criticism from immigrant advocates and human rights organizations—Amnesty International USA charged in a 2005 press conference that codifying "highly subjective credibility factors, including a person's 'demeanor,' as a basis for denying asylum" means that the "Passage of [the] Real ID Act ultimately will amount to grave danger for asylum seekers"—the practice remains in place.

Whereas nonverbal communication may be obscured in the hearing transcripts that scholars often analyze when studying the asylum process, reflections from the published work of the attorneys who represent asylum seekers reveals the prominent role it plays in asylum hearings. Attorney Alina Das, codirector of the Human Rights Clinic at the New York University School of Law, writes about how she communicates nonverbally with her clients during hearings when it is not possible to talk directly with them. Describing the asylum hearing for a domestic violence survivor named Luisa, Das explains that after the judge ruled Luisa eligible to be considered for a waiver that could help protect her from deportation, "I caught Luisa's eye and gave her a small smile, willing her to understand that this was good news."[22] Das also tries to interpret her clients' nonverbals during court hearings to gauge how they are doing and what they may need. For instance, when the judge turned his attention to Luisa for her testimony, Das writes,

> The silence in the room was thick. Luisa kept her eyes downward. I spied her rocking slowly back and forth. A panic attack was beginning. . . . Luisa took a deep breath. She brought her hands to her face, running them across her forehead, her eyes, her cheeks as if to wipe away the tears before they came. [She said] "Violence. That's what I remember. The violence." The tears came flooding down. But she shook her head, as if to tell us that she could do this.[23]

Das's short reflection on this one hearing points to a multitude of meanings communicated through several nonverbal behaviors—making eye contact, smiling, silence, fixing a gaze downward, rocking, deep breathing, face touching, tears, and head shaking. None of these nine behaviors would be evident in a hearing transcript, and yet each was perceived, interpreted, and, in Hall's words, "put to a use"—that is, employed to make meaning in Luisa's case. In the hearings that I have observed, it is frequently clear that applicants' attorneys act as nonverbal liaisons between the judge and the applicant, frequently looking back and forth between the two and responding to nonverbal cues from each, as Das describes.

When I interviewed Dr. Hawk Smith, who sometimes conducts trainings with asylum personnel about the lasting psychological effects of trauma, he explained, "We've done trainings with immigration judges, with asylum officers in the past, and sometimes they'll ask that question, 'What does a torture survivor look like in an emotional sense?'" Hawk and his team explain that because trauma affects different people in different ways, it is not possible to determine who has survived torture and who has not merely by observing their nonverbal demeanor. This desire to know what kind of archetypal "look" a torture survivor might have bolsters Agnes Woolley's charges that the asylum process depends on "an idealized version of refugeehood" in which officers and judges measure applicants not just according to their unique narratives but also by how those narratives align with the officer or judge's expectations about how forced migrants should behave.[24]

The experiences collected here leave little doubt that perception and interpretation of nonverbal communication are multidirectional in the asylum process; asylum seekers, officers, judges, and attorneys are watching and making meaning from each other's behaviors. Officers and judges rely on more than just verbal descriptions of persecution to understand the details of a case, and asylum seekers use the nonverbal communication of immigration personnel as a resource to understand how the unfamiliar process is going.

Putting nonverbal communication to use for interpretive purposes is common and neither surprising nor specific to the asylum process. However, looking more closely at one group of nonverbal behaviors in particular—eye contact and eye movement—shows that in some cases nonverbal interpretation goes beyond just momentary sensemaking. These behaviors hold the power to influence credibility determinations and, consequently, case outcomes so that the futures of migrants fleeing persecution hang in the balance.

Eye Contact and Eye Movement: Credibility and Confidence

Observing even a single asylum hearing makes clear that eye contact and eye movement serve several interactive functions in the courtroom, including indicating to whom a question is directed, demonstrating interest or a willingness that a person continue talking, and accompanying the beginning and end of speaking turns for an interpreter. The interviews I conducted reveal that beyond these more easily observed pragmatic communicative functions, eye contact also serves a more consequential purpose, indiscernible by mere observation: both asylum seekers and judges link eye contact and movement with credibility and confidence, and judges formulate interpretations and base their determinations about deservingness of protection on more than what an applicant reveals verbally.

Before an officer or judge can determine whether an individual's experience meets the definition of a refugee, they first make a determination regarding the applicant's credibility. In the asylum hearings I have observed or served as an expert witness, the determination of credibility is often the first finding a judge offers when declaring a "decision"—whether a person's application for asylum has been approved or denied. Credibility is the linchpin of the asylum process. If it is not established, none of the details of an asylum seeker's narrative can benefit the case.

Having personally witnessed dozens of asylum seekers' cases denied, Aisha knows intimately the significance of credibility. She works at a nonprofit in Manhattan that helps African immigrants navigate the asylum process. A certified translator fluent in six languages, she has been present for many asylum interviews and hearings, and she was the first to explain to me why immigrant-serving organizations that prepare asylum seekers for interviews and hearings may devote a good deal of time to raising applicants' awareness of the importance of eye contact.

"You see, in Africa, when I talk to you, it's not respectful when I'm talking to you to look right in your eyes," Aisha described. "So, many clients wouldn't want to look at you when they are explaining their stories because they feel that it's disrespectful to talk to people. But the lawyers [who represent some of the asylum seekers] tell them, 'Look, I understand—I know it's the culture, but the person you're going to meet during the interview will not understand that.'" In these instances, asylum seekers are asked to adapt their communication style to the immigration personnel's or risk threatening their credibility determination.

Attention to the relationship of eye contact and credibility is not specific to asylum cases with African applicants. In a study of participants from fifty-eight countries, the Global Deception Research Team found that "the most common belief about deception worldwide is that liars avoid eye contact."[25]

Amadeo, who fled Peru after facing persecution related to his membership in a particular social group, did whatever he could to look the officer assigned to his case in the face throughout his asylum interview because, he believes, "Body language, I guess, means a lot. Especially for them, because they can probably tell that way if you're being honest." At one point the officer who was interviewing him asked Amadeo a question he was not sure how to answer. Although his lawyer was seated just to his left and Amadeo knew that a quick glance at the expression on his lawyer's face may help to clarify how he should answer the question, he forced himself to resist the urge to turn away from the officer, worried it would make the officer think he was not being truthful. "I needed to see him straight in the eye," he determined.

It is not possible to know whether Amadeo's eye contact impacted the officer's interpretation of his veracity, but his hunch that asylum personnel regularly interpret even the most minute nonverbal behaviors was unambiguously confirmed by the judges and officers I interviewed. Judge Honeyman explained how he used nonverbals during his time on the bench as a means of telling how complete someone's testimony is—"Sometimes it looks like they're going to want to say something, but they retreat"—but affirmed that it is difficult to know for sure what a particular nonverbal communication means. He used the example of an asylum applicant "moving their feet nervously under their chair or wetting their lips"— actions that may "look like nervousness to the judge." In reality, he stressed, "There could be all kinds of reasons why an individual might be doing that, and not because [of] a fabricated claim." Honeyman is right to suggest that differing internal and external factors may lead to the same nonverbal behavior, so it is not possible to conclusively trace a nonverbal behavior to a definitive origin or impetus.

Well aware of the likelihood of misinterpretation, Aisha and her colleagues often explain to the lawyers with whom their clients work that eye contact may not mean what it seems to mean: "Sometimes they will just look at [a lack of eye contact] as maybe the person is not credible, but it's not that. It's just a cultural difference. . . . We try to explain to them that it's a cultural thing, that's why they're not looking. We can work on it." Working to change a lifelong sociocultural understanding of eye contact and to adapt one's nonverbal communication to a more normative expression during what is likely one of the most stressful situations in one's life may seem like an unnecessary burden to ask an asylum seeker to bear, especially considering that the DOJ's training materials for officers explicitly recognizes that "there may be cultural reasons why an [applicant] will not maintain eye contact with an Asylum Officer during an interview. . . . This is a product of culture, not necessarily of credibility."[26] But considering that an adverse credibility determination in most cases leads to deportation, it is clear why Aisha and other advocates sometimes spend a good deal of time and effort to ensure that asylum seekers know how to perform the kind of eye contact likely to reinforce rather than diminish their credibility.

Interestingly, while both Aisha and the DOJ reference and try to disrupt the common inference that eye contact is positively correlated to credibility, existing nonverbal communication research suggests that individuals who are lying are *more* likely to maintain deliberate eye contact than individuals telling the truth, so the correlation between eye contact and credibility is the inverse of what is commonly assumed. In a study of eye contact's relationship to deceit, Samantha Mann and her coauthors found that liars go to greater lengths to make eye contact with their interlocuters both to convince the listener of their veracity and to judge whether the listener is convinced.[27] Timothy Levine, Kelli Jean Asada, and Hee Sun Park found in their research that listeners who were told in advance that a message would contain lies "reported observing significantly less eye contact" than if they were not told in advance about the veracity of the message: "That is, although a person's nonverbal behavior affects the extent to which they are seen as dishonest, it is apparently also the case that the extent to which they are perceived as dishonest affects how people see a person's actions."[28] This research suggests a clear link between eye contact and perceived credibility, but Charles Ruby and John Brigham's earlier work complicates these findings by emphasizing that ethnic bias may affect one's ability to detect deception.[29] Ultimately, it seems, people are more certain than they should be that they can tell whether someone is lying based on their eye contact.

Aisha told me that in her experience, the perceived relationship of eye contact to credibility is built on perceptions of confidence. "If you don't look at them when you speak, they think you're not confident, you're not telling them the truth," she explained concisely. "Because if you are not confident in what you are saying, what happened to you, the way you talk about it, if you are not confident, somebody might not believe you." In Aisha's view, confidence and credibility are mutually constitutive—a reality further illuminated by Hall's view that a message "must become a 'story' before it can become a communicative event." Before a message can be "put to a 'use,'" Hall writes, "it must first be appropriated as meaningful discourse and be meaningfully decoded."[30] The Global Deception Research Team found that people worldwide decode the nonverbal behavior of gaze aversion as shame.[31] Pairing Aisha's, Hall's, and the Global Deception Research Team's findings shows that asylum personnel interpret applicants' nonverbal behavior according to a narrative (e.g., avoiding eye contact means a person may not be confident in what they are saying) before putting this nonverbal communication to use in a credibility determination (e.g., perhaps the person is not able to be confident because they are ashamed about not being truthful).

These concerns take on additional weight when applied to hearings where an interpreter is present. In the interpreted hearings I observed, applicants were more likely to look at their interpreter while responding to an inquiry from the judge than they were to look at the judge. The interpreter would typically look back at the applicant while listening, then would turn to look at the judge to deliver the interpreted message, during which time the majority of the applicants kept their eyes on the interpreter or looked down at the table in front of them. Sustained eye contact between a non-English-speaking applicant for asylum and their judge was infrequent and unusual.

"I'd like to think I got it right"

Whereas no existing research has quantitatively measured the ways asylum officers and judges decode nonverbal communication, some evidence suggests that personnel in other sectors of government-appointed work might not be more skilled at successful decoding than anyone else. Lucy Akehurst and her coauthors, for example, determined that police officers had just as many false beliefs about nonverbal cues to deception as laypeople.[32]

Perry Rhew, former judge and chief of immigration appeals at the Department of Homeland Security, is fairly confident in experienced judges' ability to accurately interpret nonverbals. Rhew remarked, "Well, after twenty years on the bench you get a pretty good idea of people's personality, of the way they act when they're talking, of how nervous they become. You wind up picking up a lot of cues from people; if their eyes are darting, if they're getting really nervous."[33] Here Rhew suggests that darting eyes and observable nervousness are "cues" that indicate some correlating reality. But when I raised this idea with officer trainer Ethan Taubes, he would hardly entertain it. Taubes believes nonverbal demeanor is "so cultural-specific that it's almost useless. I can be interpreting your lips or your kind of like little smile or your eyes looking in a certain way and can be completely off." He is fully unconvinced about officers' and judges' ability to draw correct inferences about asylum narratives through eye contact or other nonverbals because these behaviors are "arbitrary and capricious, depending on what your culture and predisposition is, your education, your frame of reference." These are serious charges considering the Real ID Act still permits officers and judges to use demeanor in their credibility determinations.

Stuart Hall suggests that similarity of experience or culture might increase one's chances of communicating a message successfully. He writes of "dominant" codes that may be "so widely distributed in a specific language community or culture, and be learned at so early an age, that they appear not to be constructed . . . but to be 'naturally' given."[34] These codes may work to the advantage of communicators from similar cultural contexts and social positions, but the asylum process makes clear how they could work to applicants' detriment because of the vast differences in cultural contexts and the inherent power imbalance between asylum seekers and the governmental personnel responsible for adjudicating their cases.

One should take into account that not every misreading of nonverbals is necessarily a result of cultural difference. Some of the narrators in this project shared with me about instances of nonverbal misinterpretation that went beyond cultural misunderstanding. Judge Jeff Chase remembers talking with another judge who recounted a case in which the asylum applicant was "moving in their chair in a way that it seemed like they were very uneasy and uncomfortable." The judge told Chase that he wondered, "Is it because they're lying?" But the answer was revealed soon enough: "After the hearing had finished, he went and sat in that chair and realized there was a loose spring or something, and that's what it was. So you have to be careful with what you're attributing nonverbal actions to." In this case, a material circumstance rather than an internal or cultural one instigated the asylum seeker's nonverbal display, revealing the diversity of impetuses that may result in nonverbal signals.

Sometimes, even a person exhibiting a nonverbal behavior does not understand why. Marcus corroborated this possibility when describing the difficulty he had controlling his nonverbal behavior during his asylum interview. "I think I was talking faster than I usually do, and I think my hands were shaking. I felt cold," Marcus told me. "I don't know why, but I moved my arms and my hands a lot when I was talking." His memory makes clear that the array of factors that incite nonverbal communication are sometimes unexplainable even to the individual displaying the behavior, emphasizing how difficult it would be for a stranger to conclusively determine an applicant's credibility from their nonverbal displays.

Because of the power they wield in this context, governmental personnel's interpretations of applicants' nonverbals prevail regardless of their accuracy. Government personnel may interpret a nonverbal symbol according to their own ideologies, incorporate the meaning of this code into their beliefs about the case's merit, act according to this gained "truth," and yet never explicitly state—or even recognize—what influenced their perceptions.

The problem of misinterpretation of asylum seekers' nonverbal communication transcends the United States: attorney Walter Kälin, representing immigrants seeking asylum in Switzerland, charged in 1986 that "too often officials assume that the way they think is also the way the asylum seeker thinks" neglecting the work of "trying to find out how the meaning in the asylum seeker's system of expression can be translated into their own. This may result in serious misunderstandings and even contribute to the denial of asylum."[35] Following an analysis of recorded nonverbal communication in asylum interviews in Finland, Eeva Puumala, Riitta Ylikomi, and Hanna-Leena Ristimäki show how one applicant's interpreter "forces his own interpretation and either unconsciously or purposefully incorporates this interpretation into the claimant's account" during an asylum interview.[36] Synthesizing the findings of her court observations of asylum hearings in the United Kingdom, Toni Johnson reveals how applicants' silence, which may result from trauma, may lead a judge to determine that the applicant is lying; Johnson argues that to avoid misinterpretation, asylum personnel "must begin to hear silence, and think through what that silence may imply."[37] Analyzing the Bosnian asylum system, Eeva Puumala and her coauthors show how an "applicant's body is read, recognized and located in terms of prevailing legislation and officials' interpretations" rather than according to culturally specific or personal realities.[38]

Despite all these warnings regarding the probability of misinterpretation, several of the asylum personnel I interviewed described instances when their interpretation of nonverbal displays guided their determination of a case—even when verbal communication did not corroborate what appeared nonverbally. Judge Chase told me he sometimes found that using his personal life experiences to interpret applicants' nonverbals led him to useful discoveries that helped him determine a case's merit. He recalled one hearing that was nearing its allotted amount of time even though he was still not yet sure whether to grant the applicant's case. Then, in response to one of his last questions, the applicant "went to answer, and then her eyes did something, and she just burst out in tears." In this moment, Judge Chase felt he knew immediately that the applicant had been traumatized because he recognized something familiar in the movement of her eyes: "I could tell from the way that her eyes moved that she had been traumatized because after 9/11, I would have this thing where, if the sky was blue a certain way or something, it's like this movie starts playing in your head of events again, and your eyes are following that, and you can't stop it, and I recognized that." Ultimately, the applicant revealed she had been sexually molested by a family friend when she was a child and had never told anyone. Adding this sexual trauma to the other instances of persecution she faced strengthened her case.

In this instance, Chase is explicit in the ways he relied on his own structures of understanding to decode the applicant's eye movement and tears. His experience complicates Officer Taubes's view that nonverbal displays are "so culturally specific" that they are "almost useless" in asylum hearings, necessitating better understanding both of individual variance in asylum personnel's reliance on nonverbal communication and of its actual ability to provide information useful to making a legal determination in an asylum case.

Many of the asylum personnel I interviewed did not shy away from confirming the difficulty of accurately determining a person's credibility from the way they communicate. Reflecting on his years on the bench, Judge Honeyman revealed thoughtfully, "I hope I get it right most of the time. The sad news is if we knew the truth about all the thousands of cases that I've heard, for example, I probably didn't get it right some of the time. I'd like to think I got it right a large proportion." Because asylum personnel were not physically present to witness the persecution applicants faced, they must depend on the way those experiences are verbally and nonverbally communicated as they work to determine who qualifies as a refugee. This is complicated by the number of cases judges are required to hear, which limits their capacity to give cases the reasonable amount of time required to make a fair determination.

Even asylum personnel who understand the challenges that prevent an accurate interpretation of nonverbals still trust themselves to follow their instincts regarding a person's affect, facial expression, or physical movement in some cases. Despite the reservations former judge Chase describes about attributing specific meanings to nonverbal communication, he admits, "I don't know, you had a sense for it, I guess, of what was significant and what wasn't." Likewise, even Judge Honeyman, who repeatedly warned of the dangers of using demeanor as evidence in credibility determinations, revealed how much he believes is lost when asylum applicants appear via video teleconference rather than in person for their court hearings: "What's lost is the human contact of being in the same room as an individual—and while I just said earlier that I'm very skeptical of many demeanor observations—it's still important I think to look at the person and have them look at you, to assess their credibility and to really not miss any part of the testimony where voice inflection, affect, or demeanor might be diluted or lost."

In all of the hearing observations I conducted, the asylum seeker was physically present. But when I serve as an expert witness, asylum seekers sometimes appear for the hearings via video, especially if they are defensive applicants who are detained elsewhere while their case is in process. Video hearings are becoming more common, and a 2017 report from the U.S. Government Accountability Office found that in half of the six immigration courts they visited, immigration personnel "stated that they had changed their assessment of a respondent's credibility that was initially made during a VTC [video teleconference] hearing after holding a subsequent in-person hearing," necessitating a closer look at the impact of the medium of live video on credibility determinations and perceptions of nonverbal communication.[39]

It is clear that throughout asylum interviews and hearings, asylum seekers, officers, and judges use their own structures of understanding to interpret both verbal and nonverbal communication. Because meanings exist in people rather than in words, asylum seekers cannot guarantee how their narratives will be understood. Viewing the nonverbal communicative interactions of the asylum process through the critical lens suggested by Carey and Hall endows behaviors such as eye movement a great deal of importance. Individuals express and assign meaning to nonverbal communication intentionally or unintentionally; instances where meaning is assigned unintentionally are both ubiquitous and more difficult to study since the process is internal and invisible. Regardless of one's intention, nonverbal behavior operates as a "sign vehicle"—a medium that delivers a message that will be interpreted in highly personal ways by every person who receives it.[40] In the context of asylum, this interpretation has the potential to directly impact an applicant's ability to secure safety from persecution.

In Their Own Words

Dr. Renée Sicalides, Psychologist

SEVERAL YEARS AGO I STARTED evaluating children whose parents were facing deportation from the United States. As part of the legal case for remaining in the United States, immigration attorneys often recommend that families seek psychological evaluations for their children and contact me, as a licensed psychologist, to conduct these evaluations. After the lawyers and I discuss the cases, I decide if I am the right person for any particular case.

The children are American citizens because they were born here. My understanding is that immigration judges consider whether an American child will experience undue hardship if their parent is deported. Undue hardship covers psychological issues, special education needs, and medical conditions, to name a few. So, for example, if a child has a medical or psychological condition and leaves the United States when a parent is deported, will the child's care in the new country be comparable to the care the child receives in the United States?

My experiences conducting these assessments range from interviewing a child and their parents and writing up a report for a

112

single immigration court hearing to conducting several evaluations for multiple hearings over several years. I also have testified in court as an expert witness. I usually meet with a child for between three to eight sessions with each appointment lasting around two and half hours. I meet with the parents privately and with their children a few times during the evaluation process.

When I first meet with the parents and children, I explain what we are going to be doing together and encourage them to tell me how they're feeling and whether they have any questions throughout the process. I let the children know it's okay to knock on my office door when their parents and I are speaking privately, if they want to see or speak with them. It's important the children have some control during the evaluation process because they have no control over the immigration process. I observe the relationship between these parents and their children, so I note whether the child hugs the parent after speaking with me and returning to the waiting area. Do they sit close to each other? Do they look at each other often? Do they separate easily from each other? If two parents come in, I note how they interact with each other; is there tension between them? How do the parents talk about the possibility of one of them being deported? Which parent does the child want to be physically close to?

I speak with the parents alone to understand the events that brought them in contact with ICE [Immigration and Customs Enforcement]. I ask about their child's life, including developmental, educational, and medical histories and the impact the parent's possible deportation has had on the child. I ask the parents to bring their child's report cards and relevant medical reports, and to give me written consent to speak with their child's teachers, doctors, and therapists. Often children speak more freely with these professionals than with their parents. Sometimes a teacher sees changes in a child's affect, behavior, and schoolwork when a family is stressed by an upcoming immigration hearing. A teacher told me the child started staying after class to help her clean up the classroom after the child learned the teacher was pregnant. This behavior coincided with the child learning her mother's immigration court date and her mother being pregnant.

I also ask about the family's plans if the parent is deported: would the child remain in the United States or leave with the parent? How well does the child speak, understand, and write the official language of the parent's country of origin? Will the family have a support system there?

The psychological evaluations consist of sections such as reasons for referral, mental status, educational and medical history, test results, clinical impressions, diagnoses, and recommendations. I describe the child's physical appearance and my observations including interactions with parents and descriptions of the child's artwork. I also conduct a mental status exam to assess things such as the child's ability to develop rapport; eye contact, speech, mood, and affect; thought content and processes; suicidality, insight, and judgment. So I'd note if a child cracks their knuckles when speaking about unpleasant material, as it may indicate anxiety, or dissociates when asked about separation-related issues and other things. I've had children ask if someone was watching and listening to us from behind a wall hanging in my office. I've observed children spill drinks after being asked emotion-laden questions pertaining to a parent's possible deportation. They also answer questions like "If you had three wishes, what would they be?" and "What's the best thing that has happened to you?"

I worked on one case for about five or six years and three or four immigration court dates. The child was in elementary school when I started working with this family and in high school when the parent's immigration case concluded. The child complained of being unable to live her life until her parent's situation was resolved. The child regressed by being more clingy than usual and with episodes of enuresis after learning of the upcoming court dates. The girl often worried her mom wouldn't be home when the girl returned from school. She feared ICE would pick up her mom, and the girl would be alone. She became anxious when she'd see a van in parking lots and on streets, especially if the vehicle was near their home. She never wanted to upset her mom because she feared her mom would leave her, so the girl wanted to be an exceptionally good child. She wanted to maintain a positive attachment with her mom.

I have heard some very traumatic experiences while conducting evaluations. During the telling of some stories the child presents the narrative in a disjointed manner, suggesting that the retelling of the event, or possibly an amalgam of events, overwhelms them. Much of these stories make sense, but there are usually gaps or small details that are a bit off. This is often the case when the person is retelling a traumatic event. Their recall memory isn't perfect, and I don't have a problem showing a child being very stressed and disorganized in their thinking. I want the stress and disorganization on the page for the judge to read and think about when arriving at their decision.

When it's time to think about the hearing, I recommend that children not be in the courtroom, so they can avoid being retraumatized by events and hearing my assessment of them. I usually advise that they sit outside the courtroom, preferably with someone they are comfortable with, like a family member. In general, I also don't recommend that children testify because of the pressure to do a good job so the family can stay together in the United States. If the judge rules against a parent, then the child is likely to think, "I disappointed my parents," or "Maybe my mom is willing to leave me here now." So I feel a big responsibility to put the child's voice on the paper. When the judge and the government's lawyer read my evaluation, I want them to have a good understanding of the child, as if they met with the child.

During these evaluations I'm trying to build a complete picture, and I have to put the child and their parent on the page, the positive and the negative. In that effort, I think it's important to quote the child verbatim because he or she is unlikely to have the opportunity to speak to the judge directly. It's important the judge hears the child in the child's own words. I have to let the child speak for themselves in the evaluation. So, I quote the child word for word whenever I think it's appropriate and think the child would want the judge to know something. I do ask each child directly what they'd say to the judge if they had the chance to talk with the judge in person.

I want the judge to get to know the child. I quote the child's response to questions around their feelings about their parent; feelings about relocating to the parent's county of origin or remaining in the United States without their parent. And if the child has had traumatic experiences, then it's important for the judge to hear the child talk about the trauma. You have to present both possible outcomes for the judge. It's critical that the judge gets to know the child. These judges make incredibly important decisions that have life-altering effects on the lives of these children and their parents.

5

Deterring Asylum

WHEN I MET HUMAN RIGHTS activist Rosa Anaya in San Salvador in early 2021, a caravan of asylum-seeking migrants from Honduras was making its way through Guatemala toward the U.S. border. A photojournalist friend traveling with the caravan was sending Rosa photos of the group while we talked. We were not surprised but concerned to see that many in the crowd were women and children. A 2017 report from Doctors Without Borders found that more than 30 percent of the Central American migrant women they interviewed reported experiencing sexual violence on their way to the United States.[1] The community of the caravan does not remove the possibility of sexual assault but does provide a semblance of safety in numbers, attracting more vulnerable migrants as well as those who cannot afford the thousands of dollars needed to hire a personal guide.[2]

Rosa considered the photos of the caravan thoughtfully and lingered over one of a young girl who had fallen asleep on the street curled into the sweater she was wearing. "As sad as this picture may be, that little girl at this point in time has something that she didn't have where she came from: hope to have a different life," she reflected. Rosa has talked with enough Central American asylum seekers who fled north to know that the driving force for most is not some kind of rose-colored American dream. "It's not like people don't understand. [They know] they're not really going to a promised land," she told me. "They know the option [to flee] is not the best option, but it's the only one they might have." When the choice is either forced migration or the possibility of violent persecution or death, those with a will to live would often leave even if they were not certain what waits on the other side.

Rosa's own experiences have afforded her empathy for the travelers. She fled home as a child and received asylum in Canada after witnessing the assassination of her father—the famous Salvadoran human rights activist Herbert Ernesto Anaya, an original member of the nongovernmental Comisión de Derechos Humanos de El Salvador, or the Human Rights Commission of El Salvador. As an adult, Rosa returned to El Salvador to continue her father's legacy of human rights advocacy by working with young incarcerated gang members to prepare them to be community leaders and promoters of peace upon their release from prison. She guides them in narrative visualization exercises to imagine what their lives in El Salvador could look like if they had all the support they needed to succeed.

In the current context, because of the many dangers facing formerly incarcerated people (regardless of gang affiliation), Rosa knows that the young men and women she works with are likely to flee the country after they complete their sentences. Her goal is for them to live in a world where immigration is only one of several viable life choices—where they have "the option to migrate because it's what they desire to do, and not because it's an obligation to be able to stay alive, to survive," she explained. She does not like to call the work she does migration deterrence, although if her program achieves its goals, that would certainly be one of the results.

The program is founded on a simple principle: "Migration is a right, and so is the right to stay." Rosa has heard people try to dissuade potential migrants from leaving the country by giving grisly details about the danger of the journey or the impermeability of the U.S. border walls and checkpoints, but she sees these tactics as too little too late: "No campaign that tells you how awful the way is, no wall, is going to be as effective as people having hope and opportunities to provide for their families and to become a positive leader in their community and to be recognized." Rosa is determined—"We need to focus more on the other part . . . what it means to stay. What your role might be, the support that you could have if you stay." Only when home becomes a viable and safe option can people really enact the right to remain.

Shortly after Rosa and I finished our conversation, the Guatemalan government—acting on a 2019 agreement they had signed after former U.S. president Donald Trump threatened them with tariffs for failing to deter northern-bound asylum seekers—interrupted the caravan and forced the migrants to turn around.[3] The young girl in the photo and her family would not, at least on that attempt, be counted among the applicants for asylum in the United States; like the thousands of others walking with them, they would not have the opportunity to set foot on U.S. soil in order to apply. What happens next—to the people in this group and the many others who set out but never reach the border—will not be part of the public narrative of asylum. Neither their bodies nor their stories will find a home in the United States.

Each year around a quarter of a million people arrive in the United States and ask for protection. Yet for every person who reaches U.S. soil there are many more facing grave violence and persecution who will be prevented from applying for the protection they need because of U.S.-funded programs and international asylum cooperative agreements designed to deter forced migrants from ever seeing the U.S. border.[4] When only the individuals who have managed to arrive in asylum-granting nations are counted in yearly asylum-tracking mechanisms, it obscures the broader narrative of everyone who has needed asylum but been deterred. To gain a clearer view of the number of people globally who determine to flee home in search of protection, we must include those who, for any number of reasons, fail to reach their intended destinations.

Stories of deterred asylum seekers are effectively excluded from the public narrative of forced migration. Because no clear paper trail of deterred migrants' attempts to escape is likely to exist, their experiences cannot be documented in a way that allows for a clear accounting of how many individuals are thwarted en route and forced to divert from their original destination to another or to return home.

This lack of record may account in part for why asylum seekers are underrepresented in public attention to migration. Compounding this deficiency is the reality that asylum seekers are also a liminal and transient group—technically, a migrant becomes an asylum seeker only when they officially present themselves to agents of an asylum-granting nation. They shed this title when they are either denied or receive immigration status.

There are all kinds of reasons many U.S.-bound asylum seekers never set foot on U.S. soil. They may be apprehended by police in countries along the way that have received financial incentives from the U.S. government to prevent the possibility of arrival; they may receive news from home that leads them to believe turning back is a more viable option than pressing on; they may be robbed, become ill, or run out of money during their journey. An advocate working with Catholic Relief Services told me about one young girl the organization recently encountered who had suffered third-degree burns on her feet from walking through the desert toward the United States without shoes. By the time she was found and deported by Mexican police, she could no longer stand.

Sometimes the reasons U.S.-bound asylum seekers do not complete the last stretch of their journey are more hopeful. Immigration advocate Rina Montti told me about one asylum seeker from Honduras she had been talking with as he traveled who never made it past Chiapas, Mexico, even though his intention was to go all the way to New York: "He got married!" Montti shared. "He fell in love, married a Mexican woman, now he has a Mexican baby, and so he is in the process of getting his documents [to be able to stay in Mexico]." Her anecdote offers a reminder that when a migration journey begins, the rest of a person's life is not merely put on hold; on the road to the United States, whole lives are taking place. Lovers meet for the first time, babies are born, older people become ill and die, homesickness overwhelms, children learn to walk and speak. Any number of developments along the way may alter one's route or destination.

Turning our critical attention to efforts to actively deter migrants from reaching their destinations helps to recover from obscurity the stories of would-be asylum seekers whose plans to leave home were thwarted altogether or disrupted along the way. Deterrence may occur through preemptive constructive efforts like those Rosa describes at the start of this chapter or via person-to-person cautionary messages from those who have been unsuccessful in their own attempts at finding asylum. Individuals may also be deterred through government-backed narrative efforts to prevent their migration. I dedicate the bulk of this chapter to this latter means of deterrence in order to illuminate the importance of the stories governments tell to prospective asylum seekers and to show how recent iterations of these narratives have harmed both asylum seekers and public perception of asylum.

Analyzing the kinds of messages sent and received in all types of deterrence efforts reveals that the decision to flee one's circumstances or remain even in the face of danger may hinge on the kinds of narratives one encounters, both before fleeing home and while en route to a new destination. Examining governmental dissuasion, in particular, shows how governments may strategically wield persuasive deterrence narratives toward politically driven ends.

Asylum Deterrence in the United States and Around the World

The governments of developed countries have used many tactics to discourage unwanted migrants fleeing persecution, including fastidious border patrol, harsh penalties for those who arrive without permission, and exclusion from legal employment and social benefits. In some notable recent cases, nations have attempted to avoid their responsibility to noncitizens through international multimedia deterrence campaigns designed to reach would-be migrants before they begin an attempt or along the way. These campaigns caution specific groups that they are unwelcome and warn of the hardships they will experience if they ignore government warnings to stay away; the more recent iterations of these efforts include graphic and textual elements appearing in both digital and print media.

Governmental asylum deterrence campaigns represent a unique convergence of political media, visual rhetoric, and international communication. Analyzing these messages uncovers how national governments characterize their responsibility to outsiders and can help identify implicit governmental anxieties about forced migration. Governmental asylum deterrence campaigns foreshadow for prospective asylum seekers the penalties their migration would provoke. They call on potential asylum seekers to visualize the bleak future that would follow their arrival and seek to persuade them to avoid future perils by curtailing their plans.

These future-visualization techniques attempt to change potential migrants' expectations. Governments often use media to address and shape refugees' expectations to ensure an easier transition post-arrival.[5] But deterrence campaigns are unique in that they attempt to alter expectations so much that forced migrants choose not to arrive at all.

The U.S. Customs and Border Protection (CBP) Know the Facts campaign, launched in 2014, included 233 billboards, posters, and bus signs featuring emotional visual appeals. Materials were disseminated in Guatemala, El Salvador, Honduras, and Mexico, and radio and television public service announcements aired 6,500 times.[6] The campaign included a website featuring links to downloadable country-specific materials and a call to action: "download them and help us disseminate this important message in a timely manner."[7]

The Know the Facts campaign corresponded to an uptick in the arrival of unaccompanied minors from Central America. In the first five months of 2014, more than 47,000 children were apprehended at the U.S.–Mexico border, a 92 percent increase over the same period in 2013.[8] While the number of immigrants from Mexico arriving in the United States has been declining for several years, increasing numbers of migrants from the Northern Triangle—Guatemala, Honduras, and El Salvador—regularly cross through Mexico, which explains CBP's decision to include Mexican bus stops and radio stations as targeted outlets for the campaign.[9]

As quickly becomes clear from a review of the deterrence efforts of other highly developed nations, the U.S. campaign is not unique. Several nations across Europe, including Belgium, Denmark, Finland, Italy, the Netherlands, and Norway, have recently employed similar tactics. The Norwegian Stricter Asylum Regulations campaign, for example, launched in November 2015 during a peak in arrivals that corresponded with the recent European "refugee crisis." Asylum seekers from Syria, Afghanistan, Iraq, and elsewhere were entering Norway via the Russian border at a rate above 2,500 per week.[10] The campaign foregrounded the message of a reduction of benefits offered to asylum seekers and was made up of print media in Afghan newspapers, posters in international transit hubs, and a Facebook page that hosted two dramatic videos about the dangers of seeking asylum in Norway.

Perhaps the most infamous of all international asylum deterrence efforts is the Australian government's Operation Sovereign Borders campaign. Operation Sovereign Borders received a substantial amount of international coverage in both news and academic discourse due in part to its predecessor: a taxpayer-funded graphic novel to visually dissuade asylum seekers that drew widespread criticism after it was revealed to have cost $15 million to produce.[11] The campaign included a YouTube video directed at would-be migrants and print media disseminated in key international settings, including Pakistan, Sri Lanka, and Indonesia. In the video, Lt. Gen. Angus Campbell appears in full military fatigues and looks directly into the camera with an unwavering frown to tell viewers, "If you travel by boat to Australia, you will *not* make Australia home. The rules apply to everyone: families, children, unaccompanied children, educated, and skilled. There are *no* exceptions."[12]

Attempts to deter migration through multimedia campaigns exist within a formidable genealogy of international public diplomacy. Understanding asylum deterrence campaigns as part of this broader historical context reveals how they play a part in larger efforts to advance national interests through media deployed abroad. Under President Woodrow Wilson's direction in 1917, for instance, the Committee on Public Information was responsible for ensuring that films produced in the United States depicted the country in a positive light; it also launched a government-produced news service. Although the committee was criticized as propaganda and dismantled shortly after the end of World War I, the Cold War gave rise to a more widely accepted tradition of nationally produced, internationally disseminated media intended to shape foreign perceptions and manage public relations.

In 1953 President Dwight D. Eisenhower established the United States Information Agency to "influence foreign publics in promotion of the national interest."[13] International public diplomacy efforts have often served an invitational function, advertising a nation's appeal in hopes of attracting desirable visitors and immigrants. Global deterrence campaigns use the same soft power mechanics to achieve the opposite goal of keeping unwanted migrants out.

Compared with countries such as Turkey, Jordan, and Colombia that physically neighbor the regions from which most recent asylum seekers have fled, the nations that produced the campaigns mentioned above approve and give immigration status to a relatively low number of asylum seekers. Data from the United Nations High Commissioner for Refugees (UNHCR) shows that the majority (85 percent) of displaced people are currently housed in developing countries; these nations are unlikely to have the financial capacity to launch expensive international public diplomacy efforts.[14] Although the UNHCR has worked to encourage highly developed nations to accept their "fair share" of migrants in need of protection, when considered in this global context, it is clear that the Know the Facts campaign functioned as an attempt by a highly developed nation to resettle even fewer asylum seekers than their already comparatively low numbers.[15]

Two theoretical principles help to illuminate the potential impact of asylum deterrence campaigns: materiality and governmentality. Materiality refers to the way physical matter informs, limits, and directs life.[16] The Know the Facts campaign's physical matter such as posters and newspaper ads may change the way individuals who encounter them communicate about migration. This conclusion is an example of how the idea of materiality, as Dawna Ballard has argued, "allows us to consider the communication consequences of material."[17] The material elements of the Know the Facts campaign include posters, billboards, websites, images, videos, and other media—all government-funded communications—that attempt to influence migration patterns. In this case, the communication inherent in the campaign materials themselves seeks to have the material effect of deterring the physical presence of asylum-seeking bodies in the United States.

Considering the material elements of migration and materiality's relationship with communication requires a marriage of media studies and migration studies. This paired perspective opens up a space for analyzing the material implications of the messages that attempt to deter migration. Some existing research points to the intersections of communication, materiality, and migration. Andrew Flanagin calls on scholars to recognize and interrogate "the fundamental interdependence of discourse and materiality."[18] Elaine Lynn-Ee Ho and Madeleine Hatfield suggest that "understanding . . . materiality as part of the experience of migration can help to illuminate migrants' everyday experiences."[19] A close reading of prior scholarship makes clear that material objects designed to influence migration patterns must be interrogated critically rather than accepted as neutral or matter-of-fact realities. In agreement with this view, I regard deterrence campaign media as situated, ideologically constructed materials that attempt to shape the idea of migrants and migration to particular ends.

To reach its intended audience, deterrence campaign material must be drafted and designed, printed and copied. Renting advertising space abroad requires international financial arrangements and local knowledge, although the internet makes it easier in many cases to transmit messages across international boundaries. Ultimately, the potential success of a deterrence campaign very much depends on whether the campaign material intercepts its intended foreign audience.

Because the Know the Facts materials are funded and disseminated not by individuals or organizations but by the U.S. government, the materials possess and represent governmental authority. The notion of governmentality illuminates how the U.S. attempts to control the international movement of bodies.[20] According to Didier Fassin's interpretation, "governmentality includes the institutions, procedures, actions, and reflections that have populations as object."[21] Other scholars have used the notion of governmentality to examine the ways governments attempt to control citizens. Here I establish how governmentality is implemented when a national government attempts to extend its reach across international borders to noncitizens.

Paring materiality and governmentality allows for a recognition of deterrence campaign media as the material apparatuses that enforce the governmentality of asylum. Material efforts to limit asylum seekers codify the perceived threat that asylum seekers pose and reify the need for policing apparatuses.

My goal is not just to analyze the stories this deterrence campaign tells potential migrants but also to interrogate the narratives governmental actors tell to warrant and rationalize the campaign itself. Analyzing how U.S. government actors talk about and justify the need for deterrence and characterize asylum seekers reveals how nations understand their own cultural values and responsibility to migrants.

Generic Archetypes

In the summer of 2015, a poster from the Know the Facts campaign began to appear in bus stations across Guatemala, El Salvador, Honduras, and Mexico. In bold black text, the mournful reflections of a regretful parent are centered: "Creí que sería fácil que mi hijo consiguiera papeles in la USA . . . Me equivoque" (I thought that it would be easy for my child to get papers in the USA . . . I was wrong). In the foreground of the image over which the text is laid, shoeprints wander a crooked path through desert sand rippled by wind. The silhouette of a single figure—too small to depict any specific demographic characteristics but ostensibly the child about whom the disembodied parent speaks—appears in the distance. The figure walks under a cloudless sky toward an expanse of desert brush and, further, mountainous terrain.

The fictional, mournful parent appears not as a specific individual but as an archetypal character in the narrative of asylum seeking. Appearing via text only rather than visually, the parent maintains a kind of unspecific anonymity, transcending human status and taking on something more mythological and paradigmatic. The parent could be from any of the four countries targeted by CBP's campaign. The juxtaposition of image and text in the poster makes clear only that this parent stayed behind as the child embarked on a journey to the United States as an unaccompanied minor.

Both the parent's words and the image of the vagrant child connote solitary and mournful reflection by expressing an assumption the parent now regrets, but a second message at the bottom of the poster conveys another tone. There a warning hails narrator and viewer into a unified goal: "Nuestros hijos son el futuro: Protejámoslos" (Our children are the future: Let's protect them). Inclusive and action-oriented, this message welcomes all parents into the shared goal of protecting children by preventing their migration to the United States.

Some existing U.S. research has chronicled the appearance of archetypal characters in media about immigrants. Most notably, Lisa Flores traced conflicting media portrayals of Mexican immigrants in the United States as far back as the 1920s and found widespread evidence of an archetype of passive "peon laborers"—a characterization used to assuage U.S. fears about the immigrants who were used to meet the labor needs that lingered in the wake of the First World War. The media Flores examines portrayed these laborers "as a docile people, unlikely to strike or to bring with them radical and un-American ideas," effectively disassociating them from the kinds of social and moral decay for which eastern European and Asian immigrants of the day were being blamed.[22] In contrast, the Opportunity Agenda, a nonprofit communication lab, analyzed popular television programs and found that 25 percent of all portrayals of immigrants from 2014 to 2016 depicted these characters engaging in unlawful acts, advancing a misleading arche-type of immigrants as criminal.[23]

When migrant characters in deterrence campaigns are portrayed as archetypes rather than individuals, they maintain a kind of non-descript anonymity and lack backstories, motivations, or voices of their own. They are effectively homogenized, characterized only by their mode of travel and their intended destinations. The archetypal character in CBP's deterrence campaign takes the form of a fictional narrator who speaks as a parent to warn about the risks of migra-tion, but no mention is made of the possibility that a credible threat might be driving this parent to send their child on a perilous jour-ney; the likely presence of traumatic push factors is verbally and visually erased.

The generic characterization has another effect: it makes room for and justifies a positive characterization of the United States. At a press conference on the banks of the Rio Grande to launch the deterrence campaign, CBP commissioner Gil Kerlikowske suggested that deterring the migration of asylum seekers is "consistent with our values as Americans." "These are hard-hitting messages," he affirms of the campaign posters. "They help [the] helpless."[24] Such language both reifies the need for the deterrence campaigns and reaffirms the nature and values of the nation struggling to keep asy-lum seekers out.

Throughout his remarks at the press release, the commissioner presented CBP as a compassionate but overworked group of heroes, exhausted by the ceaseless flow of incoming migrants. "I've seen them respond to these difficulties with professionalism, but also with compassion. They've made heroic efforts to help these kids they've rescued," he claimed. While "rescue" may seem an unusual verb to describe the process of seizing and detaining a minor, the commissioner leaned heavily on this language throughout the press conference. "Frankly, it's a way that comes from their heart," he shared. "I couldn't be more proud of the Border Patrol and the fact that in many ways they've gained trust from these communities and these people . . . they look to these border patrol agents for help."

Asylum seekers crossing the Mexico–U.S. border may believe that voluntarily presenting themselves to CBP for mandatory detention upon arrival is their best chance to present an asylum case and, in turn, receive immigration status that will allow them to remain in the country. But despite Kerlikowske's insistence that migrants "look to [his agents] for help," one imagines that the fact that an encounter with CBP may lead to asylum does more to encourage migrants to approach them than does any general trust in heroic CBP agents.

The archetypal characters that appear in this effort to deter asylum seekers show the campaign to be self-contradictory. It paints a picture of migration as too dangerous for a reasonable person or loving parent to attempt and at the same time reifies the U.S. national brand as a safe harbor with kind-hearted civil servants who excel at serving migrants.

Humanitarian Versus Nationalist Ends

A 2015 report from UNHCR suggested that "high levels of public anxiety about immigration and asylum" are "partly due to an increase in the numbers and visibility of migrants in recent years."[25] The report analyzed press coverage of refugees and migrants across five nations in the European Union and found that while some outlets focused on humanitarian themes such as the problems asylum seekers face, most common in the United Kingdom, Spain, and Italy were threat themes that focused on the problems asylum seekers could themselves cause. The report cited personnel from humanitarian organizations arguing that "this approach fails migrants by predominantly focusing on the challenges posed to the EU, rather than on those faced by the human beings whose lives continue to be lost."[26] This focus on nationalist concerns operates in contradiction to the original tenets of asylum, which calls on nations to see their humanitarian responsibilities toward those who have been forced to flee their homes as extending beyond their own borders.

Drawing the logic of this UNHCR report into the context of asylum deterrence raises the question of how the Know the Facts campaign depicts and defines who is at risk: asylum seekers facing humanitarian threats or nations threatened by migrants? Asylum seekers occupy an unusual social position. They may be represented in public discourse either as victims of the crimes that spurred their migration or as criminals themselves for migrating. These binaries— innocence/victimhood versus guilt/criminality—also appear in governments' explanations for developing deterrence campaigns.

We have already seen how the Know the Facts campaign establishes that asylum seekers are at great risk when they migrate. Operating in willful ignorance of the fact that migrants have judged the risks of migration to be less dangerous than those of remaining in their nations of origin, this presentation also ignores a significant source of the peril of seeking asylum: governments themselves. Prolonged detention, family separation, and disqualification of asylum seekers with certain criminal records all work to compound the danger facing migrants fleeing persecution.

It is clear that asylum seekers are at risk as a result of the persecution they faced in their home countries, from the dangers during their migration, and because the governments tasked by the 1951 Refugee Convention to protect them instead regularly inflict additional violence. However, global deterrence campaigns including Know the Facts discount these harms as they introduce and prioritize another purportedly imperiled population: citizens of asylum-granting nations. Deterrence campaigns work to convince citizens of the threat migrants pose. To justify preventing the migration of individuals who have faced persecution in their home countries, governments claim the need to protect nations against asylum seekers via apparatuses of governmentality. In these messages, the ways governments describe the potential harms of migration reveal clearly who they believe is at risk.

Populations of asylum seekers in the swath of developed nations that produce deterrence campaigns are so small relative to the rest of the population that most citizens are unlikely to encounter an asylum seeker firsthand. As Paul Hodge contends in an in-depth analysis of the press releases that accompanied Australia's recent asylum deterrence campaign, "For many Australian citizens who will never know an asylum seeker beyond the frame furnished by OSB [Operation Sovereign Borders], the camera works to solicit and recruit 'vulnerable publics' structuring the visual and discursive field of human mobility flows as 'security threats' and 'national emergencies.' "[27] The effect of such a structuring is not merely psychological. Hodge argues, "By reconstituting the plight and bodies of asylum seekers as security issues, clandestine practices and acts of degradations *become* necessary and defensible."[28] In other words, the campaign's discursive ideological framing of asylum seekers establishes and justifies the need for protection against the threat asylum seekers pose. Once the threat is clearly established, apparatuses of government control can appear on the scene as a welcome protective force against harm.

At the press conference launch of the U.S. campaign, CBP Commissioner Kerlikowske made repeated, unambiguous references to the harm that may befall migrants in search of asylum. The visible physical context of the Rio Grande where the press conference took place served as a place-based, material reinforcement of a message about the dangers facing migrants.[29] Kerlikowske stood at the site where migrants enter the United States, literally and symbolically replacing their bodies with his own, to speak publicly about the print and digital media created and intended to deter asylum seekers. "We chose this location because we wanted to highlight the dangers to get across not only this river, but as you can see from some of our other posters, getting across the desert," he began.

Kerlikowske announced that the number of migrant lives lost in the process of attempting to cross the border had been "significant," and he emphasized the likelihood that women would be raped during the journey by people smugglers. But this concern for the dangers asylum seekers face during migration overlooks the threats that forced them to flee their homes in the first place. The exclusive focus on dangers that occur after migrants leave their homes rather than before occludes the possibility that credible threats force asylum seekers to seek protection across borders.

Later in Kerlikowske's speech, what appears at first to be a description of humanitarian threat resolves into a threat to the nation: "When these children arrive, they are not only malnourished, as I said, they're also oftentimes, uh, are, uh, have a disease, have something that needs to be treated by a physician. The Centers for Disease Control, the public health service that is represented and the coast guard corpsmen that are all here are tremendously helpful in helping us to deal with this disease issue." Here the commissioner begins with a humanitarian concern: children arrive malnourished from their long journey. But his ambiguous reference to the "disease issue" connotes the danger of migrants spreading a sickness to citizens who may encounter them.

In fact, the affiliation of migrants with disease is widespread in U.S. public discourse.[30] The commissioner never identified which disease the migrants have contracted or offered any evidence of its existence. It would be nearly five years before the discovery and spread of COVID-19 would temporarily close the U.S.–Mexico border. The ways deterrence campaigns foreground the material harms that asylum seekers cause the nations to which they arrive emphasizes that the campaigns' primary goal is to insulate the governments that created them.

Strategic Omissions, Strategic Ignorance

Scholar Shannon Sullivan contends that ignorance is not the opposite of knowledge. Rather, it is "an active production of particular kinds of knowledges for various social or cultural purposes."[31] It is clear that the Know the Facts campaign puts strategic ignorance to work. Cultivating ignorance through omission about the rights of asylum seekers—both at home and abroad—paves the way for governments to attempt to deter even those migrants with credible asylum claims.

Article 14 of the Universal Declaration of Human Rights grants that "everyone has the right to seek and to enjoy in other countries asylum from persecution." The United States voted in favor of the declaration in 1948. The United States is also a signatory on the 1967 Protocol Relating to the Status of Refugees, which extended protections originally established in the 1951 Refugee Convention by stipulating that nations should not penalize forced migrants for illegal entry or illegal stay, regardless of where and when the migrants were forcibly displaced. Although the Universal Declaration of Human Rights and the 1967 Protocol are clear in this regard, the Know the Facts campaign obscures the reality that the nation approves and grants status to thousands of asylum seekers each year. Instead, the campaign suggests that the right to seek asylum in the United States does not exist.

At its kickoff, Kerlikowske stated the intention of the U.S. campaign plainly, clarifying that "if you cross the border illegally, no matter what your age is, you are not going to get legal papers. There is no—so there is no permission to stay." In fact, at the time of Kerlikowske's remarks, the United States was granting permission to more than twenty thousand asylum seekers every year, many of whom crossed the border without legal immigration status. Migrants who are granted asylum receive work authorization and social services and become eligible for a path to citizenship.

As the CBP commissioner, Kerlikowske is no doubt familiar with the nation's practice of granting asylum. But his statement is not an unintended error; he reaffirms it several times. "If you cross illegally into the United States, you're not eligible to earn a path to citizenship . . . no legal papers or path to citizenship awaits anyone who crossed illegally," he stresses. Later, he underscores that "whatever has caused some of this messaging to [make some] believe that once you come to this country you'll actually be allowed to stay, has been totally false." CBP's website states that the aim of the Know the Facts campaign was "clearly and simply stating the facts behind U.S. immigration policies." But the campaign only offers *some* of the information directly relevant to seeking asylum; the rest is systematically obscured. By wielding ignorance, Kerlikowske's statements and the campaign at large advance particular kinds of knowledge to discursively fashion a reality in which the right to seek asylum does not exist.

Reading asylum deterrence through this lens reveals how the Refugee Convention and 1967 Protocol, while useful for establishing international cooperation regarding the global responsibility that the signatories share in theory, cannot ensure humanitarian follow-through on the tenets of the convention. Whereas charges about failure to comply with the United Nations' directives have often been made against singular nations, government agents around the world stand in front of asylum seekers of all origins fleeing persecution of all kinds and use similar strategies to avoid responsibility for what they consider the burden—or threat—of asylum seekers.

Migrants are always characterized and defined according to nations' anxieties and aspirations. Across the globe, asylum seekers often appear as both victims and suspects.[32] The language that characterizes immigration status and fashions the seemingly stark lines between legal/illegal and regular/irregular migration is porous and politically constructed.

It is clear that nations' racial, ethnic, and religious anxieties lead to exclusionary migration policy under the guise of national security. Deterrence campaigns operate as apparatuses through which governments attempt to control migration through material communications. The migrant characters in these campaigns typically maintain a kind of nondescript anonymity. They are counted in numbers and referred to en masse, without backstories, motivations, or voice. This anonymity exists in contrast to the reality of the lived experiences of foreign-born individuals in new cultural contexts, who are regularly called out and discriminated against according to identifiable characteristics that render them "other."

Asylum seekers are a liminal and vulnerable population whose right to seek protection may be compromised through the dissemination of materials that characterize them as faceless crowds of wrongdoers who threaten the security of nations. When these materials simultaneously obscure the possibility of successful asylum claims, the nations that create them risk failing to fulfill the responsibilities determined by international refugee law.

Because deterrence campaigns attempt to predict and stop an action before it occurs, and because they operate in conjunction with other security and punitive tactics that similarly threaten the rights of asylum seekers, it is impossible to accurately measure their impact. At the launch of the U.S. campaign, Commissioner Kerlikowske emphasized, "We need to make sure that these messages are appropriate, that they're effective, and that they've been tested." When pressed by a journalist to predict the campaign's impact and explain how its effectiveness would be tested, Kerlikowske backpedaled: "If I was able to predict, I'd be a highly paid consultant instead of [working for] the Customs and Border Protection."

Acknowledging the existence and power of governmental asylum deterrence campaigns like Know the Facts can reveal the lengths to which developed nations will go to absolve themselves of the international obligation to care for forced migrants. But it cannot show the lived impact of these messages on their intended audience. Only through direct inquiry with potential, current, and past asylum seekers themselves is it possible to understand the effect of any message aimed at migration deterrence. None of the asylum seekers I interviewed for this book had encountered the Know the Facts campaign—many migrated before the campaign's launch, and many of the more recent migrants were from areas where Know the Facts was not in effect. The asylum seekers I interviewed instead returned again and again to the importance of interpersonal deterrence messages to their asylum experiences.

Interpersonal Deterrence

On a hot afternoon in the small town in El Salvador where I lived in 2021, I sat with my neighbor Marisol on her patio as she shared with me about her thwarted attempt to acquire asylum in the United States. Rather than having experienced a single devastating encounter with persecution like some asylum seekers, Marisol faced hardships over the course of her life in El Salvador that gradually piled up and complicated her ability to safely live, work, and care for her two daughters as a single mother. Finally, she reluctantly decided she had to consider a more viable option for herself and her children. Marisol's sister begged her to take her teenage niece along, and the four began a journey north in early 2019.

Marisol's brother had fled El Salvador just a couple of months earlier and was still making his way through Mexico to the U.S. border when Marisol set off; she and the three young girls followed his route and benefited from advice he shared from his own experiences along the way during phone calls. They had enough money to make it through El Salvador and Guatemala on a series of buses over the course of a couple weeks. In southern Mexico, the way forward became less clear, and she called her brother for direction.

Marisol's brother had been in the U.S.–Mexico border town of Matamoros for a few days when she phoned. She was shocked when, instead of offering her advice for the next phase of their trip as he had done just weeks before, he forbade her from continuing and asked her to turn around. He had seen too many horrors along the way since the last time they talked, he told her. There were women violated in the street and people murdered for seemingly no reason at all.

Marisol was torn—she had already sold what few possessions she owned at home and said dramatic goodbyes to her family, unsure if she would ever see them again. She was responsible for preventing the three young girls in her care from experiencing the same trials she had faced growing up and knew that living in the United States could offer them chances she had not had. But her brother was insistent, and Marisol made the hard decision to turn around; her niece cried when Marisol broke the news.

After returning to El Salvador, Marisol stayed with her sister and became more and more depressed. Seeing how much the experience had affected her, her sister asked, "Why did you return if you were so close?" and Marisol wondered whether she had made the right decision. When I asked her how she managed a way through the depression, her answer was grim: "By not thinking about it. I mean, to just like, resign."

The disruption of her thwarted attempt to make it to the United States has left Marisol jaded and pessimistic about others' chances of success. She now shares her cautionary tale of deterrence with whoever is willing to listen. "I had a[nother] niece that wanted to go, but I told her—I explained everything," Marisol shared. Similar to the messages of the Know the Facts deterrence campaign, she asked her niece to visualize the potential harms she could encounter. "Imagine if something happens to you on the way," Marisol instructed her. She was relieved when her niece finally agreed to stay home.

As I left Marisol's house that day, we paused in her small garden to look at some flowers she had planted. A few women were cooking outside on a *comal* at the neighbor's house. "She wanted to go recently," Marisol told me under her breath, pointing with her lips in the Salvadoran way at one of the women. I understood she meant that the women had made plans to go north. "I told her '*no vale la pena*'"—it's not worth it.

Person-to-person communicative deterrence efforts like the ones Marisol describes have mixed success. Potential migrants are, in many cases, talked out of taking a chance at migration through interpersonal communication with friends and family members. But in other cases even grave warnings cannot deter a person who feels they have no other choice.

In a conversation with Mexican journalist Alberto Pradilla, Bartolo Fuentes—who, despite his insistence that it was a democratic and collective effort without leadership, is largely credited with organizing the 2018 migrant caravan from Honduras—revealed that for as many people as he had helped to make the trip north, his preference would have been for them to stay home. "In fact," he told Pradilla in Spanish, "what I tell them is that they shouldn't go, that they should stay to change their country. But once a person has decided, what can you do, abandon them?"[33] Fuentes's experiences of shepherding thousands of immigrants through Central America toward the United States have led him to believe that once a person has determined they must leave, there is little that might persuade them otherwise. Contrasting his experiences to Marisol's narrative of being convinced by her brother to turn back even well into her journey underscores the variance in effect of deterrence messages.

As advocacy organizations, governments, and potential migrants' friends and families all produce messages about the dangers of migrating or the benefits of staying home, individuals who consider making the journey themselves receive multiple and sometimes conflicting messages about whether an attempt at asylum is likely to be successful. These narratives overlap and intertwine, influencing decisions about whether, where, and how to migrate. Their influence is indefinite, and it is not possible to measure in a precise way their impact on the landscape of U.S. asylum. It is certain, however, that the narratives potential asylum seekers receive, either interpersonally or from more organized efforts, play integral roles in their conception of the journey and have the potential to deter a person from finishing—or even starting—their intended journey to the United States.

Analyzing deterrence shows that the power of storytelling not only suffuses the post-arrival asylum process but also seeps deeper, saturating the decisions one makes as various actors attempt to influence those decisions long before a migrant's potential arrival on U.S. soil. A more panoramic view of migration affirms that confining migration narratives from one's arrival in the United States until their asylum case is decided leaves out the stories of all those left behind, dissuaded, diverted, or impeded along the way.

Considering the search for asylum as a process that exclusively takes place on U.S. soil also obscures from view the lived realities of the majority of those who apply for asylum but are denied and deported. Welcoming those who do not achieve the goal of U.S. protection into consideration reveals this group to be much larger than it initially appears. Making space for the narratives of forced migrants' experiences before and after their time on U.S. soil exposes both the variables that inhibit asylum narratives from ever being heard in U.S. courtrooms and, as the next chapter elaborates, the underreported hazards of life after deportation.

In Their Own Words

Jeffery Chase, Former Immigration Judge

I ALWAYS SAY I WAS BROUGHT UP Jewish at a certain time when I was told I could be anything I wanted to be as long as I wanted to be a doctor or a lawyer. I didn't want to be a doctor, but I didn't really know anything about law and ended up going to law school and really saying, "What am I doing here?" in the first year. But my wife was from Iran, and when I was in law school, wondering what I was doing there, a lot of my wife's Iranian friends and family would say, "Oh, you're in law school. How do I get a green card? How do I apply for asylum?" I said, "I don't know. I'll take the class." There was one class in those days at Hofstra Law School where I went, and it was taught by a sitting immigration judge. . . . I took the class, and I just immediately said, "This is it. This is what I want to do."

I think in those days, nobody was saying, "I want to be an immigration lawyer." It was like law schools wanted you to go to work for corporate firms that made them look good. When I said to the placement person at the university, "Immigration law," they kind

141

of looked at me like I was crazy. I was really left to my own devices in terms of plotting my career path and finding a job.

I remember there was a movie that Robin Williams was in where he played a Russian who defected here. He was approached by this guy in the shadows who said, "Psst. You want a green card?" To me, that stood for how immigration lawyers were viewed at that time; these kind of shady, in-the-shadow-y type of characters.

I was an immigration attorney for almost seven years. At that time, there was large-scale hiring of immigration judges. I was chosen, and I started in March of 1995.

It's funny because I'm very change averse. I'm very stuck in my ways. I don't like to change or take risks, but for this one I just said that that's the right thing because I was very good at the law part [of being at attorney] but very bad at the business part. . . . I thought being a judge would give me a chance to interpret the law in ways that I think are more fair. Sometimes you think you have a brilliant argument, and the judge just really isn't listening. I felt, if I was the judge, I could be in the position to make those decisions. I always wonder if I had taken another path where I would have ended up.

I think being Jewish, you were always very aware of the Holocaust and of the fact that Jews were outsiders. The Passover holiday I always call the refugee holiday. I think it's something you're very conscious of, and you say, "We Jews went through the Holocaust. Now there are other groups that are suffering and need assistance." [My father always told me,] "You're really lucky . . . You owe it to do something to give back to those that were less fortunate." I think it was the combination of all of that. . . . [I knew the immigrants I would see in court were] people who just, due to circumstances, were in this horrible situation and really needed help. You could really make a huge difference in people's lives.

[But] I didn't like [being a judge] pretty much from the beginning. It was a tough job. It was something where everybody is pressing you from a different direction. It's very difficult to ever do something that everybody is happy with. When you're on one side or the other, it's a lot easier. But when you're trying to be neutral in the middle, it's just a very difficult place to be. You feel like you can't really be yourself either because you're a judge . . . I mean, [I'm retired now, and] now I'm pretty outspoken . . . I don't hesitate to say what I think. But when you work for the government, you can't do that.

When you see some of the asylum decisions in Charlotte, North Carolina, or in Atlanta, which is notorious for having the absolute worst asylum grant rate—I mean, some of those judges I think have a 98-point-something-percent denial rate—and some places in Texas, I think there's a judge in Dallas who has begun just denying asylum without even allowing people to have a hearing. . . . A lot of the new hires have no immigration background at all. . . . I would say that that might be intentional, to bring in people that don't know anything and then train them in a way that "you don't grant this and that and that." So I think all of that is troublesome. . . . And more of these hires under this other way, where they're being brought in, told that you're on probation for two years, told that you've got quotas to meet, told that we don't think that [certain] kinds of cases are worth being granted. What kind of pushback are you going to get from judges who feel that their job stability would be at risk if they were going to grant a certain case or give a person more time to develop their case? Whereas many of the older judges are at the point of "Let them fire me. I'm going to do what I think is right."

When I talk to judges who are still on the bench, they tell me, almost across the board, "You have no idea how bad things are. You can't even imagine. Whatever you can imagine, it's 100 times worse." And I say, "Look, I hear a lot of things, I can imagine," and they go, "No, no, no, you have no idea." And I hear that over and over. . . . Many of them talk about being treated like assembly line workers. . . . They're in strong self-preservation mode, and they don't want to do anything that's going to draw the negative attention [of] their higher-ups.

The immigration judges' union and a lot of other groups feel that the courts should be taken out of the Department of Justice because of . . . the susceptibility to political pressure. As the union often says, the Department of Justice is an enforcement-based agency that's not designed to be neutral and that's not designed to be transparent in everything it does because of the nature of its investigative and prosecutorial functions. And yet it houses judges who are supposed to be both neutral and operate in a transparent manner. And I think, particularly under [the Trump] administration where immigration is such a part of its agenda, a certain point of its view on immigration is that it's something we have to stop and enforce, and the fact that these judges are completely under the control of an attorney general . . . who was so clearly anti-immigrant and had such a strong point of view on it, it just doesn't make sense. It's wrong to have a court that's supposed to be neutral and fair and protect due process operating under [those conditions]. . . . That's not the way that law or justice is supposed to be.

6

The Return

ALEX WAS BORN IN EL SALVADOR in 1989, one of the bloodiest years of the country's civil war. Because his grandfather was the controversial and outspoken mayor of a prominent town outside the capital, his family was targeted several times during the war. When Alex was a year old, someone threw a grenade through one of the open-air windows of his family's home. The explosion burned the left side of Alex's face, and his family fled to the United States to avoid further violence.

He has no memory of the explosion or of the medical treatments he underwent after the attack. By the time his mother told him the story when he was a young teenager, they had received permanent residency in the United States and had been living comfortably in Texas for over a decade; Alex's face had healed without much scarring.

When he was nineteen Alex had a run-in with the law. He was detained and, to his surprise, placed into removal proceedings— Alex would have to go in front of a judge who would determine if he was eligible to be deported. He had heard of people without papers being deported, but as a legal permanent resident of the United States for almost two decades he had never thought of himself as deportable.

The idea of being returned to El Salvador was surreal. "It's a country I've never known anything about," Alex told me. Without any memories of his own, all he knew about the country where he was born was from news reports and the stories of family members who had been there: "You know, what everybody talks about is the gangs, the gangs, the gangs." Considering the violence his family had endured during the first year of his life and how hard they had worked to get him out of the country, Alex was inclined to believe people when they talked about how violent the country was. He was willing to do whatever it took to stay away from El Salvador. He told the Immigration and Customs Enforcement (ICE) officer in charge of his case that he wanted to apply for asylum. The officer referred him to a judge, and his court date was set for almost two years later; he would remain in jail while he waited.

When his court date finally arrived, the judge looked over his case and said, as Alex remembers it, "This is going to be denied because you haven't spent any prior time in El Salvador. You can't actually qualify for asylum. When you apply for asylum, you need to have proof. You know, you need to have evidence of your claim." Alex had no evidence that he would be personally targeted if he went to El Salvador—even the life-threatening attack his family had experienced in their home was not enough to support his case since they did not know who was responsible and therefore could not prove they had been deliberately sought out. Alex was escorted back to his cell after the hearing and tried to imagine living as a stranger in a country he had never known.

He tried to convince himself that after having been in jail for twenty-three months, maybe being free to live as an unincarcerated citizen in El Salvador would feel like a relief. He called his mother collect and told her resolutely: "As long as I'm not in jail anymore,

I don't care where I get out." His mother cried on the other end of the line.

The day of his deportation, ICE officials handcuffed Alex to a deportee named Romeo and loaded the two of them onto a small airplane along with ten others. He remembers, "I was handcuffed to this other dude who was actually pretty cool. And the whole ride there he was telling me, 'Well look, check it out bro, I'm from the MS-13, and there's few things you need to know about this country.'" MS-13 and 18th Street, the two major rival gangs operating in El Salvador, sprang up in Los Angeles in the 1970s and 1980s as small groups of young, disenfranchised immigrants from Central America who coped with discrimination, loneliness, and attacks from other local gangs by forming their own makeshift cliques. Shortly after the 1992 close of the civil war in El Salvador, the George H. W. Bush administration began a crackdown on gang violence. "I want gangs to be treated like the criminal enterprises they are," Bush announced.[1] Thousands of members of MS-13 and 18th Street were rounded up and jailed together, then deported from the United States. In the much smaller country of El Salvador, their allegiances and power strengthened, and so began the gang culture that now permeates Salvadoran life.[2]

The MS-13 member he was handcuffed to during his deportation flight did not fit the violent descriptions of gang members Alex had grown up hearing. Romeo was kind and helpful; he told Alex how to dress to look like a local Salvadoran and which neighborhoods to stay away from to avoid gang violence. He explained that he had been deported before and shared some lessons he had learned the hard way. If he had to be shackled to someone, Alex told me he was glad it was Romeo, although it was embarrassing when they had to cram into the little airplane bathroom together after the guard refused to momentarily uncuff them.

When the plane reached the airspace over El Salvador, the twelve deportees on board were unshackled—their incarceration had officially concluded. They landed at El Salvador International Airport and were transported to El Centro de Atención Integral para Migrantes, known throughout El Salvador as "La Chacra." At La Chacra, the groups of deportees who are flown in from the United States and bused in from Mexico daily are given a few pupusas and some juice, have their tattoos examined and recorded by police officers—this took a while in Alex's case; he has a lot of tattoos—and sit through a short orientation about getting an identification card and how to look for work.

I knew about La Chacra from watching a film by El Salvador–based photojournalist and friend Neil Brandvold. Brandvold had spent months standing outside the doors of La Chacra filming conversations with family members who were waiting for deported loved ones to arrive. As he returned to the location day after day, he learned how perilous the facility's placement is for unsuspecting deportees. "La Chacra is in a super dangerous neighborhood," Brandvold told me. "They don't explain this to the poor migrants, [but] if you take a right when you go out, you're in an 18th Street neighborhood and if you take a left, you're in an MS[-13] neighborhood. So you have to just get on a bus and get out right away." For a disoriented deportee without family to guide them, turning left, turning right, or lingering on the spot are all unwittingly risky decisions.

In a film he made for Al Jazeera, Brandvold documents the managers of call centers who sometimes stand outside of La Chacra and recruit new English-speaking deportees to provide customer service for huge international companies like Expedia and Verizon. "We pay $600 a month!" one of the recruiters tells an arriving deportee in Brandvold's film.[3] "Don't go back [to the United States]. Why would you go back? You can make $600 and help your mother. She came to pick you up, right?" the manager asks a bewildered-looking young man.

Alex was intercepted by one of these recruiters and, without any other ideas of what to do for work in El Salvador, agreed to an interview. Like many other deportees from the United States, he is now a call center employee. He's glad to have income, but instead of the relief he was hoping to feel at not being in jail anymore, he usually feels depressed. "Your first year here is usually you're in denial that you're here. You're thinking about what you left behind," he told me. Growing up in the United States around many other immigrants, Alex had felt at home walking around his Texas neighborhood. He was accustomed to greeting his neighbors when he saw them outside. His experience in El Salvador is different: "Over here you say, 'Hey, how's it going?' and they just look at you like you're gonna rob them or something." Alex has heard random passersby insinuate under their breath that he's a gang member.

The Salvadoran police and military patrols regularly stop Alex in the street and question him for seemingly no reason at all. This is common practice in El Salvador. Salvadoran-American journalist Roberto Lovato interviewed one heavily tattooed deportee who had tracked the number of times he had been stopped by police since his 2012 deportation: 230.[4] Alex will boldly ask the police why he is being singled out when they stop him. They reply, "Oh, it's because of the way you're walking," he told me. "It's because of the way you carry yourself—we can tell [you are not from here], you know? We thought you were up to something."

Alex was one of several deportees who had mentioned to me the idea that the way they walk may cause them to be singled out, so I asked him how exactly a deportee walks. He stood up to show me. "Somebody that's deported kind of has a slouch on their upper back. Walks kind of fast, and kind of like—how can I describe it? Kind of like, if you see Eminem on TV walking, or like when he's performing a show, like some rapper performing a show, I'd say. You just walk with this, kind of like *swag*." Alex said he can instantly spot another deportee in the street this way. He also explained that something just as telling in the appearance of these strangers is the same listlessness he recognizes in himself. "We just aimlessly wander the streets," he told me. "Day in and day out. With a blank look on our face, just thinking, you know, trying to find a purpose in your life again. Trying to find what you're meant to be here—what you're going to do next. How you're gonna form a life again. You try to think, 'What did I do wrong?' "

Alex is not shy about how he copes with the crippling nature of these thoughts. "Well, most of us, to tell you outright, most of us find a way out through substance abuse and alcohol," he told me matter-of-factly. "It's what happens. I don't really know anybody that works at a call center that doesn't use on a daily basis." Out of the thirty-six people who work with him, Alex knows of only one or two who don't use drugs. The most common preference is crystal meth because of its availability and affordability; Alex was amazed the first time someone asked him for just three dollars to pay for what would have been a twenty sack in Texas.

Deportees' use of crystal meth even at work is widely known. Alex's boss at the call center—even his boss's boss—knows that their employees keep meth in their desks. "They don't care," he confirmed. "You just do it right there on your desk or in the bathroom, under the desk, whatever. [The boss says,] 'As long as you make the sale, cool. Get on the phone and sell.' " I asked Alex if using drugs really helps take away some of the depressive feelings he had been telling me about. "Ohhhh yes," he answered, laughing at the question. "Most definitely. Most definitely. I mean, I'm just going to tell you straight: Yes they do."

At the end of our conversation, Alex and I talked about my work with immigrants in New York who are facing the possibility of deportation. He wanted to pass on some advice to them for managing post-deportation life: "Tell them to stay out of trouble, don't get any type of record down there because that will definitely make it very difficult for you to come back [after being deported]. . . . Just don't lose hope. Yeah, don't lose hope. Have faith that maybe one day, if God allows it, you'll be able to be back to your old life, back to a life in the United States." A person is banned for ten years, or sometimes for life, after being deported from the United States.[5] I knew Alex knew this and asked him if he plans to attempt to reenter the United States without being detected at the border. He did not hesitate: "I am dying to return." He has already begun making plans.

As if That Were the End of the Story

When immigrants are deported, they tend to fall off the U.S. immigration advocacy docket; when notable instances of failed asylum cases appear in U.S. news, deportation is usually the end of the story. It would be a mistake to chalk up the absence of post-deportation life in U.S. public discourse to only disinterest, although there is undoubtedly some willful ignorance involved. Deportees are also pragmatically difficult to follow. They are all but unreachable during any time they spend detained in the United States before being removed, and when they come out the other side of deportation day, they have to establish new modes of communication. A new phone with a new international number may take weeks or months to access or afford.

Even highly coordinated efforts to locate deportees who are eager to be found can be exceedingly difficult in remote and hard-to-reach areas.[6] This is the case for immigrants deported for any reason, but for forced migrants who are deported after fleeing home and being refused asylum, the effect of the absence of their post-deportation lives in U.S. public imagination is particularly grave. The lack of attention and resulting lack of publicly available stories about post-deportation outcomes obscures instances where former asylum seekers have succumbed to the violence that they reported fearing in their asylum application, minimizing awareness of how often this occurs.

The absence of these stories, no matter the reason, has material consequences not just for those who have been deported but also for asylum seekers in the United States still fighting to have their cases approved. International refugee law prohibits the United

States from refoulement—that is, sending asylum seekers back to life-threatening harm. Specifically, the UN High Commissioner for Refugees defines the principle of nonrefoulement as prohibiting nations from "removing individuals . . . when there are substantial grounds for believing that the person would be at risk of irreparable harm upon return, including persecution, torture, ill treatment or other serious human rights violations."[7]

I serve as an expert witness in asylum cases for applicants from Central America. The effectiveness of the declarations I write depends on being able to show in any particular case the likelihood that a deportation would constitute refoulement. Because this is the case, my declarations rely on and directly cite the partial but integral reports of post-deportation violence and death that exist. Without documentary evidence of past instances of post-deportation harm, it is much more difficult for expert witnesses, attorneys, and asylum seekers themselves to invoke the principle of nonrefoulement in asylum cases. Only when stories about the risk of irreparable harm are carefully followed, well documented, and publicly accessible can they assist those whose lives depend on receiving the protection of asylum.

Successful attempts to create records of the dangers deportees face have revealed grave truths, like Jeremy Slack's 2019 study finding that immigrants deported to Mexico are frequently subjected to extreme violence, including systematic massacres.[8] Also in 2019 Beth Caldwell found that even when deportees to Mexico do not face immediate danger from others, they are alarmingly prone to depression, homelessness, drug use, and suicide. This likelihood, Caldwell found, is especially prevalent in the case of veterans who had been deported after serving in the U.S. military, effectively cutting them off from the military aid and mental health support that many veterans rely on in the United States.[9]

Amnesty International reports that immigrants deported to Eritrea have been charged with treason for fleeing the country to apply for asylum, then forced under torture or the threat of torture to reveal what they said about Eritrea in their asylum applications.[10] In an eighteen-month longitudinal study, a team of researchers from the Refugee Support Network conducted more than 150 interviews with former asylum-seeking children who had been forcibly returned to Afghanistan. The researchers learned that pursuing an education post-deportation was nearly impossible for the children, who instead were forced to focus assiduously on survival; they were being doubly targeted and victimized, subject at once to the circumstances that led to their original asylum claims and facing additional scrutiny related to their new identities as deportees.[11] These crucial studies paint a grisly but fragmented view of post-deportation stories; their appearance in academic journals and white paper reports tends to limit their reach to those already actively searching for such evidence rather than new or larger audiences.

These efforts to tell the stories and build a record of immigrants who are harmed, suffering, or murdered after their deportation are critical. But because the work is so logistically difficult to coordinate across international borders, and because cases of harm are only rarely identified, recorded, and made discoverable when they occur, such efforts may have the ironic effect of rhetorically minimizing rather than clarifying the likelihood of post-deportation danger—of making what stories we do hear seem like unfortunate outliers.[12]

The implications of this challenge are already clear in other widespread but underreported global harms such as gender-based violence. In a twenty-four-country international study published in the *American Journal of Epidemiology*, researchers found that women victims of gender-based violence reported the crimes to formal authorities in just 7 percent of cases.[13] What's more, regional variations in rates of reporting showed that in national contexts where gender-based violence is more normalized and more prevalent, victims may be even less likely to report it, so the disparity between crime and awareness is widest in the most critical contexts. This observation of less rather than more reporting of harms in the most harmful contexts is almost certainly the case in the context of deportation as well.

A commendable 2020 Human Rights Watch (HRW) report documented 138 cases in El Salvador alone of migrants who had been killed after deportation from the United States since 2013.[14] The report reveals that the researchers confirmed these cases by talking with family members they identified by searching court files and press accounts. These are the most obvious sources for such a survey, but it must be understood that in El Salvador, stories of murdered deportees are unlikely to appear in either court files or press accounts;[15] an estimated 95 percent of crimes in the country are uninvestigated and unsolved.[16]

Rick Jones, senior technical adviser for Latin America and the Caribbean for Catholic Relief Services, told me that after a few decades working in El Salvador, he has no shortage of stories he could add to a report like the one from HRW if only there were some documentary evidence. Even in the last couple of years, he shared, "I know of at least four cases of people who said [in U.S. immigration court], 'If I go home, I'll be killed,' and they ended up killed here in El Salvador." None of these four cases has been reported in any news outlet, in El Salvador or internationally. "The police know about the cases, but they never appeared anywhere in the press," Jones added. Even the best-funded, most widely visible narratives of post-deportation danger likely only scratch the surface of the ugly reality below.

It is clear, then, that available narratives of the dangers of post-deportation life are far from comprehensive. However, documenting the extent to which these harms are underreported, the material and immaterial factors that impede a more complete narrative, and the full consequences of this narrative absence requires direct insights from deportees and those who work with and advocate for them.

Reynaldo left El Salvador as a two-year-old and received asylum in the United States as a derivative benefit of his parents' successful claims based on violence they had been victim to during the country's civil war. Deported in his late twenties after being arrested for selling drugs, he has struggled to rebuild his life. When I mentioned to him the number of murders recorded in the HRW report, he was unfazed. "Those are just the ones that you know about," he replied. "Because a lot of these guys also end up disappearing and nobody knows anything about them." When I asked Reynaldo later in our conversation if he spends time with other deportees and could tell me how they are doing, he answered, "There's not that many of us because those guys, they keep on dying. I don't know what they do, but they keep on dying."

Rick Jones and his team have mapped at least seven currently active Salvadoran death squads—groups who are available for hire to kill others. These groups "almost always involve somebody from the police," Jones revealed, so journalists publishing anything about the specifics of the group's actions or makeup would be asking for trouble. Even if someone were willing to take the risk and identify the embedded state actors, the difficulty of proving that the death squads are responsible for the murder of specific individuals perpetuates a dangerous silence. In this context, the combination of cultural normalization of stigma-fueled violence against deportees and the systemic underreporting of crimes in general often proves deadly.

The thin record of stories about the dangers of post-deportation life is a problem not easily solved. To be clear, the issue is not primarily a lack of data about the act of deportation itself. Formal processing at the point of deportation ensures that at least the rudimentary details of deportees' cases are documented both upon their departure from the United States and upon their arrival in the country where they were born.[17] The more sweeping problem is the lack of narrative insight into asylum seekers' experiences while incarcerated in the lead up to deportation and the difficulty of tracking deportee narratives after the immediate moment of return.

Brief glimpses into the seclusion of asylum seekers' detained lives sometimes incite a flicker of public attention, as when the *BBC* published a February 2021 handwritten letter to Congress from a Salvadoran girl detained with her asylum-seeking mother in Dilley, Texas, for 531 days and counting: "I have spent two Christmases here," the nine-year-old writes in Spanish.[18] She pleads with the recipient to do something so she can be out of prison by her tenth birthday. Although this story and the poignant visual of the child's handwritten note drew wide attention, those concerned for the girl after hearing her story have few leads to follow: she is obscured by a pseudonym and locked behind bars in a remote detention center an hour's bus ride outside of San Antonio. If she is deported, the public would be unlikely to find out.

Rick Jones confirmed as much about the Central American context: "The fact that there are two or three flights a week and buses almost on a daily basis bringing people back into the country— what happens to them is not really covered. So, it's like they left, and they're gone forever from the public imagination. . . . It just sort of ends with, 'Oh. Too bad they didn't make it [in the United States],' as if that were the end of the story." The lack of available stories of post-deportation life means that asylum case decisions are rendered based on an incomplete understanding of what happens to people after deportation.

In 2021 I lived in Central America with funding from the Fulbright Association to conduct oral histories of people who had been deported to Guatemala, El Salvador, and Honduras. Before relocating from Brooklyn, thinking I would need help gaining access to some furtive world of deportees who would likely be reluctant to talk, I established academic and nonprofit-affiliated contacts who were willing to facilitate introductions. While these contacts were helpful and generous during my stay, within a few months of my arrival I had learned that deportees were all over my community— the waiter at the bar where we would watch the sunset over a nearby surf break, my neighbor's sister, my Spanish tutor's father,

the woman who ran a *pupuseria* down the street—almost everyone I got to know had a story of a family member going "north";
many had painful stories of life after a return.

Approximately sixty thousand to eighty thousand individuals are
deported to Central America every year.[19] In talking with deportees, the children of immigrants currently in removal proceedings
in the United States, and family members of undocumented immigrants who returned to the United States after deportation because
life at home was untenable, it became clear that there is no such
thing as a harm-free deportation to Central America.

Because Central American kids who grew up in the United States
and were deported as young adults in the 1970s and 1980s are considered responsible for the introduction and evolution of gang culture in Central America, deportees cannot shake the social stigma
that they are dangerous criminals. In his extensive work at Catholic Relief Services throughout the Northern Triangle, Rick Jones and
his team have found that only 10–12 percent of deportees reenter-
ing Central America have a criminal record.[20] Among that group,
Jones revealed, most of the crimes were minor, committed when a
person drove through a red light, jaywalked, had a traffic violation,
or were apprehended for having an open container of alcohol. These
are not hardened criminals, Jones stressed.

Still, the stigma persists. As a result, deportees may not be offered
jobs even when well qualified, may struggle to form meaningful
relationships with friends and romantic partners, and may face a
range of microaggressions as they go about their daily lives. Reynaldo told me he sees it all the time: "People are actually very racist against us deportees . . . I don't know what it is. I have no idea
why. Maybe they think we came and we messed up the country
because of the gangs and stuff like that. They think it's us, [that]
we probably started all this stuff." We talked about how each side
blames the other—U.S. political and news discourse regularly faults
Central America for the presence of gangs in the United States even
as Central American public discourse blames the United States for

fueling the rise of gang culture in El Salvador, Guatemala, and Honduras. "And that's probably why people don't like us," Reynaldo concluded. "They see the tattoos and they're like, 'Oh, that's a deportee. They came and messed up the country.'" The supposition is difficult to dispel, and few can thrive working to rebuild a life while simultaneously bearing the weight of the social responsibility for gang violence one may have nothing to do with.

A 2021 report written by political scientist Sonja Wolf and published by the Mexican nonprofit Centro de Investigación y Docencia Económicas details the range of damage a person endures during a forced migration.[21] The report makes clear that the homes, cars, personal effects, family relationships, sources of income and savings, educational pursuits, romantic relationships, and long-term goals lost in the process of migration are not simply recovered when a person is deported "home." Instead, these losses are compounded by the psychosocial impact of the failed migration attempt and often a significantly worse financial situation, leaving deportees with what Wolf's report calls a sensation of *desarraigo*—uprootedness.[22] "It's an emptiness that one carries daily," one of the report's informants described in Spanish. "A thought that one does not leave behind."[23] Approaches to deportation research that consider only the material or psychosocial effects miss the ways in which these two intertwine and affect one another.

The ubiquity of post-deportation hardship makes the lack of stories on record all the more unsettling. Rick Jones told me he is confident that these narratives, if they were to make it into the public eye, would not only assist in the asylum claims of current applicants but would also incite some shift in public sentiment: "Storytelling—that's one of the best ways that people can actually access what has happened to these people, why they've left, what the forces are that are shaping their lives, and then also what happens to them when they may return," Jones offered. "We've been sitting around fires telling stories for thousands and thousands of years as a way to not only communicate what's happened but deeper insights as well. So, I think story really is a way for people to access what's actually happening and connect to it." Jones believes that stories of deportees could foster a connection that would lead to a sea change in American public understanding of the harms of U.S. immigration policy. But it may be that dismantling the public's current acceptance of deportation as a logical response to unwanted immigration will require something more.

The idea that the U.S. immigration system is "broken" is, in contemporary public discourse, fairly uncontroversial—even bipartisan. But the narrative of brokenness obscures the reality that the system is in fact working as designed. As César Cuauhtémoc García Hernández points out in *Migrating to Prison: America's Obsession with Locking Up Immigrants*, "The system hasn't malfunctioned. It is intended to punish, stigmatize, and marginalize."[24] That is, somewhere along the way, U.S.-born citizens accepted the idea that returning undesirable migrants to countries widely known for their violence is a sensible and maybe unavoidable part of U.S. immigration policy. For as long as that is the case, it is difficult to imagine that better access to post-deportation narratives alone will trigger some widescale antideportation movement.[25]

Rather, protecting immigrants from post-deportation danger by requiring the United States to uphold its legal obligation to nonrefoulement will require as a first step the defamiliarization of high-risk deportation as a viable option. Interrogating the "taken-for granted meaning structures underlying what is most routine," sociologist Ryan Gunderson contends, is necessary before any kind of significant reimagining of a normalized practice can take place.[26] The insidious norming of the horrific failure to protect immigrants beyond the boundaries of the United States obfuscates the reality that any other way is possible. Replacing passive acceptance of the grisly realities of the U.S. deportation process with narrative inquiry and a critical approach, one can begin to defamiliarize the current status of deportation and envision an alternative. The first step is recovering from obscurity the stories of how real humans with complicated lives find themselves at the exit door of the United States.

The Winding Path to Deportation Day

Hank's deportation story began when, as a teenager, he broke a window in an abandoned factory in the small town where he lived, leading to a charge of criminal mischief. His judge was sympathetic, and the case was dismissed, but the charge itself was enough to give ICE license to initiate removal proceedings against Hank, despite the fact that he had been living as a legal permanent resident in Texas since he was three years old.

Hank was incarcerated in a detention center where he applied for asylum as a defense against removal. Multiple members of his immediate family had been murdered during El Salvador's civil war. He arranged for the records and news mentions of their deaths to be sent to his attorney so he could use them as evidence in his asylum hearing, but they arrived so close to his court date that there was no time to have them translated from Spanish by a certified interpreter, so the judge refused to admit them.

"It was devastating," Hank told me. To be holding the part of his life story that he believed could lead to a successful asylum case in his own hands in front of a judge who was unwilling to postpone his case for a few days so it could be translated and admitted as evidence was infuriating. "Maybe he didn't care," Hank considered. "I think he just wanted to get it over with and get it done. The caseloads that they have, I'm pretty sure it's a lot."

Hank's experience of not being allowed to present what he considered to be critical evidence is just one of the innumerable ways an asylum seeker's narrative may be deemed "inadmissible" in court and thereby rendered powerless. As Hank sees it, it is too common for judges to "overlook prominent details that [could make all the] difference for the person that is filing an application for asylum."

When pieces of a narrative do not arrive on time, or the applicant cannot afford to have them notarized or translated, or even when a document lacks a crucial detail like a date because of being placed askew on a photocopier, the impact may be dire. Any one of these practical misfortunes can change the trajectory of a person's life. Understanding the many bureaucratic and arbitrary reasons a person may find themselves at the mercy of deportation is one way of beginning to defamiliarize the U.S. deportation system and uncover the violence it inflicts.[27]

There are many paths to deportation, and a failed asylum claim is only one of them. A person may be deported after entering the country without detection and being found by CBP, for overstaying their student or tourist visa, or as punishment for committing even a minor crime after living the majority of their life as a legal permanent resident in the United States.

Long-term residents of the United States have been increasingly targeted for deportation and placed into removal proceedings in recent years.[28] It has become more likely, then, for a person being deported to have long-term friendships, employment experience, English language ability, family ties, and other affiliations in the United States when they are expelled. This experience results in a much different narrative from those of individuals who receive a negative outcome to their asylum claim and are deported just days or months after they arrive in the United States—a circumstance that has become more probable since 2018, when the Trump administration instituted the "last in, first out" policy.[29] The policy changes the order of asylum processing so that some asylum seekers arriving at the southern border can be rushed into legal proceedings then promptly returned to their countries of origin while others who filed their applications before 2018 and who may already have been waiting in limbo for years must now wait even longer for their own cases to be processed.

When recently arrived asylum seekers are rushed into hearings to determine their deportability, they may have too little time to prepare a strong legal case, gather important evidentiary documents, and find a lawyer; these shorter turnarounds increase the likelihood that a person who fled a life-threatening situation just days or months before is likely to find upon their quick return that the threat is still very much present and active.

While last in, first out facilitates the deportation of removable individuals before they form viable connections to life in the United States, the first five deportees I interviewed had been removed after living almost their whole lives in the United States and were so young when they left their countries of origin that they had absolutely no memory of the place to which they were returned. Matthew, who was deported to El Salvador, had never even lived there. When his parents fled El Salvador via the infamous Central American train "La Bestia," Matthew's mother was four months pregnant. Matthew was born almost two months premature in Mexico before his parents carried him across the border into the United States when he was a year old. He was granted U.S. residence in addition to dual Mexican/Salvadoran citizenship; his "home country" was a place in which he had never set foot until his deportation to El Salvador at the age of thirty following a failed asylum case.

Not all failed asylum seekers are returned alive. In *Caravana*, author Alberto Pradilla offers a crushing account of the morning he spent with a small group of mothers waiting at the area of the Ramón Villeda Morales Airport in Honduras designated for the repatriation of human remains. They were mothers of migrants who left San Pedro Sula to join the 2018 caravan of asylum seekers headed to the United States but who starved in the desert, were attacked by wild animals, or were murdered for their few possessions. Their bodies must be identified, sometimes after having been found in remote areas many days after their death. "This is not a place for hugs and goodbyes," the author writes in Spanish. "But for transactions: 'Here is your container. Here is your packet. Here is your casket.' "[30] Because these migrants died before they could reach their destination and submit claims for asylum, their narratives are all but erased from public asylum discourse. They are not counted in the numbers of those who arrive and submit a claim; as a result, the global magnitude of the number of migrants who flee their homes in a desperate search for safety is rhetorically minimized.

Death before arrival is just one of many ways the stories of those who need asylum becomes muffled and muted in global consciousness. And while no one could ensure the safety of every asylum seeker making a dangerous journey, there are more proactive and delusory ways that the scope of the narrative of asylum is diminished. Sometimes asylum seekers unwittingly agree to deportation even when being returned to their nation of origin is their worst nightmare. One young mother named Marcela, who fled gang violence in Guatemala with her fourteen-year-old son, found out only after she had been deported without him that one of the English documents she was asked to sign in the detention center despite not understanding English had indicated not only her agreement to be deported back to Guatemala but also her willingness to leave her son behind in the United States.[31] "They didn't even give me an opportunity," Marcela remembers through tears. Her case was never heard before a judge.

Although it seems impossibly cruel, this practice is not uncommon. The American Immigration Lawyers Association filed a complaint with the Department of Homeland Security in 2018 after recording the details of seventy-six parents who revealed they were verbally and emotionally abused and coerced into signing documents they could not read, some of which rescinded their rights to be reunited with their children or attested their willingness to be deported even as they were actively working toward pursuing an asylum claim.

Practices like these make clear that deportation is not merely the carefully considered legal result of an insufficiently convincing asylum case. Rather, individuals in grave danger with viable claims to asylum that fit squarely within the boundaries of immigration law are being deported all the time, even before they have a chance to present their narratives in court. This injustice results from proactive attempts by U.S. governmental actors to intercept and obscure asylum seekers' narratives, preventing them from reaching either impartial judges or the American public. The current system depends on silence; any narrative visibility threatens the status quo by uncovering common practices so inhumane that they cannot even feign alignment with the protections afforded by international refugee law.

Not all asylum seekers forcibly expelled from the United States are officially deported. As a result, published yearly statistics of deportation are misleading. Some migrants are granted the possibility of "voluntary departure"—a phrase that suggests a firm distinction from deportation that is rarely evident in practice. A 2013 class action lawsuit brought by the American Civil Liberties Union against the acting secretary of the Department of Homeland Security revealed that immigration officers in California were pressuring and threatening immigrants into accepting voluntary departure even when other forms of relief may have been available to them.[32] The tactic is not original; a 1985 case in which a sixteen-year-old was arrested and "voluntarily" expelled without understanding his rights charged that U.S. immigration officials' "policy and practice coerces [unaccompanied minors] into unknowingly and involuntarily selecting voluntary departure, thereby waiving their rights to a deportation hearing or any other form of relief."[33] In a chronological analysis of U.S. deportation practices, historian Adam Goodman found that 85 percent of the expulsions from the United States that have occurred over the last 125 years were legally "voluntary"; Goodman charges that any definition of deportation that excludes these supposedly freewill departures is grievously misleading.[34] Using the word *voluntary* to describe circumstances in which forced migrants have little choice but to return to the very danger they fled rhetorically occludes the magnitude of the United States' role in refouling vulnerable populations.

I spoke with several forced migrants in Central America who had returned to the countries of their birth after agreeing to voluntary departure despite being at a high risk of persecution, torture, or other violence. As a result, like Goodman, I consider these instances deportation by another name. While some of these returnees had not been aware that they may have had other options, several others became so exasperated by the labyrinthine uncertainty of the U.S. immigration system that after years of trying, often while detained in inhumane circumstances, they eventually lost their will to continue to pursue their own safety. "That's the intention," immigration advocate Rina Montti reminded me. "[That] people give up . . . due to the difficulties or the trauma of the process." In these cases of voluntary departure, giving up on the possibility of safety becomes rhetorically inoculated as a choice; the desperation and despair that mark these circumstances are effectively erased in the renaming.

Rewriting the Narrative

A forced removal is unlike any other form of international relocation. Understanding deportation's individual impact requires the sort of long-term biographical view rarely afforded by mainstream narratives. As Rick Jones offered during our conversation, "The larger narrative about migration [is] that it's sort of a one-way street. People migrate, they leave, and they're gone, and they're gone forever, and then they send money back home. But this whole idea that this is circular, and that people are coming back and not being successful . . . that there's a life that needs to be rebuilt and put together again, that part of it rarely gets told." What Jones describes applies in a range of deportation contexts, but in the case of deportation after a failed asylum claim, the work of piecing a life back together is complicated by having to confront anew the dangers one fled.

Deported asylum seekers do not merely pick up their lives where they left off when they were forced to leave home. "You have no assets to build," Hank emphasized. "Like a home or a car, or even a phone—anything. So you have to start from zero. And a person that hasn't been here, that doesn't know the territory . . ." he trailed off, but his meaning was clear and echoed by several deportees I met in Central America. It takes a while to learn which gangs control which areas and how to evade the danger they pose. There is no manual to consult, and it is easy to wander into the wrong place at the wrong time. Where this sort of mistake may be less immediately life threatening for the average Central American, for a heavily tattooed man like Hank, who dresses and walks like a deportee, it could be a death sentence.

Reynaldo told me has made that mistake more than once:

> I've gotten stabbed, I've gotten robbed, I've gotten beat up, and all because deportees—a lot of people see us very bad. Over here, there's a lot of racism about that. If you go to work and you're working with the natives and stuff, they actually start hating on you. They don't like you. It's very, very difficult to fit in because a lot of people are like, "Oh, you're a deportee." There's a lot of hate for deportees. Not only with gangs and stuff like that, but with people [in general] it's kind of tough. It's really tough.

Reynaldo's invocation of the word *native* to describe the Salvadorans he works with indicates the identity distinction he feels from this group. His lifetime in the United States has marked him—he is a Salvadoran "native" in name only.

Without the money he would need to live in one of the more secure gated communities of middle- and upper-class Salvadorans, Reynaldo has had to move several times to avoid trouble. He now lives in an area that's widely known to be dangerous, and he feels he is just biding his time until the next terrible thing happens to him. "There's a gang right here that, they don't like anybody—no deportees. They don't like deportees, they don't like tattoos, they don't like anything like that. So they'll just kill anybody. They don't really care. They're actually very vicious." A few months before I met and interviewed him, a man that he did not recognize jumped Reynaldo and stabbed him in his side multiple times just minutes from home in the middle of the day. The wounds were shallow enough not to be life threatening but did not heal well; the mass of small scars on his side looks like the skid of a tire.

After that day, Reynaldo changed his daily habits. "I just stay home. I go to work, stay home, go to work, stay home," he told me. It is a far cry from his life in Whittier, California, where his days were full of time spent with his girlfriend caring for their children—"It is lonely, trust me. I get lonely a lot of times." During the COVID-19 pandemic, Reynaldo lost his job. The lack of a routine has amplified his feeling of helplessness. He shared, "I'm not working, so I'm here all day. You can imagine how boring it gets. So yeah, it is boring [and I] have no family to come home to. I wish my mom, or my sister, I mean somebody . . . but nope. I just come home and that's it." I asked Reynaldo what his life would look like ten years from now if everything went his way. The simplicity of his quick reply saddened me: "What I want to do is just pretty much have a home and just have my little family."

The Spanish word often used disparagingly to describe deportees who lived for long periods of time in the United States is *creido*—a person who thinks they are better than others and behaves in a conceited way. Deportees are accused of being *creido* for having lived and earned money in the United States—this label can persist long after a person has lost whatever capital they may have gained in the United States through expensive legal battles and months or years without working while one is detained. At the same time, in a cruel catch-22, several deportees told me they feel like they are unfairly compared to others who receive asylum or another type of legal immigration status in the United States, as though they were offered the same chance to improve their situation and somehow failed to lay hold of it.

Deportation is a trauma both preceded and followed by other traumatic events. When deportees have been away for many years, they may return as near-strangers to any community they still have in the area. Some are ostracized by family members who had been depending on their success in the United States to survive financially. Rick Jones suggests that "the idea that these people are carrying trauma back with them [is an issue] that's hardly ever addressed" as the more immediate public focus tends to stay on material and visible concerns. When a person does not have the capacity to address and work through the trauma of a failed forced migration, it is likely to fester and intensify. "The potential for suicide is also extremely high because their whole life project has now been dashed," Jones shared.[35] "The fact that they can go for months without work, that they suffer from discrimination within their own family—[these realities are] not part the general societal narrative. But almost everybody who knows somebody can tell you a story about this."

Jones's perspective shows how narrative realities can have material consequences. When the harms that deportees face are left out of the "general societal narrative," advocates and nongovernmental organizations may be less aware and therefore less likely to include deportees in their initiatives, with the compounding effect that efforts to attend to the needs of deportees receive less visibility and funding. Moreover, narrative silence can perpetuate psychological harm by fostering a sense of isolation; when one's experiences are not reflected in public narratives, they may have a sense of being alone in their challenges rather than as though they belong to a group who has faced similar challenges and may have the capacity to understand and support each other. Finally, the rhetorical minimizing of post-deportation harms likely skews asylum case decisions by occluding from judges' view the life-threatening harms that frequently occur after one is denied asylum.

As a result of the stigma they face from their family and community members, the fear of danger that permeates their daily lives, the trauma of their experiences of expulsion from the United States, and the perpetual narrative erasure in public discourse of their post-deportation challenges, deportees as a demographic group are not doing well. It is not difficult to understand, then, why so many would be eager for a second chance of escape.

Dying to Return

Angelica and her little brother, Denis, spent almost all their time together until, at fifteen years old, Angelica moved to the United States to join her U.S.-resident father in the task of making money to send back to the small town in Honduras where the rest of the family lived. Denis stayed behind, and the family celebrated when he found work driving for a local Honduran trucking company. But the job required him to drive into neighborhoods where, on at least three occasions that Angelica knows about, he was threatened by gangs and only narrowly escaped with his life. Knowing he was testing fate by continuing on the same daily route and without other options for work, he left his few possessions behind and made his way north to join Angelica in the United States.

She worried about him making the trip. Angelica's own journey had been harrowing, and Denis was more of a sensitive and kind type than a rugged survivalist. "Truthfully, I didn't agree with his decision to come in that way," Angelica told me, "Because, well, it's scary. I know that it's also scary to be in Honduras, but it's scary to take that journey because they were walking." Denis could not afford to hire long distance transportation for his migration, so he walked day after day as far as he could manage before looking for a place to rest for the night. The route was a popular one for others making the same journey, and he met some traveling companions along the way.

Denis had a cell phone with him, and Angelica would call often to make sure he was okay and learn where he was. "And he would tell me that he was doing well, that it was worse to stay in Honduras. He'd say, 'I know that I'm going to make it. Don't worry, I'm okay,'" she remembers. As the journey went on, he sounded less enthusiastic. His feet started to hurt from all the walking and there were days he did not have water or food. He sometimes walked with other migrants whose children were starving and he felt powerless to help. On more than one occasion, he passed makeshift memorials for others who had died along the way.

Once, while walking along the side of a busy highway, Denis witnessed a man split in half by an oncoming truck. "And despite seeing all of that—suffering through all of that, he didn't want to turn back," Angelica told me. "Because he was so afraid to return to Honduras and of what would happen to him there."

To her relief, Denis finally arrived at the U.S. border, where he presented himself as an applicant for asylum. She was hopeful that the nightmare he had been living had reached its end.

It was early 2017, and the rate of asylum denials had already begun to climb during former president Trump's first year in office.[36] Denis's case was denied, and he was swiftly deported. But life in Honduras was no longer an option. When the gang that had threatened him learned that he was back in the country, they began actively pursuing him; he had to leave again almost immediately. Knowing asylum was impossible, he would attempt to enter the United States without being detected.

His second journey benefited from the lessons he had learned the first time, but Denis was unfamiliar with the safest route on the U.S. side of the border, and CBP apprehended him just steps inside Texas. The detention center they took him to was already over capacity; he had to sleep in the facility's bathroom. A conversation I had with former Border Patrol Officer Josh Childress confirmed this was not unusual—at the detention processing facility where Officer

Childress was stationed at in Arizona, he told me, "we were over-capacity on a regular basis."

Denis was deported to Honduras a second time, out of money and without a plan. Then, on September 26, 2018, like a sign meant especially for him, a message of hope appeared on his Facebook feed:

> MIGRANTS: IT IS BETTER TO GO TOGETHER
> TO AVOID RISKS

> People keep leaving Honduras. For the grave economic situation or for the violence. They are exposed to risks of all types on the journey. . . . It would be better to leave together and organized from Honduras, showing our face, without hiding. To leave shouting to the world that we go because here we have been robbed of opportunities and because those that should protect us the most have become threats to our lives. If we go together, we can mutually support each other, protect ourselves from threats, and demand respect for our rights. . . . The governments that persecute undocumented immigrants are to blame for thousands that have died on the way, those who have been mutilated and those whose fate we do not know because they have lost communication with their family. If you have plans to go, do not go alone. MIGRATION IS NOT A CRIME.[37]

Denis did not need to be convinced. There were no preparations to make; he waited patiently in San Pedro Sula for the group to leave. On the twelfth day of October 2018, around 160 people set off; over the next few days the numbers quickly grew to more than 500 as the caravan made its way through northwest Honduras. In Guatemala, more joined. Several international news crews started following along and reporting on their whereabouts. Angelica watched for daily updates on Univision.

Reporters working for the *Washington Post* interviewed several members of the group who were deportees from Central America making their way to the United States for the second, third, or even fourth time.[38] Their words reveal why the caravan appealed to deportees—some had left children or spouses in the United States who they were desperate to return and see; others had faced such violence traveling north alone before and believed in the safety in numbers; many had spent all their savings hiring the coyotes who guided their failed past trips, and the caravan was a much less expensive option.

The group formed a kind of makeshift community. Denis would call Angelica and tell her about the people he was meeting. One woman was traveling alone with three kids; he took turns with a couple other men carrying the kids on his back.

When the group entered Tecún Umán near the Guatemala–Mexico border on October 18, their numbers counted at least five thousand. That day Donald Trump tweeted a series of rapid-fire condemnations:

> I am watching the Democrat Party led . . . assault on our country by Guatemala, Honduras and El Salvador, whose leaders are doing little to stop this large flow of people, INCLUDING MANY CRIMINALS, from entering Mexico to U.S. . . . In addition to stopping all payments to these countries, which seem to have almost no control over their population, I must, in the strongest of terms, ask Mexico to stop this onslaught—and if unable to do so I will call up the U.S. Military and CLOSE OUR SOUTHERN BORDER! . . . Hopefully Mexico will stop this onslaught at their Northern Border. All Democrats fault for weak laws!

Mexican journalist Alberto Pradilla, who was with the group as they neared the Mexican border, later wrote in his book *Caravana* about the ironic result of those tweets: "What Trump did not know was that . . . with his furious messages, [he] amplified the power of the caravan's message. He had told hundreds of people who were waiting for an opportunity with their backpacks ready that there were others in their same situation."[39] Rather than dissuading the group, Trump had emboldened them.

The day of Trump's tweets, Mexican police scrambled to erect barricades at the bridge over the Suchiate River that marks the boundary between Mexico and Guatemala, but the migrants were unwilling to be deterred. The following day thousands were forced to wait as Mexico allowed only a couple of migrants through the border at a time. A few threw rocks in desperation; the police responded swiftly with rubber bullets and tear gas.

Angelica was watching the chaotic scene unfold on a live stream posted to Univision's Facebook page with her grandmother; they both scanned the crowd frantically for signs of Denis. She called him, and her heart sank when he answered the phone crying. He was right in the heart of the conflict; one of the kids he had been helping to carry for the last several days had ingested the tear gas and was struggling to breathe. "I told him that I could hear a lot of noises, like things being thrown. Or like, shots. And I told him, 'Can you please leave? It's not worth it. Move. Leave.' 'Yes,' he told me. 'I'm going to leave, because this is getting ugly.'" On the phone and on the livestream, Angelica could hear the government's helicopters hovering low.

The violence escalated rapidly. Angelica waited a few uneasy minutes and called Denis again to make sure he had gotten of harm's way. When he didn't answer, she had a sick feeling. "Since my grandmother was here, I withheld the feeling," she remembers. "I started to call him, and call him, call him . . . and nothing." The livestream was now her only source of information.

And then, suddenly, Denis was there on the screen: Laying on the ground with his face partially obscured by a handkerchief, unmoving. "I recognized his body," she told me. "But I said, no, I have to be mistaken. It's not him."

She stood frozen in front of the screen and jumped when her phone rang in her hands a few moments later. It was her aunt in Honduras, and she was hysterical. She told Angelica she had just received a call from Denis's phone, from one of the friends he had made on the journey. Denis had tried to run away from the scene, the friend told her, but a woman near him got shot in the chest with a rubber bullet and Denis hesitated, moving toward her while turning to see where the bullet had come from. In that split second, a shot from the helicopter struck him on the side of the face; it took him a few minutes to die.

"I don't know how this could have happened to him," Angelica told me through tears. "Someone who was like he was. He was a very precious person. He was so loved. He was very sweet. He liked to help people. He was a person everyone loved. It's true. Many people loved him, and that was clear when his body arrived to Honduras. A lot of people cried and wondered how it was possible, because he was a good person."

My conversation with Angelica grew quiet as we both sat under the weight of the end of her story. She finally said quietly, "The people that come from Honduras . . . they're risking their lives. And if you're willing to do that, it means that you are not safe in your home country." I have heard this sentiment many times in many forms—"No one leaves home unless home is the mouth of a shark," refugee poet Warsan Shire writes.[40] It is one thing to hear and understand this sentiment in the abstract; hearing it from Angelica after Denis's death, it became incontrovertible.

Denis had known what it was like to be without food or water on his journeys north. Even on his first attempt, he had watched others slowly suffer through starvation and dehydration on the way and been witness to one sudden violent death. He knew the humiliation of detainment and the weight of a failed asylum case. And *still* he decided to return. It was not the "best" option; it was the only option.

I ask every deportee I interview if they are planning to return to the United States. More often than not, the answer is maybe or yes—sometimes tentative and a little sheepish, other times resolute and uninhibited. The director of Casa del Migrante, a deportee-serving organization in Guatemala, found in a 2018 survey of their clients that 95 percent plan to return to the United States.[41]

Over breakfast at a restaurant on the beach one morning, my Salvadoran neighbor Fernando told me the hellish story of his own journey to the United States. He was threatened at knifepoint after attempting to prevent the rape of one of his traveling companions and later spent several days shut inside a suffocatingly hot, pitch-dark shipping container hitched to a semitruck with dozens of others wearing adult diapers to mitigate the mess and smell—just a few months after our conversation, a similar truck carrying over one hundred migrants to the United States in December 2021 would crash in Mexico killing more than fifty of the people who were crammed into its dark trailer.

In the detention center where he was held in Texas before his deportation, Fernando thought he would freeze to death, and the guards humiliated him with racist slurs. But, as is common, the "package" he had purchased from a coyote to guide him on this journey included three attempts; it cost Fernando all of his savings and some money he had borrowed from his uncle. "I still have two attempts," he told me, shrugging. Not taking advantage of them would be a waste of money and possibility. He plans to leave again this fall.

It would be a mistake to think of deportation as the climax of a linear, round-trip journey leading to and away from a failed asylum case. Deportation is the end of one story but the beginning of another: a single point in an asylum seeker's often cyclical odyssey. Although rendered all but invisible to the U.S. public eye, deportees are returning every day to their countries of origin, where they must work to re-envision their lives and decide their next steps, often under duress.

The lack of public attention to post-deportation life, trauma, and danger is more than an unfortunate humanitarian blind spot.

Detailed documentary evidence about the lived experience of post-deportation difficulties has the potential to save other potential deportees' lives. Just as asylum seekers' narratives are integral to their own chances of asylum at the start of a case, the narrative of the hard realities of post-deportation life long after an asylum case has been denied offer support to future migrants' pleas for protection. Harnessing and wielding that power may be the difference between life and death.

Asylum seekers are an already vulnerable population whose deportation back to dangerous contexts puts them considerably more at risk. The perpetuation of silence around their lives and outcomes is a problem with effects that range beyond the lives of deportees themselves and helps to perpetuate and justify an asylum system in which only a precious few receive the protection they need. Because the narrative absence of post-deportation harms precludes current asylum seekers from having the evidence they would need to build cases strong enough to prevent refoulement, the problem self-perpetuates, with material and grave consequences for the world's most vulnerable immigrants.

In Their Own Words

Rafael, Detained Asylum Seeker

November 7, 2020

Good Morning Sarah,

My friend, I hope you find yourself well in these moments, in a perfect state of health alongside your family and others, enjoying the triumph of our new president. On my end, I will tell you that I am healthy, despite the difficulties in which you find me. But I'm certain that I will be better soon, and back alongside my loved ones. Today, the United States begins a new life, with a new president that has begun to unite the people and I hope he follows through on all of the promises he has made.

In this letter, I will begin to recount my experiences as an immigrant, and the events that occurred in the prisons that I had to go through because of ICE and the government wanting to instill fear in the people who seek asylum in this country.

I am a Cuban citizen. I abandoned my country in July 2018, with the objective of arriving to the United States of America, a country where democracy exists and there is freedom of speech and respect of human rights. I turned myself in to the border post with my wife, who was pregnant.

It was on this day that I began to live a terrible nightmare. Donald Trump's government implemented a zero-tolerance policy and said that all of us immigrants were delinquents, drug-addicts, etc., giving ICE and all immigration officials a free pass to mistreat and discriminate against all of us who came to this country to seek asylum.

That's when our hopes got more complicated due to the family separation policy that the president had in place. After having my wife in detention for four days, in a cell without any type of comfort, sleeping on the floor, they released her and took me to a prison in El Paso. They had us in a cell that they call the *hielera* due to the immense cold. We couldn't complain to anyone, though some of the officials that work there are children of Cuban immigrants. They verbally mistreated us, laughing and making fun of the conditions we were in. We were there, freezing cold, for approximately twelve hours without any type of comfort.

After a while, they transferred us in the early morning, our arms and legs shackled as if we truly were criminals, to another detention center. We were in that detention center for fifteen days, and the officials there, some of whom were Mexican, treated us better. Just when we thought that everything would be resolved here in this detention center, the absolute opposite was the case. They removed us in the early morning and took us to an airport. They put us on a plane, shackled by our hands and feet, to a prison in Tennessee. That's where they did our credible fear interview, sometime during the twenty-six days we were detained there.

This prison is for high-risk criminals, with drug problems, murder charges, and more. They locked us up there in two-person cells, as if we were inmates that had committed a crime. This began to take a psychological toll on many who were like me. I began to feel depressed, due to the stress caused by the ICE officials, due to the orders given by the government, due to President Donald Trump . . . after twenty-six days they again removed us in the early morning and distributed us to various prisons—Pine Prairie, Winn, Roswell, LaSalle in Olla, River, among others. Prisons where we all lived cruel moments, due to the mistreatment and discrimination from the officers and immigration judges because we were Latino.

Specifically, I was sent to a center that is in good condition and hygienic. But the hate and mistreatment from some of the officers and the boss in charge of the center was unacceptable. On top of that, the medical unit was mismanaged; the doctors there only care about the money that ICE pays them. To be seen by a doctor, you had to fill out a request form and you could only get medical attention seventy-two hours after submitting it no matter how serious your illness was . . . and in most cases, all they would give you is Ibuprofen. In many of the cases, such as mine, they took bloodwork and never told me that I had diabetes, nor gave me treatment for the illness.

The judges that oversaw the asylum cases for the prison were totally racist. They verbally mistreated me during the hearing. If your case is good and you apply for asylum, they say "I believe you but I won't give you asylum." The government-driven objective is to not give asylum and instead to deport all immigrants.

It's good to point out that most of the immigrants seeking political asylum that come from our country are university graduates: doctors, engineers, licensed technicians, etc. We left Cuba in search of democracy, freedom of expression, respect of human rights. And we found ourselves in a country transformed due to the current president and government representatives. They are incapable of analyzing the injustices that are being committed, due to discrimination, selfishness, and the hate that this president has against Latino immigrants.

After being in that prison for nine months, where we suffered violent mistreatment from the officials on occasion—they would spray pepper spray in our face when we would request our right to conditional liberty (which the ICE officials had denied us in order to keep us in these prisons). These prisons are businesses, made to fill the pockets of a few corrupt members of this state of Louisiana, where most residents are racist.

In these prisons we have been through hell. The mistreatment of officials, discrimination, punishment in cells called *el pozo*— "the pit"—where we had friends who took their own lives and others who cut their veins due to the acts of violence they experienced despite not having committed a crime.

They took me to another prison. I compare it to a concentration camp. We lived there eight more months, and we kept being victims of hate, selfishness, and discrimination. The same mistreatment from the officials, doctors, nurses, and all of this combined with the ICE officials and driven by the representatives of this government.

I've had to live a long and intense period. Thanks to the help of God our Lord, we have been given the strength to endure all this injustice, put in place by the authoritative government of Donald Trump, just to be able to reunite with my wife and child, born in this country—a U.S. citizen. This is the worst state of this county, where people are incapable of thinking for themselves, and where they live from dirty money at the cost of immigrants, without thinking about the psychological, social, and human harm that they cause people who are the same as them.

Until now, I have written you the most bitter experience that I have ever lived, and I wish I could forget it. I have summarized my lived experience. I would have liked to write something positive, but there wasn't anything, except for the call of our Lord Jesus Christ, for the communion with God, Amen. I hope what I have written will be useful. You know that you can count on me unconditionally. That's what friends are for. I hope that this new era with our new president is fruitful and that we can have a nice and enjoyable life.

Without more to write,
Your friend that cares for you
and hopes to meet you in person

Postscript

ON THE ONLY DAY OF HARD SNOW during the winter of 2019 in New York City, I was supposed to accompany a young Guatemalan family to their asylum court hearing. I was already running a few minutes late when I learned there had been an accident that was disrupting service on the subway. The F Train was running express to try to mitigate the congestion, so I had to transfer three times to different trains, doubling my commute time. Despite a decade of living in the city, I often find myself turned around, and when I finally arrived at a station downtown, I had to use a navigation app to direct me to the familiar courthouse a few blocks away. The distraction kept me from seeing the ice in an intersection I was trying to rush across before the light changed; I slipped, breaking my fall with the hand clenched around my cell phone before landing on my back in the crosswalk.

Stunned from the shock of the fall before realizing I wasn't badly hurt, I could only manage to defeatedly shake my head when a sympathetic construction worker called to me from across the street asking if I needed help. After getting back to my feet and taking stock of the scrapes on my hand, I finally found my way to 26 Federal Plaza, through the airport-style security, and up to the 14th floor for the hearing. My heart sank when I saw the judge had requested the door be closed and the hearing had already begun. I waited in one of the bolted-together plastic chairs under the fluorescent lights of the waiting room. As my hand bled into a crumpled tissue I had found in the bottom of my bag, I surveyed the damage to the new iPhone I had received as a gift just a couple weeks earlier—the glass across the face of the screen had deep scrapes that would soon splinter. I pitied myself for the bad morning I was having.

It was impossible to hear how the hearing was going from the muffled sound of voices through the door, but just before the judge read her decision, one of my volunteer colleagues poked her head out of the courtroom and motioned for me to come in. I settled into one of the wooden benches in the small courtroom just in time to hear the judge deny the case and explain to the family how their deportation process would proceed. The trivial frustrations of my morning receded as the reality of what I was witnessing set in. I watched the young Guatemalan mother struggle to hold back tears as she gave her daughter a squeeze of reassurance. As the family comforted each other, I felt the weight of all the asylum cases that would be denied on that floor of the courthouse that day. This family did not have a lawyer and would be very unlikely to pursue an appeal; they would ready themselves for their deportation, and there would be another family for us to accompany to court the next day, as goes the endless cycle.

I have never faced the prospect of fleeing from my country because of a threat to my life. The United States of America granted me jus soli citizenship just for having been born on U.S. soil, so I have never had to prove to a government official that I am of "good moral character," demonstrate my working knowledge of U.S. history and civics, swear an oath of allegiance, or be subjected to any of the other preconditions required of immigrants attempting to gain U.S. citizenship.[1] Although I have spent much of my adult life studying and writing about forced migration, I do not understand the experience of living it. Sometimes when an attorney emails me to say that an asylum case I testified for was denied, I experience a kind of self-preserving numbness. Engaging emotionally with the life-threatening implications of each deportation is overwhelming.

Deciding to become an expert about something one has not experienced personally is always problematic, and the questions it raises have only complicated answers. My view of forced migration is only partial; my citizenship privilege clouds my understanding of the ways my country has benefited from the subjugation of immigrants from its inception. It is important for scholars in my position to linger over the implications of these problems with the goal of advancing the ongoing conversation about ethical research design. I want to end this book by engaging explicitly with the challenges this kind of work presents and acknowledging the guides who have helped to illuminate the way. No research design is neutral, and my work has benefited immensely from the generosity of scholars who have been explicit about their social positions and ethical choices rather than rendering them invisible in the works they produce. I hope that my own contribution to the ongoing conversation around the challenges intrinsic to this kind of work can be of use to others.

Privilege, Responsibility, and Scholar Advocacy

As far as I am concerned, the best essay on the matter of writing about or working with groups to which one does not belong is still Panamanian-American philosopher Linda Alcoff's 1991 "The Problem of Speaking for Others," although many others have joined the conversation since then.[2] The most pressing troubles, in Alcoff's view, involve the threat of muffling rather than amplifying marginalized voices, the danger of assumption, and the likelihood of perpetuating instead of dismantling power structures that admit only voices from preferred social locations. In a recent article about allyship, Tsedale M. Melaku and her coauthors illuminate through several examples how "privilege is a resource that can be deployed for good."[3] In an economy of privilege, the resource can be hoarded, spent, or shared. One modest way to put privilege to work for good and to ethically navigate the problem of speaking for others is through scholar advocacy.

As Alcoff establishes, and as is likely already clear to most readers, the answer to the thorny question of how to write about groups to which one does not belong cannot merely be to avoid the practice altogether. One cannot really circumvent the practice or the problem of speaking for others, although many attempt it as a means of skirting both responsibility and criticism. Avoidance perpetuates the marginalization of already disenfranchised voices and allows privileged actors to evade culpability for harms going on around them—harms they may, wittingly or unwittingly, perpetuate.

As Rosa Anaya told me as we discussed her human rights work in Central America, "There are no innocents. We've all been part of this cycle of perpetrating violence—by action or omission." Just as those with racial privilege may perpetuate the status quo or choose to work toward the dismantling of racism, citizens of privileged nations to which persecuted individuals flee have an integral role to play in the future of forced migration.

The damage the United States has inflicted and continues to inflict on developing nations through resource exploitation, covert political intervention, and the funding of unjust wars can be addressed and engaged not only by the victims of those horrors and their decedents but also by those living within the United States and enjoying the privileges of its citizenship. In his introduction to an edited collection of essays written by refugee authors, Việt Thanh Nguyễn charges: "Refugees are ignored and forgotten by those who are not refugees. . . . We who do the ignoring and forgetting oftentimes do not perceive it to be violence, because we do not know we do it. But sometimes we deliberately ignore and forget others . . . like threatening ghosts whose fates we ourselves have caused and denied. No wonder we do not wish to see them."[4] However common and innocuous it may seem, ignoring rather than engaging the humans at the center of one of the most widescale human rights abuses of our time perpetuates invisible harm against them through a failure to dismantle the status quo.

This caution against ignoring abuses, however, does not give privileged members of dominant groups ethical license to speak indiscriminately on the behalf of others. We are not exempted from criticism or absolved from the consequences of our words merely because we have ethical intentions; on the contrary, we should be held to account for both our motives in speaking about others and for the results. Alcoff's guidance on this matter, which has been central to my design of this project, is "to create wherever possible the conditions for dialogue and the practice of speaking *with* and *to* rather than speaking for others."[5] Meaningful dialogue can mitigate—but not remove altogether—the danger of assumption and of muffling already underrepresented voices.

The prolific work and dramatic lives of scholar activists like W. E. B. Du Bois, Angela Davis, Jane Addams, and Ignacio Martín-Baró offer a wealth of methodological models to be mined by scholars who aspire to use their platforms to engage the work of underrepresented groups and simultaneously advance some practical good. Their ethical guidance and determination inspired me as I leaned into the sharpest corners of my own work: soliciting and receiving funding from the U.S. State Department to investigate the results of harms perpetuated by the U.S. government; the prospect of benefiting professionally from publishing a retelling of others' persecution; and the knowledge that the writing of a book would likely have little tangible impact on the suffering of the humans whose stories it tells.

It is probably better for scholars to think too little of their work's ability to do good than too much. There is more than enough grandiosity to go around in academia, accompanied by an implicit but powerful view that writing itself works some justice by allowing a reader access to a perspective they would not have had before. Nguyễn writes:

> Yearning to hear the voiceless is a powerful rhetoric but also potentially a dangerous one if it prevents us from doing more than listening to a story or reading a book. Just because we have listened to that story or read that book does not mean that anything has changed for the voiceless. Reader and writers should not deceive themselves that literature changes the world. . . . Literature does not change the world until people get out of their chairs, go out in the world, and do something to transform the conditions of which the literature speaks.[6]

This charge should lead writers and readers alike to ask what good their reading and writing might do, and to question rather than take for granted the ways that engaging with the narratives of a vulnerable group can be an impetus for change.

Writer Aleksandar Hemon, who became a reluctant asylum seeker when the Bosnian War broke out while he was vacationing in the United States, suggests, "What literature does, or at least can do, is allow for individual narrative enfranchisement. The very proposition of storytelling is that each life is a multitude of details, an irreplaceable combination of experiences, which can be contained in their totality only in narration."[7] In Hemon's view, telling the stories of those whose lives and displacement have been overlooked and diminished is a radical beginning. The stories themselves carry the seed of future change, but that seed must be nourished to affect the future.

While this project was in its developmental stages, I made a list titled "What I Want My Work to Do." It became clear that some of the items on the list—engage the work of refugee authors, foreground the voices of asylum seekers—were things the writing itself could accomplish. Others—encourage advocacy, not be indifferent to suffering, prepare asylum seekers to know what to expect from their court hearings—would require actions beyond the publishing process. And so alongside the project of gathering and telling the stories found in these pages, I pursued several concurrent endeavors that allowed me more firsthand interactions with asylum seekers and that broadened my understanding of a range of perspectives while also serving some goals that superseded book writing: I volunteered in a weekly pro se asylum clinic, worked on the immigration advocacy team of a Brooklyn nonprofit, wrote country condition reports and testified in immigration court as an expert witness, served as the communication coordinator for a group of volunteers that provided practical and emotional support for the families of detained immigrants, and began corresponding regularly with some asylum-seeking pen pals in detention through snail mail. I say more about each of these efforts in the appendix.

The ways a scholar might find to act as an advocate are many, limited mostly by the availability of the scholar and the scope of the problem they are addressing. My own efforts have been made possible by a tenured position in a department that values community engagement and leaves me some time to do it. Whether one has one or many hours to devote to it, advocacy work that runs alongside scholarship is valuable both for the perspective it lends one's academic pursuits and for reasons having nothing at all to do with scholarship. Scholar advocacy can amount to more than doing volunteer work at the same time one pursues related academic projects. Advocacy can be built into the design of the research, as in the pursuit of funding that can be used to pay interviewees who are struggling financially for their time or the participant observation of some community service that advances the goals of the group whose experiences are being studied.

Scholars need not succumb to the pressure to act as neutral and removed examiners of cultural phenomena. As scholarship on feminist research design has clearly taught, neutrality is a ruse.[8]

Disengagement with one's research subjects may even be detrimental, preventing researcher and participant from seeing each other as humans engaged in a power-laden social interaction.[9] Research that has the potential to work some practical good is interactive, collaborative, and human. It must not ignore out of professional habit the possibility that researchers can work, in ways large or small, to ameliorate some facet of the problems they are studying.

There is so much good work to be done that scholars of all stripes are especially well-equipped to do, if only we can give up the notion that our expertise is bound up in our ability to dispassionately hover above a problem rather than becoming personally involved. The academic skills of critical thinking, methodical problem solving, and collaboration have endless applications in advocacy work that will ultimately benefit the scholarly project through added perspective and protect the work from producing knowledge that cannot be put to some use.

Recommendations and Resources

There are currently around 3.5 million asylum seekers across the world—the highest number that UNHCR has ever recorded. Displaced individuals often flee to neighboring areas, so about 85 percent of displaced people reside in developing regions that are often missing the material resources and long-term social services necessary for a high-functioning asylum system.[10] But even in highly developed nations like the United States, the human rights of asylum seekers are regularly threatened and violated.

Asylum is in a state of crisis. In the year 2000, more than 32,000 individuals were granted asylum in the United States; by 2019, even though UNHCR reported more displaced people worldwide than ever before, the number of individuals granted asylum in the United States had dropped almost 40 percent, to about 19,800.[11] As individuals pursue the possibility of safety though a legal asylum claim, challenges arise at every turn. Many experience sexual or other physical violence on their way to the United States. Families arriving at the southern border are routinely separated from each other and held in freezing cold detention centers with too little food and inadequate medical care.[12] Once their cases are finally scheduled to be heard, a new series of obstacles presents itself.

The majority of the nation's current immigration judges were hired under the Trump administration and offered lifetime appointments. An analysis by Reuters of eight hundred thousand immigration cases found that "judges appointed under Trump ordered immigrants deported 87% of the time, compared to 58% for all other judges over the last 20 years."[13] Forty-two percent of the new hires have no former immigration experience; the more prevalent backgrounds are as law enforcement, former prosecutors, or military personnel. Former immigration judges have charged that these new judges have a "lack of basic understanding of immigration law and policy," and the American Bar Association has charged that "due to lack of thorough vetting," the hires could be "underqualified or potentially biased."[14] President Joe Biden seems to be continuing this trend; almost all of the immigration judges hired under his administration so far have backgrounds as prosecutors, military personnel, or government immigration officials previously tasked with deporting immigrants.

Under these circumstances, asylum seekers are not able to fully enact their right to seek asylum before fair and impartial judges. This is the case in part because the immigration court currently exists under the executive branch of the U.S. government, so judges are appointed through the U.S. attorney general and report through the U.S. Department of Justice to the White House rather than existing in the judicial branch, where they would have more independence and protection from politicized efforts to sway outcomes.

The odds are stacked against asylum seekers to such a degree that only a small fraction end up living safely, free from harm, in the United States. And asylee status itself is not a cure-all. Many residents and citizens of the United States who arrived as asylum seekers still carry trauma that impacts their ability to be in healthy relationships, hold jobs, or sleep peacefully. Many face the loneliness of being geographically distant from their parents or children, and some face the exact kind of gang recruitment or extortion in the United States that they fled in their home countries.

So what can be done?

I highly recommend those seeking to take action that will benefit forced migrants to first read existing accounts that highlight the range of political changes that would be necessary at the national and international level to uphold the right to seek asylum in practice rather than only in theory. For those eager to engage in the big-picture work, I especially recommend the last chapter of Alina Das's 2020 *No Justice in the Shadows*; the work of Sean Rahaag out of the Canadian Refugee Law Lab; and the essay collection *Refugee Roulette: Disparities in Asylum Adjudication and Proposals for Reform*, edited by Jaya Ramji-Nogales, Andrew Schoenholtz, and Philip Schrag.[15] Individuals, organizations, and political actors can draw inspiration from the historic U.S. abolitionist movement and from considering the present-day practices of nations such as Canada that have more progressive refugee policy as they envision a future where immigrants are not criminalized for seeking safety.

This kind of existing big-picture work is admirable and ambitious. It is clear that dismantling and rebuilding the United States immigration system is feasible but will take a considerable amount of time and political circumstances that may or may not occur in our lifetimes. Certainly, there are actions that individuals and organizations can take even within the confines of our current circumstances as we work toward these more ambitious goals.

First, Americans of all ages would benefit from learning about the United States' role in contributing to, if not engineering, the very circumstances from which asylum seekers flee. While reading about American history may feel like a passive way to involve oneself in the plight of forced migrants, this foundational step proffers exactly the kind of perspective an individual needs to be able to understand why nations produce refugees and what would be necessary to create a sociopolitical climate in which remaining at home was as viable an option as fleeing. Gaining this historical perspective can protect well-meaning but tentative would-be advocates from retreating to an "America First" perspective at the slightest challenge and can help undermine the idea that only irreproachable and blameless folks are deserving of asylum. U.S.-funded conflicts in Central America and Eastern Europe in particular have exacerbated the kind of "kill or be killed" atmospheres in which protecting oneself has sometimes required the exact kind of violence that disqualifies applicants from asylum.

Second, individuals in a range of academic and community contexts can create opportunities for sharing immigrants' stories and commit to radical listening. Jesuit priest and founder of Homeboy Industries Gregory Boyle has been working in rehabilitation and post-incarceration reentry for gang members for more than three decades; he writes powerfully about the transformative power of storytelling he has witnessed. Boyle facilitates opportunities for former members of gangs to share in long form about their life experiences. "The moment one says, 'This is what it was like for me,' a rebirth occurs," Boyle writes. "Locating our wounds leads us to the gracious place of fragility, the contact point with another human being."[16] Creating spaces where stories are honored with attention and care can have powerful effects for both speaker and listener.

The importance of creating platforms for immigrant storytelling is bound up in the reality that stories of forced migration have been grossly underrepresented and underpreserved. News media and political discourse render immigrants faceless and voiceless in portrayals that show them only as problems to be solved; "to deprive them of their stories is a crime against humanity and history," Hemon charges.[17] Listening can be coalitional—a show of solidarity, a recognition of the speaker's expertise, and a form of reparation for the institutional historical silence around forced migration.

Nguyễn offers: "The people we call voiceless are actually talking all the time. They are loud, if you get close enough to hear them, if you are capable of listening."[18] To be capable of listening is not merely a matter of time or attention. Although we live in a culture that favors and rewards speech over silence, listening works to cultivate humility and to oppose performative allyship. Listening must be responsible and ethical. I recommend the writing of Shannon Moore on the relationship of radical listening to restorative justice and of Nicki Pombier on practices of narrative allyship.[19]

Zimbabwean refugee author Novuyo Rosa Tshuma suggests that stories serve a function of self-actualization wherein "we can try to understand ourselves and our new landscapes beyond the flattened news versions of ourselves."[20] Narrative allyship in the form of coalitional listening is not merely for those who have not had to flee their homes to better understand those who have. Creating and maintaining spaces where forced migrants can listen to and share with each other can be therapeutic and transformative. Recovering the stories of forced migration that have been ignored or intentionally silenced requires forethought and care. The organizational and administrative work of generating platforms, audiences, and community agreements to protect the speakers may be done on behalf of the storytellers rather than left to the storytellers themselves.

In her brilliant essay "The Ungrateful Refugee," Dina Nayeri writes, "It is the obligation of every person born in a safer room to open the door when someone in danger knocks. It is your duty to answer us, even if we don't give you sugary success stories. Even if we remain a bunch of ordinary Iranians, sometimes bitter or confused."[21] Although the trend has been to seek out and amplify narratives that reveal only the most heartrending or heartwarming tales of resilience, there must be space made for stories of ordinary lives that highlight that immigrants have much more to say than just a recounting of the worst things that have ever happened to them.

When oral historians and others gather stories of forced migration for research purposes, they should seek the consent of the storytellers to archive those stories in public libraries where they can be accessed by future students and scholars to mitigate the scarcity of national records of firsthand experiences of forced migration and bolster the multifaceted historical record of these experiences.

Beyond creating new spaces for story sharing, prospective advocates can seek out and patronize those that already exist: *The Bare Life Review* is a literary journal dedicated to publishing immigrant and refugee authors, and collections like Nguyễn's *Displaced: Refugee Writers on Refugee Lives* are instrumental for recognizing the scope of and differences between migrants' experiences.

Third, asylum seekers need much more support than is currently available to them during the wait for their cases to be decided. Defensive applicants often spend their waits detained alongside the homegrown perpetrators of the kinds of crimes from which asylum seekers escaped. One of the challenges facing those who want to support detained asylum seekers in practical ways is that a good deal of the money raised for this purpose ends up back in the hands of the exact government entities that perpetuate forced migrants' oppression. Paying bond for incarcerated immigrant mothers so they can be reunited with their children, for example, is a worthy cause that organizations like Immigrant Families Together and RAICES have worked tirelessly and admirably to support. Still, the volunteer-raised funds must be delivered to the Department of Justice. Even small acts of kindness like filling the commissary accounts of detained migrants put more money in the hands of the prison industrial complex where for-profit prisons thrive on the suffering of captive human beings. Still, these actions have direct and beneficiary impacts on the lives of asylum seekers.

Encouraging letters sent to immigrant detainees can curb loneliness and offer encouragement. Organizations like First Friends of NJ & NY, the Queer Detainee Empowerment Project, and Freedom for Immigrants keep running databases of detainees who would like to receive letters and the languages they speak.

Affirmative applicants and applicants with young children are less likely to be detained but still likely to have to wait several years for their cases to be decided—a wait that often leaves people living in limbo, feeling like they are "in the air," as one applicant described to me. Asylum seekers who are not detained must currently wait at least 180 days after submitting an asylum application to become legally eligible to work in the United States. Even then, depending on their language ability, childcare responsibilities, health, and skillset, it can be difficult to locate work in a new place where one may have few connections. Communities can help immensely by providing cash assistance, basic home goods, local knowledge about safe and inexpensive places to access necessities, and connections to social service organizations and potential employers. Asylum seekers need friends and kind neighbors to offer kinship during their transition to U.S. life. Initiatives like the national Hello Neighbor Network facilitate connections, but of course this work can be done individually as well.

Those who wish to support of the rights of asylum seekers can work to raise more general awareness about the injustices that are intrinsic to the U.S. asylum process. Detention centers are purposefully hidden from public view, in remote locations or tucked without signage into busy metropolitan areas to diminish the reality and scope of their presence. Frequent transfer of detainees makes it difficult for advocates and family members to keep track of their location, provide commissary support, and know how to reach them.[22] My interviews with deported asylum seekers revealed that some were transferred so frequently, they did not always know which state they were being held in; because of language barriers or simply the withholding of information, detainees sometimes do not know if they are being transferred to another facility or deported until the move is complete.

Seeking out and raising public understanding about the kinds of distressing conditions families are made to live in points out the absurdity of relegating those who need protection to the dangerous and volatile prison industrial complex. Should Americans, after pulling back this curtain, become alarmed at the amount of "criminal aliens" detained across the country, a historical lesson in exclusionary U.S. immigration policy can help. "Immigrants didn't suddenly decide to start breaking the law," Alina Das reminds us. "Rather, America chose to criminalize immigrants."[23] Immigrants are first made into criminals and then punished for being criminal. Because immigrants' coalitional potential is restricted on account of their tenuous legal position, those of us who have not been criminalized and detained for the actions we have taken to keep our families safe should consider advocating and caring for those who have. Organizations and initiatives like the Global Detention Project, the International Detention Coalition, and Freedom for Immigrants rely heavily on individual donations and volunteer organizers to create a vision of the world in which immigrant detention is not an uncontested norm.

Finally, an ode to immigration attorneys and a call for more advocacy work to connect asylum seekers to vetted and reliable representation: Immigration attorneys are highly skilled at assisting asylum seekers in the process of writing and telling their narratives of persecution to immigration officers and judges. But many applicants navigate the process without counsel despite the fact that, in every asylum case, a government attorney is present to represent the interests of U.S. Immigration and Customs Enforcement. An effective attorney is a massively influential factor in the determination of whether a case that fits the boundaries of asylum law is granted or denied. According to the American Immigration Council, between 2007 and 2012, 63 percent of immigrants in deportation proceedings—including 86 percent of those in detention—endured the process with no legal representation; depending on detention status, those with representation were between 3.5 and

10.5 times more likely to be granted relief from deportation, including through asylum.[24] According to Kids in Need of Defense, children without representation during their immigration legal process are five times more likely to be deported.

In New York, asylum seekers are more likely to have access to representation because of a network of legal nonprofits and, for detained applicants in particular, a city council–funded program called The New York Immigrant Family Unity Project that provides public defenders for immigrants facing deportation (the program does not extend to nondetained migrants). Whereas 54 percent of asylum seekers nationally are unrepresented in court, in New York City only 18 percent are unrepresented. This context offers a model— albeit imperfect—that could improve conditions in other areas.

It became clear over the course of my interviews that good immigration lawyers do much more than offer legal representation. Attorney Liz Markuci described a case in which she was fearful for her client, a transgender woman who had been significantly traumatized before fleeing to the United States. Liz felt uncertain about the client's ability to recount her story to an officer without retraumatization. The night before the interview Liz recommended some mindfulness techniques to ward off the threat of trauma and advised her client to take a bath and write in her journal. Knowing that nerves often keep people from eating, Liz met her client early in the morning on the day of the interview to buy her breakfast. When I talked with her about these compassionate practices, Liz emphasized the importance of doing "nurturing things, because it's a very alienating experience . . . you feel exposed, and so anything that you can do that is comforting I think is really important." Liz's willingness to devote extra time to nurturing her client's mental health needs despite the other demands in her sizable caseload had a noticeable effect on the client's demeanor the day of the interview, and Liz was further relieved when the officer conducting the interview demonstrated a surprising amount of respectfulness and patience. "I know that's not the case across the board, [so] I'm very grateful that we had an officer that was patient and spent the time to really deep down, dig deep and gave our client a break because she was clearly nervous. She knows how much is riding on this moment," Liz remembers. These cases reveal that even as immigration attorneys face increasing caseloads and judges and officers are pressured to hear the testimonies of more and more applicants in a day, compassionate interactions with immigration attorneys and government personnel have marked positive effects on applicants' mental health during the harrowing experience of the asylum interview and hearing.

Unfortunately, fraudulent and extortionary legal advice runs rampant, especially in big cities like New York, where "travel agencies" and "*notarios*" sell and submit fake asylum narratives on behalf of uninformed migrants that often lead to the detainment and deportation even of individuals with credible histories of persecution. It is not always easy know the difference between a credible and corrupt attorney, especially in cases where the latter has a bona fide law degree and years of experience working with asylum seekers. Extorting unsuspecting forced migrants is unfortunately a lucrative choice of career, and there is no shortage of disreputable attorneys preying on this population.

I listened to two neighborhood friends of mine in Brooklyn who are sisters talk about interactions with their immigration lawyer on multiple occasions before I began to suspect the man was extorting them. I was able to connect them with a skilled and benevolent pro bono attorney from Volunteers of Legal Service, who determined after just a short interview about their experiences and look through their paperwork that they were being scammed. The tears in their eyes as they came out of the appointment made my stomach turn. I knew they had already paid the disreputable attorney everything they had saved for their case, and even borrowed some money when his fees exceeded their expectations. There was nothing left.

Luckily, thanks to herculean efforts by local and national non-profit organizations and big law firms who have prioritized pro bono representation for immigrants in their corporate social responsibility goals, the rate of asylum seekers with access to legal counsel is increasing. TRAC Immigration, an immigration data initiative out of Syracuse University, found that in 2019 almost 85 percent of decided asylum cases were represented by legal counsel compared to 84 percent the year before, 78 percent two years before, and 76 percent five years before.[25] This steady climb is good news but still leaves out many of the most vulnerable applicants—due to the time and expertise required to do it well, the expense of legal representation, and the reality that representation is still most likely for asylum seekers with money, community support, and access to information. TRAC's numbers do not include cases that do not yet have a decision, including the vast majority of immigrants subjected to the Trump-era Migrant Protection Protocols ("Remain in Mexico") program, who were seven times less likely to be able to access legal representation than those applying for asylum from within the United States.[26]

The right to seek asylum is protected by the Universal Declaration of Human Rights, and access to legal counsel is necessary to uphold that right—especially considering the labyrinthian nature of the asylum process and the long record of human rights abuses involved. More pro bono attorneys are necessary to address the needs of asylum seekers without monetary resources, especially in the more rural areas of the United States and along the U.S.–Mexico border. The remote geographic location of some detention centers and the inhumane practice of requiring some applicants to wait in Mexico has purposefully kept attorneys and asylum seekers physically distant, making the prospect of meeting together to carefully build a case much less feasible.

When asylum seekers appear in court with poorly prepared cases because they did not have access to expert counsel, judges may feel they have little choice but to deny their cases. As Judge Bruce J. Einhorn explains forthrightly, "An adequate supply of adequate counsel would make it just as easy for even busy immigration judges to grant asylum as to deny it."[27] Asylum seekers need more information about their rights and clearer ways to discern fraudulent attorneys from scrupulous ones. Initiatives like the Immigration Advocates Network work to vet attorneys and keep a running geographic database of available counsel, but asylum seekers must know about and be able to access these digital resources in order for them to be effective.

Advocating for immigrants is not an endeavor only available to a particular skill set, profession, legal status, or political party. There are ways big and small that those concerned about the well-being and rights of forced migrants can involve themselves; I have mentioned only a few. The recent ways the U.S. government has managed those seeking asylum is likely to go down in the nation's history as one of the worst systems of human rights abuses of our time; citizens' coalitional attention is integral if we are to imagine a future that prevents further violence.

Methods and Trauma-Informed Research Design

An interdisciplinary project of this scale demands careful methodological forethought and design. Further, research design benefits if scholars are transparent about their methodological choices so that future projects can make use of the resulting insights. In what follows, I explain each of the methodologies used to produce this book.

My primary goals in this project were to (1) interrogate the power and limitations of narrative, (2) explore from a communication-centric perspective the intercultural transfer of culturally bound storytelling conventions, and (3) foreground the voices of asylum seekers themselves, providing a look behind the closed doors of the legal asylum process. To those intertwining ends, I used a qualitative mixed methods approach.

Methodologies

Court Observations

I observed nine court hearings from December 2018 to March 2020, when the New York City immigration courts closed because of COVID-19. These observations were possible because I volunteered with a nonprofit organization that arranges for volunteers to accompany asylum seekers to court; once there, we use our citizenship privilege to bear witness to hearings and stand in solidarity with applicants.

These accompaniments offer a perspective that is unique from the immigration hearings I attend as an expert witness. The goal of accompaniment is threefold: to provide moral support to the person whose future is being decided in the hearing so they do not have to attend court alone; to access, witness, and record the ways governmental personnel interact with immigrants and handle their cases; and to demonstrate to the judges, officers, and ICE attorneys present that the asylum seeker whose fate they are deciding is a part of a community who supports them and stands opposed to their deportation.

Because this act is not merely observational but is rather an act of immigration advocacy, it makes some sense to consider it through the lens of Michelle Rodino-Colocino's notion of *participant activism* rather than just observation or participant observation.[1] Participant activism provides unique insight into research contexts via the researcher's position as both analyst and advocate. For Rodino-Colocino, participant activists "ac[t] in multiple roles simultaneously—as both scholars and activists."[2] However, the court observations I conducted make two notable departures from the method Rodino-Colocino describes. First, many of her examples and applications show researchers playing a vocal and active role in organizing, protesting, and raising awareness of social problems; court accompaniment is quiet and still. We sit silently during hearings, taking detailed notes but otherwise offering just the physical presence of our bodies without comment.

Second, the "participant" side of participant activism may implicitly connote that researchers are in the same social location as those for whom they are advocating. This is not the case in my work. I am not and have never been an asylum seeker, and while I am physically present with asylum seekers during these court observations, my presence has contrasting implications. Some of the asylum seekers are brought to court from detention wearing prison clothes and shackled at the wrists and ankles; after the hearing they are promptly returned to their cells, often without even being able to share a short conversation with us. In every hearing I observed, the asylum applicant's fate hung in the balance—mine did not. My future and my family's future have never depended on the outcome of an asylum hearing, and therefore my participation in this space was a matter of physical presence rather than shared ramifications.

I recorded fieldnotes during each observation, prioritizing things that would not be included in the transcripts of the audio recordings created during each hearing: nonverbal greetings, eye contact and movement, posture, vocal tone, emotional displays, silence, arm and leg movement, and the demeanor of all participants before and after the official hearing begins and ends. The goal of the observations was simple: to get a sense of the typical or atypical verbal and nonverbal behavior of the participants. Typically present in each asylum hearing is a judge, the asylum seeker (usually called "the Respondent"), and an attorney who represents the government's interests. When the Respondent does not speak English, an interpreter is also present; in cases where the Respondent speaks a less common indigenous language or dialect, two interpreters may be required for relay interpretation. The Respondent may have an attorney present to represent them or may represent themselves— this is called "pro se" representation, from the Latin for "on one's own behalf."

An asylum seeker may appear in asylum hearings telephonically rather than in person when (1) the applicant is detained, (2) the applicant lives far from the courthouse where their case is being heard, or (3) the government redistributes an overage of cases to less busy immigrant courts. In all of the hearings I observed, the applicant was physically present.

Oral History Interviews

From 2018 to 2021, I conducted fifty-eight oral history interviews. Thirty-two of the interviews were with present and former asylum seekers (seventeen men, fifteen women): eleven from Central America (El Salvador, Guatemala, and Honduras), eight from South America (Venezuela, Colombia, and Peru), three from North America (Mexico and Cuba), four from Africa (Nigeria, Mali, and Gambia), and six from Asia (China and Japan). Of these thirty-two, at the time of the interviews, ten had been granted asylum, fourteen were still awaiting a decision in their case, seven had been denied and deported or offered voluntary departure, and one had returned home before making it to the United States.

In addition to these, I interviewed the sister of an asylum seeker who had been killed on the way to the United States, seven attorneys, three current and former immigration judges, three former asylum officers, two former officers from Customs and Border Protection, three doctors who provide psychological evaluations of asylum seekers, six representatives from U.S. and international nongovernmental organizations that work with asylum seekers and deportees, and a photojournalist who accompanied one of the recent caravans of asylum seekers as it made its way to the U.S.–Mexico border from Honduras.

Oral history involves conducting long-form autobiographical interviews with open-ended questions that follow the narrative lead of the interviewee. I consider the narrators experts in their own lives who collaborated with me for this project to produce partial accounts of their experiences, mediated by language.[3] I recruited participants through my own immigration advocacy work, through my affiliation with local immigrant-serving organizations, and through snowball sampling. Federal regulation 45 CFR 46.102(l) excludes oral history research from institutional review board (IRB) review because the method does not seek to produce general knowledge claims from a representative sample of participants. To confirm that this regulation applied to the current project, I submitted it to the IRB officer at my university who determined it exempt from review. In lieu of the protections the IRB would provide, the project followed the best practices published by the Oral History Association, the governing body for this method.[4] The interviews were conducted in English and Spanish with paid interpreters for participants who are speakers of other languages.

In adherence with trauma-informed interviewing practices, I avoided asking the asylum-seeking participants about the circumstances that required them to flee their homes. This choice shielded those who only wanted to share about life after their arrival in the United States, but the nature of oral history interviews is such that interviewees have a good deal of opportunity to steer the conversation themselves. Several of the narrators chose to tell me about why they left home despite not being asked, and in those cases I worked to present the results of the conversations carefully and ethically. To protect all of the asylum-seeking and formerly asylum-seeking narrators' identities, I asked them to choose pseudonyms, and we talked after each interview about whether there were any parts of the interview that they wanted to restrict from the project. I have excluded identifying information about these participants' places of work, ages, and, in some cases, current immigration statuses.

For the chapter content that focuses on asylum interviews and hearings, I prioritized asking participants about oral testimony given during asylum interviews and hearings rather than the written testimony that accompanies the I-589. Because of its more ephemeral nature and the methodological hurdles associated with access, oral testimony has received less attention than written testimony in asylum research. Oral and written testimony may work in tandem in cases where credible fear interviews are transcribed and then the transcription is used by judges during the hearing of oral testimony in order to check for consistency and discrepancy.

I asked asylum seekers questions such as, "How did you prepare to tell your story during your asylum interview?" and "Could you describe your interactions with the immigration judge present in your hearing?" I asked attorneys questions such as, "How do you navigate situations where your client is not able to recall or effectively recite the types of hardships that are likely to lead to a successful application?" I asked judges and asylum officers questions such as, "How important are nonverbal displays of emotion to your interpretation of an applicant's story?" The interviews were audio recorded and professionally transcribed in English. I provided cash incentives to each asylum seeker who participated; the attorneys, judges, doctors, and officers donated their time. A research assistant coded the data from both the asylum applicants and the governmental or legal personnel thematically, placing them into a single spreadsheet to facilitate considering these perspectives side by side.

Because I was explicit in my interview recruitment about my goal to assert the right to seek asylum, and because government immigration personnel are not permitted to be interviewed without the explicit permission of their office, my interviews with asylum officers and judges produced an overrepresentation of retired, left-leaning immigration personnel. To gain access to a broader array of governmental personnel's perspectives, my ethnographic observations of asylum hearings were especially useful.

When COVID-19 arrived, this project had to make some immediate and integral changes to move forward. New York City immigration courts closed, disallowing accompaniment. My oral history interviews became remote. This required changes both to how I paid participants—formerly, in cash; after, via mobile apps or wire transfer—and how I obtained their informed consent (formerly, via a handwritten signature on a hard copy deed of gift; after, via digital signatures or emails that operated in lieu of signatures). Curiously, COVID-19 also made some facets of data gathering easier. It became simpler, for example, to schedule interviews and coordinate interpreters where necessary since we were meeting in a digital space. It encouraged me to interview individuals regardless of their physical location, so several months before I arrived in Central America for a Fulbright research award that was meant to allow me to recruit and interview deportees, I was able to identify and phone interview several participants. Findings from Patrick Risan and his coauthors suggest that interviewing survivors by phone may be beneficial in contexts where interviewees have experienced trauma, although in-person interviews are still privileged as a preferred norm in oral history contexts.[5]

Once it became clear that COVID-19 was not a momentary interruption, many other mid-project oral historians made the switch to video interviews that produced both an audio and video recording. In order to maintain the anonymity of the asylum-seeking participants and because the internet bandwidth required for video calls with quality audio would have posed a challenge for some international participants, I chose to conduct audio recordings via phone instead of video calls.

Critical Narrative Analysis

In chapter 5 I employ a method of critical narrative analysis to interrogate "Know the Facts," the U.S. government's international asylum deterrence campaign. Critical narrative analysis is a method of investigating how stories are told within media artifacts such as texts and images. I follow communication scholar Sonja Foss's guidelines for this method, which include identifying the dimensions of the narrative (e.g., the setting, characters, causal relations, and so on) and discovering an explanation for the narrative—in other words, illuminating the explanatory value of the artifact through a series of pointed questions.[6] The pursuit of explanatory value interrogates, for instance, the fidelity of a narrative, the cultural tropes it employs, its omissions, and the potential counternarratives it condones or represses. Using narrative analysis as a method in this context demonstrates how power, images, and language are inextricably linked within the contexts of materiality and governmentality.

Supplemental Practices

Beyond observing court hearings, conducting interviews, and analyzing asylum deterrence texts, this project led to me to several concurrent advocacy endeavors that allowed for more first-hand interactions with asylum seekers and illuminated facets of the asylum process that would not have been available otherwise. I include them not because they resulted in concrete data but rather to highlight that the insights they afforded both were integral to this book's design and also offered a perspective beyond its scope.

First, I served for about a year as a volunteer in a weekly pro se asylum clinic. Unlike most defendants in American criminal courts, asylum seekers do not have a legal right to a court-appointed attorney and as a result often have no choice but to represent themselves if they cannot afford to hire a lawyer.[7] Pro se clinics have been developed in conjunction with law schools and nonprofits across the country to help asylum seekers complete their applications and prepare for court in response to clear data that shows the negative impact of a lack of representation.

In the clinic, I worked on small teams of volunteers who met with and explained the asylum process to applicants who were referred through nonprofits or friends and family. The team worked to gather and arrange the data required by the I-589 Application for Asylum. We listened to applicants tell their histories of persecution and worked to organize these histories into chronological order, drawing out details likely to be asked by immigration judges or Department of Homeland Security attorneys during a hearing. We connected these applicants to resources that could help them meet their immediate needs in the face of the United States' utter failure to care for the basic needs of persecuted migrants while they wait for their cases to be resolved. Some experience food insecurity, unmet physical or mental health needs, unstable living situations, or domestic violence. One need not be an expert in immigration law to serve as a volunteer at an immigration clinic. Roles range from this kind of narrative work to data entry to appointment scheduling to interpreting; pro bono immigration attorneys are often available to answer difficult questions.

I am also on the board of directors of a Brooklyn-based immigrant-serving organization called Mixteca. Mixteca acts as a community center, connecting immigrants without legal status to education, mental and physical health services, and information about their rights. We train young people to be immigration advocates and plan actions around local and national policy changes. Immigrant-serving nonprofits across the country are regularly looking for reliable and willing volunteers who will serve in capacities ranging from tabling at community events to grant writing.

Until COVID-19 redirected our funding and shifted the organization's priorities, I worked as the communication coordinator for a group of volunteers in Brooklyn that provided practical and emotional support for the families of detained immigrants. We raised money for monthly care packages for detained loved ones and for small cash grants to their families trying to make ends meet after unexpectedly losing a source of income. Because undocumented family members are at risk when they accompany children to detention centers, we facilitated monthly visits between children and their detained parents by arranging U.S. citizen drivers to take children to see their parents in detention centers in New Jersey.

The work with families of detained migrants opened my eyes to the loneliness of detention and, remembering how my Mennonite grandmother used to write and send encouraging letters to incarcerated young people, I began to correspond with some pen pals in immigrant detention through snail mail. This is how I met Rafael, who gave me permission to publish one of his letters in this book. These pen pals share with me about conditions in the detention centers and their frustrations with U.S. immigration policy and practice. They also sometimes write about their hometowns and families, ask questions about the work I do, send poetry, and talk about what they would like to do in the United States if they should receive a favorable outcome in their asylum cases. I send stamps and refill their commissary accounts when possible and tell them that there are many Americans who are frustrated with the current state of U.S. immigration policy and who work in support of immigrant rights. Especially in cases where the detainee does not have access to the internet, I share news and updates about current events in the United States and in their home countries.

Finally, I serve as an expert witness in immigration hearings and provide testimony about the harms of deportation in particular. Medical practitioners, mental health experts, and scholars who have lived and worked in asylee-producing nations and have deep knowledge of even just one of the kinds of persecution that causes individuals to flee can assist attorneys and nonprofit legal clinics by providing country condition reports that get submitted with an asylum seeker's other documents and used by the judge deciding the case.

Engaging Survivors of Traumatic Experiences

This project involved interviews with individuals who have been shot, sexually violated, tortured for information, beaten, abandoned by their families, and imprisoned, among other harms. Not being a trauma psychologist does not preclude or exonerate a scholar from carefully planning and enacting trauma-informed interviewing practices in projects that involve conversation with individuals with histories of persecution and victimhood. While interviewers should be cognizant of the effects trauma might have on the reliability of an interviewee's memory (see chapter 2), it is also crucial to consider the potential effects of the interview on the traumatized individual.

A formidable amount of scholarship—a good deal of it from the contexts of health care and policing research—offers direction on the topic. Much of this direction is pragmatic and readily applicable. For example, clinical psychologist Chris Brewin asserts that interviewing an individual too soon after a traumatic event may interfere with their ability to recover and that it is best to wait until the event is more than one month in the past.[8] Beyond considering the immediacy of the trauma, Patrick Risan, Rebecca Milne, and Per-Einar Binder offer that although interviewing a person who is in the process of recovering from trauma has the potential to be retraumatizing, the interview can also promote greater well-being by offering the interviewee the opportunity to establish a sense of control over their own narrative.[9] Interviewees who feel that both they and their interviewer are well prepared and that the interview itself might have a positive effect on society have been shown to have more positive experiences than participants who encounter lines of questioning they have not expected or who do not feel they have a social responsibility to be interviewed.[10]

The following are the trauma-informed practical procedures I employed. I frame them here as recommendations in the hope that they can be of future use to those pursuing related work:

1. Researchers working with and interviewing traumatized individuals should be explicit in their recruitment invitation. A written invitation to interview participants should

be provided in the participants' language that explains the intention and scope of the project and offers examples of the types of questions that will be asked. A traumatized participant should never be surprised by the intimacy of the questions they are asked mid-interview.

2. Leave as much room as is feasible for a flexible methodology rather than insisting on a rigid adherence to particular research practices for the sake of standardization. I have been conducting research with forced migrants for over a decade and have never gotten pushback from a publisher or peer reviewer for explaining that I prioritized the safety of my participants by making my methodology flexible rather than rigid. Be forthright with participants about the kinds of flexibility that are available—offering multiple meeting location options for an interview, providing the ability to choose between video or audio recordings, or giving the opportunity to review and suggest interview questions ahead of time can communicate to a participant that their opinions and comfort are more important than a particular outcome. If a project has successfully used a flexible methodological design, researchers should write about it in what they publish. This additional labor will offer a model for others, normalize transparency, and promote research design that foregrounds participant safety over convenience or standardization.

3. Design interview questions that allow the interviewee to choose avoidance of or engagement with difficult topics. An interviewer can inadvertently retraumatize either by pushing someone to share something they are not ready for or by removing that possibility for someone who would like to share, especially if their voice has been silenced before in other contexts. Research that errs on the side of being overly careful not to retraumatize can still be open and designed thoughtfully enough to leave

room for participants for whom talking about difficult experiences is a cathartic way of regaining agency over their story.[11] An interviewer can facilitate this by leaving lots of space in the design of open-ended interview questions and not rushing from one to the next. One should recognize and accept that traumatization is possible and even likely in poorly planned interviews. The same trauma can cause different reactions, and researchers should be prepared to address different needs.

4. Pay participants or offer another tangible benefit. Finding a $50,000 grant for a project may be unfeasible, but a project with fifty participants only needs $2,500 of funding to pay each participant $50 for their time. Seek out microgrants from foundations, academic associations, and libraries, or (if applicable) your own university. Don't avoid the work of applying for funding to pay participants because of the likelihood that it might be rejected. Marginalized populations like refugees, asylum seekers, and asylees are chronically underpaid for their labor. Counteract that pervasive reality by paying generously for people's time whenever possible. Paying interviewees provides the auxiliary benefit of a sense of mutual incentive. A researcher may feel more comfortable taking the time to conduct an interview well if they do not need to rush because of a feeling that the interviewee is doing them an uncompensated favor.[12]

5. Match and mirror the participant's communication style. Pay attention to the way an interviewee communicates and take some time before beginning the recording to build rapport and gather insight on their communication style. During the interview, match their pace: if they're moving slowly and softly through the narrative, leave some extra time between speaking turns and offer encouraging nonverbal feedback but do not interrupt; if they are quick, move a little faster through the material. Mirror the

nonverbals you observe. This sometimes means resisting the impulse to look horrified when someone tells you something horrifying if they are not displaying that emotion themselves. In these cases, it can be sufficient to say empathetically, "I'm so sorry that happened to you." Remember that interviews are not merely the performance of a methodology but also two-way conversations between humans who affect and learn from each other.[13]

6. Circulate transcripts and drafts back to participants; accept every requested change. This is a matter not every author agrees on; some even firmly contest it.[14] But working with vulnerable populations requires an understanding that sometimes trauma may cause someone to say something they later regret, or to worry about the consequences of their language, even if such worry does not seem serious to the interviewer. Circulating transcripts back to interviewees and allowing changes takes a long time and will frustrate even the most patient of writers, but giving traumatized interviewees an opportunity to edit their words is a researcher's way of demonstrating that they respect the interviewee's ownership over their own story.

7. Finally, those who work with traumatized individuals should take care of themselves. I have found trainings on how to manage vicarious trauma quite helpful not only to help me manage the weight of the narratives I encounter in my research and expert witness work but also to treat the individuals sharing those narratives with more thoughtful care. It is important for researchers who work on traumatic research subjects to create and foster a place where they can process, perhaps with a colleague or with someone who has done similar work.[15]

When researchers engage traumatized individuals in their methodologies, they have a responsibility to do that work ethically and without harm. One should not use a lack of knowledge or experience as an excuse to circumvent responsibility for the well-being of a project's participants. If vulnerable interviewees' mental health and well-being are not at the top of a project's priorities, the project should be suspended and redesigned.

Despite the reality that English-speaking scholars often refer to research participants as "subjects," projects that prioritize the humanity of rather than subdue participants is most likely to be ethical and generous. Of course, there is no one "right" way to design research, and each project that involves other people may require its own unique set of considerations and affordances.

Notes

1. Halted Expectations

1. Matt Stieb, "Everything We Know About the Inhumane Conditions at Migrant Detention Camps," *New York Magazine*, July 2, 2019, https://nymag .com/intelligencer/2019/07/the-inhumane-conditions-at-migrant-detention -camps.html.

2. "Asylum Seeker Commits Suicide on US-Mexico Border Bridge," *Al Jazeera*, January 9, 2020, https://www.aljazeera.com/news/2020/1/9/asylum -seeker-commits-suicide-on-us-mexico-border-bridge.

3. "Fact Sheet: Immigration Detention in the United States by Agency," American Immigration Council, January 2, 2020, https://www.americanimmi grationcouncil.org/research/immigration-detention-united-states-agency.

4. Arjun Appadurai, *Modernity at Large: Cultural Dimensions of Global- ization* (Minneapolis: University of Minnesota Press, 1996), 35.

5. Both affirmative and defensive applicants submit an I-589 application that may be supported by additional documentary evidence of persecution, if available. Affirmative applicants participate in an interview with an officer who may either approve their case or refer them to a judge. Defensive applicants, too, undergo an interview with an asylum officer to recount their histories; if the officer determines that the applicant has a credible fear of persecution, the applicant appears in a hearing before an immigration judge and an attorney

from Immigration and Customs Enforcement (ICE) and must once more orally present the details of their past.

6. The Trump administration imposed stricter limits on B2 tourist visas for Cubans in 2019. See U.S. Embassy Havana, "Decreasing B2 Visa Validity for Cuban Nationals," *U.S. Embassy in Cuba*, March 15, 2019, https://cu .usembassy.gov/decreasing-b2-visa-validity-for-cuban-nationals/

7. Transactional Records Access Clearinghouse, "Contrasting Experiences: MPP vs. non-MPP Immigration Court Cases," *TRAC Immigration*, December 19, 2019, https://trac.syr.edu/immigration/reports/587/

8. Chris Jennewein, "Report: Few Migrants Granted Asylum Under 'Remain in Mexico' Program," *Times of San Diego*, December 16, 2019, https://timesofsandiego.com/politics/2019/12/16/report-few-migrants-granted -asylum-under-remain-in-mexico-program/

9. "The Out Crowd," *This American Life*, November 15, 2019, https:// www.thisamericanlife.org/688/the-out-crowd.

10. The number of refugees allowed into the United States has dramatically declined to fifteen thousand people in fiscal year 2021, a drop of over 80 percent since Trump took office. See Julie Watson and Matthew Lee, "Trump Plans to Slash Refugee Admissions to US to Record Low," *U.S. News & World Report*, October 1, 2020, https://www.usnews.com/news/us/articles /2020-09-30/trump-set-to-miss-required-deadline-for-2021-refugee-quota.

11. Donica Phifer, "Donald Trump Calls Asylum Claims a 'Big Fat Con Job,' Says Mexico Should Stop Migrant Caravans from Traveling to US Border," *Newsweek*, March 29, 2019, https://www.newsweek.com/donald-trump-calls -asylum-claims-big-fat-con-job-says-mexico-should-stop-1379453.

12. Ryan Baugh, "Annual Flow Report, Refugees and Asylees: 2019," US Department of Homeland Security Office of Immigration Statistics, September 2020, https://www.dhs.gov/sites/default/files/publications/immigration -statistics/yearbook/2019/refugee_and_asylee_2019.pdf. When a judge denies a case, the applicant may appeal; defensive applicants who are ultimately unsuccessful are placed into removal proceedings.

13. U.S. Department of Justice, "Asylum Decision Rates by Nationality," Workload and Adjudication Statistics, 2020, https://www.justice.gov/eoir/page /file/1107366/download.

14. Baugh, "Annual Flow Report, Refugees and Asylees: 2019."

15. Jeremy Slack, *Deported to Death: How Drug Violence Is Changing Migration on the US–Mexico Border* (Oakland: University of California Press, 2019); and "Deported to Danger: United States Deportation Policies Expose Salvadorans to Death and Abuse," Human Rights Watch, February 5, 2020, https://www.hrw.org/report/2020/02/05/deported-danger/united-states -deportation-policies-expose-salvadorans-death-and.

16. Agnes Woolley, "Narrating the 'Asylum Story:' Between Literary and Legal Storytelling," *International Journal of Postcolonial Studies* 19, no. 3 (2016): 378, http://dx.doi.org/10.1080/1369801X.2016.1231585.

17. Amy Shuman and Carol Bohmer, "Representing Trauma: Political Asylum Narrative," *The Journal of American Folklore* 117, no. 466 (2004): 406. See also Jacqueline Bhabha, "Independent Children, Inconsistent Adults: Child Migration and the Legal Framework," *UNICEF Innocenti Research Centre*, May 2008, https://www.unicef-irc.org/publications/503-independent-children -inconsistent-adults-international-child-migration-and-the-legal.html; Sam Dolnick, "Immigrants May Be Fed False Stories to Bolster Asylum Pleas," *New York Times*, July 12, 2011, http://www.nytimes.com/2011/07/12/nyregion /immigrants-may-be-fed-false-stories-to-bolster-asylum-pleas.html; and Katherine Fobear, "I Thought We Had No Rights": Challenges in Listening, Storytelling, and Representation of LGBT Refugees," *Studies in Social Justice* 9, no. 1 (2015): 102–117, https://doi.org/10.26522/ssj.v9i1.1137.

18. Sharvari Dalal-Dheini and Michael Turansick, "AILA Policy Brief: USCIS's 'No Blank Space' Policy Leads To Capricious Rejections of Benefits Requests," *American Immigration Lawyers Association*, October 22, 2020, AILA Doc. No. 20101990, https://www.aila.org/File/DownloadEmbeddedFile /86619.

19. Walter Kälin, "Troubled Communication: Cross-Cultural Misunderstandings in the Asylum-Hearing," *International Migration Review* 20 (1986): 230–241.

20. Laura Smith-Khan's formidable critique of the policy documents that Australian officials use to attempt to standardize asylum narratives, for example, determines that such attempts are misguided since cultural and individual characteristics of asylum seekers make variation in their stories inevitable. Laura Smith-Khan, "Telling Stories: Credibility and the Representation of Social Actors in Australian Asylum Appeals," *Discourse & Society* 28, no. 5 (2017): 512–534, http://dx.doi.org/10.1177/0957926517710989; and Laura Smith-Khan, "Contesting Credibility in Australian Refugee Visa Decision Making and Public Discourse" (doctoral dissertation, Macquarie University, North Ryde, New South Wales, Australia, 2018). In subsequent work, Smith-Khan argues that prospective refugees arriving in Australia are held responsible for "performing credibility" but are at a disadvantage from the start as they must do so within a discourse that is not their own—and often presumes their dishonesty—and illuminates the ways varying amounts of communicative skill and differing narrative choices made by asylum seekers' attorneys affect case outcomes both positively and negatively. Laura Smith-Khan, "Migration Practitioners' Roles in Communicating Credible Refugee Claims," *Alternative Law Journal* 45, no. 2 (2020): 119–124, http://dx.doi.org/10.1177/103

7969X19884205. Jan Blommaert's work shows an existing contrast between the amount of narrative context asylum seekers attempt to include in their application narratives and the lesser amount of context the Belgium asylum procedure has the capacity to permit. Jan Blommaert, "Investigating Narrative Inequality: African Asylum Seekers' Stories in Belgium," *Discourse & Society* 12, no. 4 (2001): 413–449, 10.1177/0957926501012004002. In a beautifully crafted study of nonverbal communication, Gillian McFadyen demonstrates how asylum seekers in the United Kingdom may use silence as a means of nonverbally claiming some agency during their asylum interviews. Gillian McFadyen, "Memory, Language and Silence: Barriers to Refuge Within the British Asylum System," *Journal of Immigrant & Refugee Studies* 17, no. 2 (2019): 168–184, http://dx.doi.org/10.1080/15562948.2018.1429697. Robert Gibb and Anthony Good demonstrate how the need for and presence of an interpreter to translate communicative data may alter the substance and outcome of asylum hearings in the United Kingdom and France, and Marco Jacquemet shows in an ethnographic study of several European countries that asylum officers heavily rely on heavy and culturally rooted communicative details to determine asylum seekers' credibility. Taken together, this work shows that it is not possible to accurately account for the results of asylum cases without an understanding of how communicative challenges pervade the entire process. See Robert Gibb and Anthony Good, "Interpretation, Translation and Intercultural Communication in Refugee Status Determination Procedures in the UK and France," *Language and Intercultural Communication* 14, no. 3 (2014): 385–399, http://dx.doi.org/10.1080/14708477.2014.918314; and Marco Jacquemet, "Asylum and Superdiversity: The Search for Denotational Accuracy During Asylum Hearings," *Language & Communication* 44 (2015): 72–81.

21. McFadyen, "Memory, Language and Silence," 168.

22. Priscilla Alvarez, "I don't want to be deported": Inside the Tent Courts on the US-Mexico Border," *CNN*, January 28, 2020, https://www.cnn.com/2020/01/28/politics/tent-courts-remain-in-mexico/index.html; Manny Fernandez, Miriam Jordan, and Caitlin Dickerson, "The Trump Administration's Latest Experiment on the Border: Tent Courts," *New York Times*, September 13, 2019, https://www.nytimes.com/2019/09/12/us/border-tent-courts-asylum.html; and Michelle Hackman and Alicia A. Caldwell, "Immigration Tent Courts at Border Raise Due-Process Concerns," *Wall Street Journal*, December 14, 2019, https://www.wsj.com/articles/immigration-tent-courts-at-border-raise-due-process-concerns-11576332002.

23. Human Rights Watch, "Q&A: Trump Administration's 'Remain in Mexico' Program," January 29, 2020, https://www.hrw.org/news/2020/01/29/qa-trump-administrations-remain-mexico-program.

24. "Amnesty International Statement for Hearing on 'Examining the Human Rights and Legal Implications of DHS's "Remain in Mexico" Policy,'" *Amnesty International*, November 18, 2019, https://www.amnestyusa.org/our -work/government-relations/advocacy/amnesty-international-statement-for -hearing-on-examining-the-human-rights-and-legal-implications-of-dhss -remain-in-mexico-policy/.

25. Lev Golinkin, "Guests of the Holy Roman Empress Maria Theresa," in *The Displaced: Refugee Writers on Refugee Lives*, ed. Việt Thanh Nguyễn (New York: Abrams Press, 2018), 68.

26. *Public Papers of the Presidents of the United States, Lyndon B. Johnson: Containing the Public Messages, Speeches, and Statements of the President, November 22, 1963 to January 20, 1969* (Washington, D.C.: US Government Printing Office, 1965–1970), 868–869.

27. Gordon F. De Jong, "Expectations, Gender, and Norms in Migration Decision-Making," *Population Studies* 54, no. 3 (2000): 307–319, 10.1080 /713779089; and John Kennan and James R. Walker, "Modeling Individual Migration Decisions," in *International Handbook on the Economics of Migration*, ed. Amelie F. Constant and Klaus F. Zimmermann, 39–54 (Cheltenham, England: Edward Elgar, 2013).

28. Sarah C. Bishop, *U.S. Media and Migration: Refugee Oral Histories* (London: Routledge, 2016), 46.

29. Bridget M. Haas, "Citizens-in-Waiting, Deportees-in-Waiting: Power, Temporality, and Suffering in the US Asylum System," *Ethos* 45, no. 1 (2017): 75–97, http://dx.doi.org/10.1111/etho.12150.

30. Haas, "Citizens-in-Waiting," 81.

31. Cultural Orientation Resource Center, "Orientation FAQs," (n.d.), http://www.culturalorientation.net/providing-orientation/faqs; I offer a detailed analysis of this curriculum in my book *U.S. Media and Migration*.

32. Rosayra Pablo Cruz and Julie Schwietert Collazo, *Book of Rosy: A Mother's Story of Separation at the Border* (New York: HarperCollins, 2020), 105.

33. Diana Bögner, Jane Herlihy, and Chris R. Brewing, "Impact of Sexual Violence on Disclosure During Home Office Interviews," *British Journal of Psychiatry* 191, no. 1 (2007): 75–81. http://dx.doi.org/10.1192/bjp.bp.106 .030262; and Katrin Schock, Rita Rosner, and Christine Knaevelsrud, "Impact of Asylum Interviews on the Mental Health of Traumatized Asylum Seekers," *European Journal of Psychotraumatology* 6 (2015): 1–9, http://dx.doi.org/10 .3402/ejpt.v6.26286.

34. Reyna Grande, "The Parent Who Stays," in *The Displaced: Refugee Writers on Refugee Lives*, ed. Việt Thanh Nguyễn (New York: Abrams, 2018), 82.

2. Long Stories Short

1. Deryn Strange and Melanie K. T. Takarangi, "Memory Distortion for Traumatic Events: The Role of Mental Imagery," *Frontiers in Psychiatry* 6 (2015): 27, http://dx.doi.org/10.3389/fpsyt.2015.00027; Steven M. Southwick, C. Andrew Morgan, Andreas L. Nicolaou, and Dennis S. Charney, "Consistency of Memory for Combat-Related Traumatic Events in Veterans of Operation Desert Storm," *American Journal of Psychiatry* 154, no. 2 (1997): 173–1777; and C. J. Brainerd, Lilian M. Stein, Ronie A. Silveira, Gustavo Rohenkohl, and Valerie F. Reyna, "How Does Negative Emotion Cause False Memories?," *Psychological Science* 19, no. 9 (2008): 919–925, http://dx.doi.org/10.1111/j.1467-9280.2008.02177.x.

2. Martina J. Acevedo, "Battered Immigrant Mexican Women's Perspectives Regarding Abuse and Help-Seeking," *Journal of Multicultural Social Work* 8, no. 3–4 (2000): 243–282, http://dx.doi.org/10.1300/J285v08n03_04; and Heather R. Hlavka, "Normalizing Sexual Violence: Young Women Account for Harassment and Abuse," *Gender & Society* 28, no. 3 (2014): 337–58, http://dx.doi.org/10.1177/0891243214526468.

3. Julia T. Wood, "The Normalization of Violence in Heterosexual Romantic Relationships: Women's Narratives of Love and Violence," *Journal of Social and Personal Relationships* 18, no. 2 (2001): 239–261, http://dx.doi.org/10.1177/0265407501182005.

4. Pamela Heller, "Challenges Facing LGBT Asylum-Seekers: The Role of Social Work in Correcting Oppressive Immigration Processes," *Journal of Gay & Lesbian Social Services* 21, no. 2–3 (2009): 294–308, http://dx.doi.org/10.1080/10538720902772246.

5. Jenni Millbank, "From Discretion to Disbelief: Recent Trends in Refugee Determinations on the Basis of Sexual Orientation in Australia and the United Kingdom," *International Journal of Human Rights* 13, no. 2–3 (2009): 391–414, http://dx.doi.org/10.1080/13642980902758218; and Héctor Carrillo, "Immigration and LGBT Rights in the USA: Ironies and Constraints in US Asylum Cases," in *Routledge Handbook of Sexuality, Health and Rights*, ed. Peter Aggleton and Richard Parker (New York: Routledge, 2010), 466–474.

6. Carillo, "Immigration and LGBT Rights in the USA," 446.

7. Sharon Dekel and George A. Bonanno, "Changes in Trauma Memory and Patterns of Posttraumatic Stress," *Psychological Trauma: Theory, Research, Practice and Policy* 5, no. 1 (2013): 27, http://dx.doi.org/10.1037/a0022750.

8. Iris M. Engelhard, Marcel A. van den Hout, and Richard J. McNally, "Memory Consistency for Traumatic Events in Dutch Soldiers Deployed to

Iraq," *Memory* 16, no. 1 (2008): 3–9, https://dx.doi.org/10.1080/09658210 701334022.

9. Dekel and Bonanno, "Changes in Trauma Memory."

10. Walter Kälin, "Troubled Communication: Cross-Cultural Misunderstandings in the Asylum-Hearing," *International Migration Review* 20 (1986): 231.

11. Transactional Records Access Clearinghouse, "Asylum Decisions Vary Widely Across Judges and Courts—Latest Results," *TRAC Immigration*, January 13, 2020, https://trac.syr.edu/immigration/reports/590/.

12. Jeffrey Chase, "The Importance of Expert Witnesses," *Opinions/Analysis on Immigration Law* (blog), August 24, 2017, https://www.jeffreyschase .com/blog/2017/8/24/theimportance-of-expert-witnesses.

13. U.S. Department of State, "2020 Country Reports on Human Rights Practices," Bureau of Democracy, Human Rights, and Labor, 2021, https:// www.state.gov/reports/2020-country-reports-on-human-rights-practices/.

14. Tarah Demant, "A Critique of the US Department of State 2017 Country Reports on Human Rights Practices," *Amnesty International USA* (blog), May 8, 2018, https://amnestyusa.medium.com/a-critique-of-the-us-department -of-state-2017-country-reports-on-human-rights-practices-f313ec5fe8ca.

15. Robbie Gramer, "Human Rights Groups Bristling at State Department Report: What's Not in the Report Is as Important as What's in It," *Foreign Policy*, April 21, 2018, https://foreignpolicy.com/2018/04/21/human-rights -groups-bristling-at-state-human-rights-report/.

16. Deniz Akin, "Queer Asylum Seekers: Translating Sexuality in Norway," *Journal of Ethnic and Migration Studies* 43, no. 3 (2017): 458–474, http://dx .doi.org/10.1080/1369183X.2016.1243050.

17. Chase, "The Importance of Expert Witnesses."

18. Qi Wang, "Culture Effects on Adults' Earliest Childhood Recollection and Self-Description: Implications for the Relation Between Memory and the Self," *Journal of Personality and Social Psychology* 81, no. 2 (2001): 220–233, http://dx.doi.org/10.1037/0022-3514.81.2.220; Katherine Nelson, "Self and Social Functions: Individual Autobiographical Memory and Collective Narrative," *Memory* 11, no. 2 (2003): 125–136, http://dx.doi.org/10.1080 /741938203; and Qi Wang, "Remembering the Self in Cultural Contexts: A Cultural Dynamic Theory of Autobiographical Memory," *Memory Studies* 9, no. 3 (2016): 295–304, http://dx.doi.org/10.1177/1750698016645238.

19. RAIO Combined Training Program, "Cross-Cultural Communication and Other Factors That May Impede Communication at an Interview: Training Module," December 20, 2019, https://www.uscis.gov/sites/default/files /document/foia/CrossCultural_Communication_LP_RAIO.pdf.

20. USCIS, RAIO Combined Training Program, "Cross-Cultural Communication," 20, 21.

21. USCIS, RAIO Combined Training Program, "Cross-Cultural Communication," 16.

22. U.S. Citizenship and Immigration Services, "USCIS Asylum Program: Information Guide for Prospective Asylum Applicants," 2012, https://www.uscis.gov/sites/default/files/USCIS/Humanitarian/Refugees%20%26%20Asylum/Asylum/Information%20Guides%20For%20Prospective%20Applicants/info-guide-for-prospective-asylum-applicants-english.pdf. Emphasis added.

23. Bridget M. Haas, "Citizens-in-Waiting, Deportees-in-Waiting: Power, Temporality, and Suffering in the US Asylum System," *Ethos* 45, no. 1 (2017): 75–97, http://dx.doi.org/10.1111/etho.12150; and Carol Bohmer and Amy Shuman, "Producing Epistemologies of Ignorance in the Political Asylum Application Process," *Identities* 14, no. 5 (2007): 603–629, http://dx.doi.org/10.1080/10702890701662607.

24. USCIS, RAIO Combined Training Program, "Interviewing—Eliciting Testimony," December 20, 2019, https://www.uscis.gov/sites/default/files/document/foia/Interviewing_-_Eliciting_Testimony_LP_RAIO.pdf, p. 13.

25. USCIS, RAIO Combined Training Program, "Interviewing—Eliciting Testimony," 13.

26. Marco Jacquemet, "Asylum and Superdiversity: The Search for Denotational Accuracy during Asylum Hearings," *Language & Communication* 44 (2015): 72–81; and Massimiliano Spotti, "'It's all about naming things right': The Paradox of Web Truths in the Belgian Asylum-Seeking Procedure," in *Asylum Determination in Europe: Ethnographic Perspectives,* ed. N. Gill and A. Good, 69–90 (Cham, Switz.: Palgrave MacMillan, 2018), http://dx.doi.org/10.1007/978-3-319-94749-5.

27. Katrijn Maryns, "Disclosure and (Re)Performance of Gender-Based Evidence in an Interpreter-Mediated Asylum Interview," *Journal of Sociolinguistics* 17, no. 5 (2013): 661–686, http://dx.doi.org/10.1111/josl.12056; and Robert Gibb and Anthony Good, "Interpretation, Translation and Intercultural Communication in Refugee Status Determination Procedures in the UK and France," *Language and Intercultural Communication* 14, no. 3 (2014): 385–99, http://dx.doi.org/10.1080/14708477.2014.918314.

28. Amir Rasoulpour, "Writing Your Asylum Story," *RIF*, n.d., https://static1.squarespace.com/static/55e65ac9e4b028016a8e7b2b/t/5e276e58775bac40e4c6afbe/1579642462314/Asylum+Story_English.pdf.

29. Maaza Mengiste, "This Is What the Journey Does," in *The Displaced: Refugee Writers on Refugee Lives*, ed. Việt Thanh Nguyễn, 129–136 (New York: Abrams, 2018).

30. Jeff Chase, "Making Your Trial Record: The Importance of Dates—Jeffrey S. Chase," *Opinions/Analysis on Immigration Law* (blog), June 29, 2017, https://www.jeffreyschase.com/blog/2017/6/29/making-your-trial-record-the-importance-of-dates.

31. U.S. Citizenship and Immigration Services, "I-589, Application for Asylum and for Withholding of Removal, 09/10/19 Edition," September 10, 2019, https://www.uscis.gov/i-589.

32. American Immigration Lawyers Association, "Call for Examples: USCIS Rejection of Forms I-589 Due to Claimed Incompleteness," December 23, 2019.

33. Charles Davis, "Bureaucracy as a Weapon: How the Trump Administration Is Slowing Asylum Cases," *Guardian*, December 23, 2019, https://www.theguardian.com/us-news/2019/dec/23/us-immigration-trump-asylum-seekers.

34. U.S. Citizenship and Immigration Services, "I-589, Application for Asylum." Applicants whose forms were rejected because of blank spaces were given a limited window to resubmit their filing or request an updated receipt "reflecting the original filing date." See U.S. Citizenship and Immigration Services, "Notice of Settlement Agreement in *Vangala v. U.S. Citizenship and Immigration Services*, No. 4:20-cv-08143 (N.D. Cal.)," 2021, https://www.uscis.gov/laws-and-policy/other-resources/class-action-settlement-notices-and-agreements/notice-of-settlement-agreement-in-vangala-v-us-citizenship-and-immigration-services-no-420-cv-08143.

35. J. Douglas Bremner and Charles R. Marmar, eds., *Trauma, Memory, and Dissociation* (Washington, D.C.: American Psychiatric Press, 1998); Jane Herlihy and Stuart W. Turner, "Asylum Claims and Memory of Trauma: Sharing Our Knowledge," *British Journal of Psychiatry: The Journal of Mental Science* 191 (2007): 3–4, http://dx.doi.org/10.1192/bjp.bp.106.034439; and María Crespo and Violeta Fernández-Lansac, "Memory and Narrative of Traumatic Events: A Literature Review," *Psychological Trauma: Theory, Research, Practice and Policy* 8, no. 2 (2016): 149–56, http://dx.doi.org/10.1037/tra0000041.

36. Steph J. Hellawell and Chris R. Brewin, "A Comparison of Flashbacks and Ordinary Autobiographical Memories of Trauma: Content and Language," *Behaviour Research and Therapy* 42, no. 1 (2004): 1–12, http://dx.doi.org/10.1016/s0005-7967(03)00088-3.

37. Belinda Graham, Jane Herlihy, and Chris R. Brewin, "Overgeneral Memory in Asylum Seekers and Refugees," *Journal of Behavior Therapy and Experimental Psychiatry* 45, no. 3 (2014): 375–380, http://dx.doi.org/10.1016/j.jbtep.2014.03.001.

38. Strange and Takarangi, "Memory Distortion for Traumatic Events," 27.

39. Bellevue/NYU Program for Survivors of Torture, "Client Demographics," 2019, https://www.survivorsoftorture.org/.

40. Grethe E. Johnsen and Arve E. Asbjørnsen, "Verbal Learning and Memory Impairments in Posttraumatic Stress Disorder: The Role of Encoding Strategies," *Psychiatry Research* 165, no. 1–2 (2009): 68–77, http://dx.doi.org/10.1016/j.psychres.2008.01.001; Kristin W. Samuelson, "Post-Traumatic Stress Disorder and Declarative Memory Functioning: A Review," *Dialogues in Clinical Neuroscience* 13, no. 3 (2011): 346–351, http://dx.doi.org/10.31887/DCNS.2011.13.2/ksamuelson; and Graham et al., "Overgeneral Memory."

41. Grace Wyshak, "The Relation Between Change in Reports of Traumatic Events and Symptoms of Psychiatric Distress," *General Hospital Psychiatry* 16, no. 4 (1994): 290–297, http://dx.doi.org/10.1016/0163-8343(94)90009-4.

42. Hamed Aleaziz, "Being an Immigration Judge Was Their Dream. Under Trump, It Became Untenable," *Buzzfeed News*, February 13, 2019, https://www.buzzfeednews.com/article/hamedaleaziz/immigration-policy-judge-resign-trump.

3. Emotional Labor

1. REAL ID Act of 2005, H.R. 418, 109th Cong. (2005).

2. *Dyer v. Macdougall*, 201 F.2d 265 (2d Cir. 1952).

3. Nicholas Narbutas, "The Ring of Truth: Demeanor and Due Process in U.S. Asylum Law," *Columbia Human Rights Law Review* 50, no. 1 (2018): 349–94.

4. *Mendoza Manimbao v. Ashcroft*, 329 F.3d 655, 662 (9th Cir. 2003).

5. *Sarvia-Quintanilla v. United States I.N.S.*, 767 F.2d 1387, 1395 (9th Cir. 1985).

6. *Shrestha v. Holder*, 590 F.3d 1034 (9th Cir. 2010).

7. Bruce Einhorn, "Consistency, Credibility, and Culture," in *Refugee Roulette: Disparities in Asylum Adjudication and Proposals for Reform* ed. Philip G. Schrag, Andrew I. Schoenholtz, and Jaya Ramji-Nogales, 187–201 (New York: New York University Press, 2009), 189.

8. Michael Kagan, "Is Truth in the Eye of the Beholder? Objective Credibility Assessment in Refugee Status Determination," *Scholarly Works* 633 (2003): 367.

9. Narbutas, "The Ring of Truth," 350.

10. Leif A. Stromwall, "To Act Truthfully: Nonverbal Behaviour and Strategies During a Police Interrogation," *Psychology, Crime & Law* 12, no. 2 (2006): 207–219, http://dx.doi.org/10.1080/10683160512331331328; and Clea Wright Whelan, Graham F. Wagstaff, and Jacqueline M. Wheatcroft,

"High-Stakes Lies: Verbal and Nonverbal Cues to Deception in Public Appeals for Help with Missing or Murdered Relatives," *Psychiatry, Psychology, and Law* 21, no. 4 (2014): 523–537, http://dx.doi.org/10.1080/13218719.2013 .839931.

11. Nina Bernstein, "Judge Who Chastised Weeping Asylum Seeker Is Taken Off Case," *New York Times*, September 20, 2007.

12. Việt Thanh Nguyễn, Introduction to *The Displaced: Refugee Writers on Refugee Lives*, ed. Việt Thanh Nguyễn (New York: Abrams Press, 2018), 13–14.

13. Liam Stewart, "Storytelling and the Lives of Asylum Seekers," *West Coast Line* 44, no. 4 (2011): 16–22; and Amy Shuman and Carol Bohmer. "Representing Trauma: Political Asylum Narrative," *Journal of American Folklore* 117, no. 466 (2004): 394–414.

14. Hannah Arendt, *Eichmann in Jerusalem: A Report on the Banality of Evil* (New York: The Viking Press, 1963), 128.

15. Arendt, *Eichmann in Jerusalem*, 28.

16. Einhorn, "Consistency, Credibility, and Culture," 191

17. Alina Das, *No Justice in the Shadows: How America Criminalizes Immigrants* (New York: Bold Type, 2020), 157.

18. See "Deported to Danger: United States Deportation Policies Expose Salvadorans to Death and Abuse," *Human Rights Watch*, February 5, 2020, https://www.hrw.org/report/2020/02/05/deported-danger/united-states -deportation-policies-expose-salvadorans-death-and; and Sarah Stillman, "When Deportation Is a Death Sentence," *New Yorker*, January 8, 2018, https://www.newyorker.com/magazine/2018/01/15/when-deportation-is-a -death-sentence.

19. Einhorn, "Consistency, Credibility, and Culture," 189.

20. RAIO Asylum Officer Basic Training Course, "Children's Claims: Training Module," December 19, 2019, https://www.uscis.gov/sites/default/files /document/foia/Childrens_Claims_LP_RAIO.pdf, p. 40.

21. Shuman and Bohmer, "Representing Trauma," 406.

22. Anjum Gupta, "Dead Silent: Heuristics, Silent Motives, and Asylum," *Columbia Human Rights Law Review* 48, no. 1 (2016): 1–52.

23. Stuart Turner, "Torture, Refuge, and Trust," in *Mistrusting Refugees*, ed. E. Valentine Daniel and John Chr. Knudsen (Berkeley: University of California Press, 1995), 64.

4. Nonverbal Communication and Credibility

1. The transcripts and audio recordings that result from asylum hearings reveal how verbal communicative interactions shape the outcome of cases;

existing research has carefully mined verbal data from these transcripts to demonstrate how asylum seekers' words may be diluted by a court interpreter (see Katrijn Maryns, "Disclosure and (Re)Performance of Gender-Based Evidence in an Interpreter-Mediated Asylum Interview," *Journal of Sociolinguistics* 17, no. 5 [2013]: 661–686, http://dx.doi.org/10.1111/josl.12056), how "transidiomatic practices come into conflict with national language ideologies in asylum interviews" (Marco Jacquemet, "Transcribing Refugees: The Entextualization of Asylum Seekers' Hearings in a Transidiomatic Environment," *Text & Talk* 29, no. 5 [2009]: 528, http://dx.doi.org/10.1515/TEXT .2009.028), and how applicants and governmental personnel may exhibit "conflicting language ideologies" that impact a case's outcome (Laura Smith-Khan, "Telling Stories: Credibility and the Representation of Social Actors in Australian Asylum Appeals," *Discourse & Society* 28, no. 5 [2017]: 515, http://dx.doi.org/10.1177/0957926517710989). The language used in asylum applications, interviews, and hearings provides a wealth of insights. There is much to gain from these analyses, but transcripts and audio recordings obscure the reality that alongside all this verbal communication runs a simultaneous and equally complex range of nonverbal and paralinguistic communication that holds a good deal of potential to affect asylum decisions. Because much of this nonverbal communicative record is absent from transcripts and audio recordings, it must be accessed some other way. This chapter's use of data from firsthand reflections and court observations is designed to recover and highlight the presence and function of nonverbal communication in the asylum process.

2. For a detailed discussion of each of the methodologies used in this project, see the appendix.

3. Fatik Baran Mandal, "Nonverbal Communication in Humans," *Journal of Human Behavior in the Social Environment* 24, no. 4 (2014): 417, http://dx .doi.org/10.1080/10911359.2013.831288.

4. Stella Ting-Toomey and Leeva C. Chung, *Understanding Intercultural Communication* (New York: Oxford University Press, 2012).

5. See Judy A. Tyson and Shavaun M. Wall, "Effect of Inconsistency Between Counselor Verbal and Nonverbal Behavior on Perceptions of Counselor Attributes," *Journal of Counseling Psychology* 30, no. 3 (1983): 433–437; and Michelle Eskritt and Kang Lee, "Do Actions Speak Louder Than Words? Preschool Children's Use of the Verbal-Nonverbal Consistency Principle During Inconsistent Communications," *Journal of Nonverbal Behavior* 27, no. 1 (2003): 25–41.

6. Tyson and Wall, "Effect of Inconsistency," 433.

7. In the first published academic study about international deception, Charles Bond Jr. and colleagues found that both U.S. and Jordanian research

participants judged people who paused while speaking and who avoided eye contact to be less truthful. Charles F. Bond Jr., Adnan Omar, Adnan Mahmoud, and Richard Neal Bonser, "Lie Detection Across Cultures," *Journal of Non-verbal Behavior* 14 (1990): 189–204. Participants were more likely to be able to correctly identify lies when told by a member of their same ethnic group (e.g., Jordanian listener observing a Jordanian speaker) than from the other group (e.g., U.S. American listener observing a Jordanian speaker). In a later report synthesizing three subsequent experiments with participants from the United States, Jordan, and India, Bond and Atoum found evidence of "cross-cultural similarities in the way that liars act and that behavioral concomitants of deception can be identified across cultures." Charles F. Bond Jr. and Adnan Omar Atoum, "International Deception," *Personality and Social Psychology Bulletin* 26, no. 3 (2000): 394; still, listeners were more likely to judge speakers as deceptive if they were speaking in an unfamiliar language rather than the listener's language.

8. See, for example, Michael Argyle, "Non-Verbal Communication in Human Social Interaction," *Non-Verbal Communication* 2 (1972); William B. Gudykunst, Stella Ting-Toomey, and Elizabeth Chua, *Culture and Interpersonal Communication* (Newbury Park, Calif.: Sage, 1988); and Abigail A. Marsh, Hillary Anger Elfenbein, and Nalini Ambady, "Nonverbal 'Accents' " Cultural Differences in Facial Expressions of Emotion," *Psychological Science* 14, no. 4 (2003): 373–376, http://dx.doi.org/10.1111/1467-9280.24461.

We know from Rachael Jack and colleagues, for instance, that the meaning of some facial expressions are culturally specific. Rachael E. Jack, Roberto Caldara, and Philippe G. Schyns, "Internal Representations Reveal Cultural Diversity in Expectations of Facial Expressions of Emotion," *Journal of Experimental Psychology: General* 141, no. 1 (2012): 19–25, http://dx.doi.org/10.1037/a0023463. David Matsumoto found that cultural dimensions such as individualism and power distance correlate to one's ability to correctly observe the intensity of a communicator's anger and fear. David Matsumoto, "Cultural Influences on the Perception of Emotion," *Journal of Cross-Cultural Psychology* 20 (1989): 92–105. Likewise, Monica Weathers and colleagues found that race "is a significant factor in the interpretation of emotion of facial expressions." Monica D. Weathers, Elaine M. Frank, and Leigh Ann Spell, "Differences in the Communication of Affect: Members of the Same Race Versus Members of a Different Race," *Journal of Black Psychology* 28, no. 1 (2002): 66, http://dx.doi.org/10.1177/0095798402028001005. Considered together, the existing research shows clearly that both displays and interpretation of some nonverbal communication behaviors are culture-dependent.

9. Scholarship exists that offers insight from those who work with or advocate for asylum seekers by, for instance, showing the adverse psychological

effects and "emotional difficulty of encountering the client narratives" experienced by those who conduct asylum interviews. Ranit Mishori, Alisse Hannaford, Imran Mujawar, Hope Ferdowsian, and Sarah Kureshi, "'Their Stories Have Changed My Life': Clinicians' Reflections on Their Experience with and Their Motivation to Conduct Asylum Evaluations." *Journal of Immigrant and Minority Health* 18 (2016): 214, http://dx.doi.org/10.1007/s10903-014 -0144-2. But work that foregrounds the firsthand perspectives and reflections of asylum seekers themselves is much more sparse. Two notable exceptions are Amy Shuman and Carol Bohmer's analysis of the ways asylum narratives are culturally constructed, based on interactions with asylum seekers in the United States, and Blommaert's analysis of interviews she and her students conducted with African asylum seekers in Belgium. See Amy Shuman and Carol Bohmer, "Representing Trauma: Political Asylum Narrative," *Journal of American Folklore* 117, no. 466 (2004): 394–414; and Jan Blommaert, "Investigating Narrative Inequality: African Asylum Seekers' Stories in Belgium," *Discourse & Society* 12, no. 4 (2001): 413–449, http://dx.doi.org/10 .1177/0957926501012004002.

10. Toni A. M. Johnson, "On Silence, Sexuality and Skeletons: Reconceptualizing Narrative in Asylum Hearings." *Social & Legal Studies* 20, no. 1 (2011): 59, http://dx.doi.org/10.1177/0964663910391205.

11. Katrijn Maryns and Jan Blommaert, "Stylistic and Thematic Shifting as a Narrative Resource: Assessing Asylum Seekers' Repertoires," *Multilingua* 20, no. 1 (2001): 61–84, http://dx.doi.org/10.1515/MULTI.2001.003.

12. Didier Fassin and Estelle d'Halluin, "The Truth from the Body: Medical Certificates as Ultimate Evidence for Asylum Seekers," *American Anthropologist* 107 (2005): 599, http://dx.doi.org/10.1525/aa.2005.107.4.597.

13. Stuart Hall, "Encoding/Decoding." In *Media Texts: Authors and Readers*, ed. David Graddol and Oliver Boyd-Barrett, 200–211 (Clevedon, UK: Open University).

14. James Carey, *Communication as Culture: Essays on Media and Society* (New York: Routledge, 1992), 23.

15. See Wendy Leeds-Hurwitz, *Semiotics and Communication: Signs, Codes, Cultures* (New York: Erlbaum, 1993); Henrik Bødker, "Stuart Hall's Encoding/Decoding Model and the Circulation of Journalism in the Digital Landscape," *Critical Studies in Media Communication* 33, no. 5 (2016): 409–423, http://dx.doi.org/10.1080/15295036.2016.1227862; and Angel-Luke O'Donnell, "Audience," *Early American Studies: An Interdisciplinary Journal* 16, no. 4 (2018): 591–598, http://dx.doi.org/10.1353/eam.2018.0022.

16. Hall, "Encoding/Decoding," 202.

17. Carey, *Communication as Culture*, 84.

18. Hall, "Encoding/Decoding," 204.

19. Carey, *Communication as Culture*, 25.

20. Hall, "Encoding/Decoding," 207.

21. Colleen Long, "Immigration Judges Say New Quotas Undermine Independence," *Associated Press*, September 21, 2018, https://apnews.com/d800 8f7a66a54562b612bd74156f2bed.

22. Alina Das, *No Justice in the Shadows: How America Criminalizes Immigrants* (New York: Bold Type, 2020), 156.

23. Das, *No Justice in the Shadows*, 156–157.

24. Agnes Woolley, "Narrating the 'Asylum Story:' Between Literary and Legal Storytelling," *International Journal of Postcolonial Studies* 19, no. 3 (2016): 378, http://dx.doi.org/10.1080/1369801X.2016.1231585. See also Ulrika Wernesjö, "Across the Threshold: Negotiations of Deservingness Among Unaccompanied Young Refugees in Sweden," *Journal of Ethnic and Migration Studies* 46, no. 2 (2020): 389–404, http://dx.doi.org/10.1080 /1369183X.2019.1584701.

25. Global Deception Research Team, "A World of Lies," *Journal of Cross-Cultural Psychology* 37, no. 1 (2006): 63, http://dx.doi.org/10.1177/002202 2105282295.

26. Jeff Weiss, "INS Guidelines for Children's Asylum Claims," *American Immigration Lawyers Association*, December 10, 1998, https://www.aila.org /infonet/ins-guidelines-for-childrens-asylum-claims.

27. See Samantha Mann, Aldert Vrij, Sharon Leal, Pär Anders Granhag, Lara Warmelink, and Dave Forrester, "Windows to the Soul? Deliberate Eye Contact As a Cue to Deceit," *Journal of Nonverbal Behavior* 36, no. 3 (2012): 205. http://dx.doi.org/10.1007/s10919-012-0132-y; and Samantha Mann, Sarah Ewens, Dominic Shaw, Aldert Vrij, Sharon Leal, and Jackie Hillman, "Lying Eyes: Why Liars Seek Deliberate Eye Contact," *Psychiatry, Psychology and Law* 20, no. 3 (2013): 452–461, http://dx.doi.org/10.1080/13218719.2013.791218.

28. Timothy R. Levine, Kelli Jean K. Asada, and Hee Sun Park. "The Lying Chicken and the Gaze Avoidant Egg: Eye Contact, Deception, and Causal Order," *Southern Communication Journal* 71, no. 4 (2006): 401, http://dx.doi .org/10.1080/10417940601000576.

29. Charles L. Ruby and John C. Brigham, "Can Criteria-Based Content Analysis Distinguish Between True and False Statements of African-American Speakers?" *Law and Human Behavior* 22 (1998): 369–388, http://dx.doi.org /10.1023/A:1025766825429.

30. Hall, "Encoding/Decoding," 202.

31. Global Deception Research Team, "A World of Lies."

32. Lucy Akehurst, Günter Köhnken, Aldert Vrij, and Ray Bull, "Lay Persons' and Police Officers' Beliefs Regarding Deceptive Behaviour," *Applied Cognitive Psychology* 10, no. 6 (1996): 461–471.

33. Perry Rhew, "Interview with Esther Kishk," *Asylum Seekers in New York City*, May 6, 2019, https://eportfolios.macaulay.cuny.edu/bishop19/2019/05/06/perry-rhew/.

34. Hall, "Encoding/Decoding," 204.

35. Walter Kälin, "Troubled Communication: Cross-Cultural Misunderstandings in the Asylum-Hearing," *International Migration Review* 20 (1986): 234.

36. Eeva Puumala, Riitta Ylikomi, and Hanna-leena Ristimäki, "Giving an Account of Persecution: The Dynamic Formation of Asylum Narratives," *Journal of Refugee Studies* 31, no. 2 (2018): 197–215, http://dx.doi.org/10.1093/jrs/fex024.

37. Johnson, "On Silence, Sexuality and Skeletons," 72.

38. Eeva Puumala, Tarja Väyrynen, Anitta Kynsilehto, and Samu Pehkonen, "Events of the Body Politic: A Nancian Reading of Asylum-Seekers' Bodily Choreographies and Resistance," *Body & Society* 17, no. 4 (2011): 85, http://dx.doi.org/10.1177/1357034X11410453.

39. U.S. Government Accountability Office, "Immigration Courts: Actions Needed to Reduce Case Backlog and Address Long-Standing Management and Operational Challenges," June 2017, https://www.gao.gov/assets/690/685022.pdf. See also Catholic Legal Immigration Network, "Motions for Telephonic/VTC Appearance FOIA Request," October 2, 2019, https://cliniclegal.org/resources/freedom-information-act/motions-telephonicvtc-appearance-foia-request.

40. Hall, "Encoding/Decoding," 200.

5. Deterring Asylum

1. Médecins Sans Frontières, "Forced to Flee Central America's Northern Triangle: A Neglected Humanitarian Crisis," May 2017, https://www.doctorswithoutborders.org/sites/default/files/2018-06/msf_forced-to-flee-central-americas-northern-triangle.pdf.

2. The likelihood of women being sexually violated en route to the United States is well documented and is so high that those who have access to birth control often take it preemptively to prevent pregnancy in case of rape. In a caravan, this likelihood is still present but may be diminished by the group's ability to protect each other.

3. U.S. Department of State, "Migration and Refugees: Agreement Between the United States and Guatemala," signed at Washington, July 26, 2019, entered into force November 15, 2019, Treaties and Other International Acts series, 19-1115, https://www.state.gov/wp-content/uploads/2020/01/19-1115-Migration-and-Refugees-Guatemala-ACA.pdf.

4. At the time of writing, President Biden had just announced plans to suspend and terminate the Trump-era Asylum Cooperative Agreements. See Antony J. Blinken, "Suspending and Terminating the Asylum Cooperative Agreements with the Governments El Salvador, Guatemala, and Honduras," February 6, 2021, https://www.state.gov/suspending-and-terminating-the-asylum-cooperative-agreements-with-the-governments-el-salvador-guatemala-and-honduras/.

5. Sarah C. Bishop, *U.S. Media and Migration: Refugee Oral Histories* (New York: Routledge, 2016).

6. U.S. Customs and Border Protection, "CBP Commissioner Discusses Dangers of Crossing U.S. Border, Awareness Campaign," July 2, 2014, https://www.cbp.gov/newsroom/national-media-release/cbp-commissioner-discusses-dangers-crossing-us-border-awareness.

7. Lorenzo Zazueta-Castro, "VIDEO: CBP Head Touts Campaign to Deter Immigrants from Illegally Crossing into US," *Monitor*, August 26, 2015.

8. U.S. Customs and Border Protection, "Southwest Border Unaccompanied Alien Children," June 4, 2014, https://web.archive.org/web/2014060 4084428/http://www.cbp.gov/newsroom/stats/southwest-border-unaccom panied-children.

9. U.S. Customs and Border Protection, "U.S. Border Patrol Nationwide Apprehensions by Citizenship and Sector FY 2007–FY 2018," March 2019, https://www.cbp.gov/sites/default/files/assets/documents/2019-Mar/BP%20 Apps%20by%20Sector%20and%20Citizenship%20FY07-FY18.pdf.

10. Audun Beyer, Jan-Paul Brekke, and Kjerstl Thorbjørnsrud, "Communicating Borders: Informing Migrants and Potential Asylum Seekers Through Social Media," *Institutt for Samfunnsforskning*, 2017, http://hdl.handle.net /11250/2452544.

11. Paul Farrell, "Revealed: How Australia "dumped so much fucking money" on Asylum-Seeker Ad Campaign," *Guardian*, July 31, 2017, https://www.theguardian.com/australia-news/2017/aug/01/revealed-how-australia-dumped-so-much-fucking-money-on-asylum-seeker-ad-campaign.

12. The video is no longer available through the Australian government, but it is still available on the *Guardian*'s story about it: "'There is no way you will make Australia home,'" *Guardian*, April 11, 2014, https://www.theguardian .com/world/video/2014/apr/11/140411nowayfromgaus.

13. William M. Chodkowski, "The United States Information Agency Fact Sheet," American Security Project, November 2012, https://www.americans ecurityproject.org/ASP%20Reports/Ref%200097%20-%20The%20United %20States%20Information%20Agency.pdf.

14. United Nations High Commissioner for Human Rights, "Committee on the Elimination of Racial Discrimination Examines Report of Norway,"

December 6, 2018, https://www.ohchr.org/EN/NewsEvents/Pages/Display News.aspx?NewsID=23986&LangID=E.

15. UN High Commissioner for Refugees, "Global Trends: Forced Displacement in 2017," June 25, 2018, https://www.unhcr.org/globaltrends 2017/, 4.

16. Karen Lee Ashcraft, Timothy R. Kuhn, and François Cooren, "Constitutional Amendments: 'Materializing' Organizational Communication," *The Academy of Management Annals* 3, no. 1 (2009): 1–64, http://dx.doi.org/10 .1080/19416520903047186.

17. Mark Aakhus, Dawna Ballard, Andrew J. Flanagin, Timothy Kuhn, Paul Leonardi, Jennifer Mease, and Katherine Miller, "Communication and Materiality: A Conversation in the CM Café," *Communication Monographs* 78 (2011): 560, http://dx.doi.org/10.1080/03637751.2011.618358.

18. Aakhus et al., "Communication and Materiality," 563.

19. Elaine Lynn-Ee Ho and Madeleine E. Hatfield (née Dobson), "Migration and Everyday Matters: Sociality and Materiality," *Population, Space, and Place* 17 (2011): 707, http://dx.doi.org/10.1002/psp.636.

20. Michel Foucault, *Security, Territory, Population: Lectures at the Collège de France, 1977–78*, ed. Arnold I. Davidson, trans. Graham Burchell (Basingstoke: Palgrave Macmillan, 2007).

21. Didier Fassin, "Policing Borders, Producing Boundaries: The Governmentality of Immigration in Dark Times," *Annual Review of Anthropology* 40, no. 1 (2011): 214, http://dx.doi.org/10.1146/annurev-anthro-081309-145847.

22. Lisa Flores, "Constructing Rhetorical Borders: Peons, Illegal Aliens, and Competing Narratives of Immigration," *Critical Studies in Media Communication* 20, no. 4 (2003): 269–270, http://dx.doi.org/10.1080/073931803 2000142025.

23. "Immigrant Representation on Television," *The Opportunity Agenda*, 2017, https://www.opportunityagenda.org/explore/resources-publications /immigrant-representation-television.

24. U.S. Customs and Border Protection, Know the Facts Campaign Launch Press Event, July 2, 2014, transcript, https://www.cbp.gov/video/opa/c1 -dangers-press-event-070214.srt.

25. Mike Berry, Inaki Garcia-Blanco, and Kerry Moore, "Press Coverage of the Refugee And Migrant Crisis in the EU: A Content Analysis of Five European Countries," United Nations High Commission for Refugees, 2016, http://www.unhcr.org/56bb369c9.pdf, p. 4.

26. Berry, Garcia-Blanco, and Moore, "Press Coverage of the Refugee and Migrant Crisis," 4.

27. Paul Hodge, "A Grievable Life? The Criminalisation and Securing of Asylum Seeker Bodies in the 'Violent Frames' of Australia's Operation

Sovereign Borders," *Geoforum* 58 (2015): 129, http://dx.doi.org/10.1016/j
.geoforum.2014.11.006.

28. Hodge, "A Grievable Life?," 129, emphasis in original.

29. Ashcraft, Kuhn, and Cooren, "Constitutional Amendments: 'Materializing' Organizational Communication."

30. J. David Cisneros, "Contaminated Communities: The Metaphor of
'Immigrant as Pollutant' in Media Representations of Immigration," *Rheto-
ric and Public Affairs* 11, no. 4 (2008): 569–601; and Kent A. Ono and
John M. Sloop, *Shifting Borders: Rhetoric, Immigration, and California's
Proposition 187* (Philadelphia: Temple University Press, 2002).

31. Shannon Sullivan, "White Ignorance and Colonial Oppression: Or,
Why I Know So Little About Puerto Rico" in *Race and Epistemologies of
Ignorance*, ed. Shannon Sullivan and Nancy Tuana (Albany: State University
of New York Press, 2007), 154.

32. Edwidge Danticat, Foreword to *We Are All Suspects Now: Untold Stories from Immigration After 9/11*, ed. Tram Nguyen, vii–xii. (Boston: Beacon,
2005).

33. Alberto Pradilla, *Caravana: Como el Exodo Centroamericano Salio de
la Clandestinidad* (Mexico City: Penguin Random House Grupo Editorial,
2019), 50. My own interpretation from Spanish.

6. The Return

1. "Bush Campaign Speech," CSPAN, 23:06, September 28, 1992, https://
www.c-span.org/video/?32800-1/bush-campaign-speech.

2. For a more detailed history, see William Wheeler, *State of War: MS-13
and El Salvador's World of Violence* (New York: Columbia Global Reports,
2020).

3. "El Salvador: Deportees Welcome: Between MS-13 & Call Centres |
Witness | Deportados Bienvenidos," YouTube video, 25:00, posted by "Al
Jazeera English," April 9, 2018, https://www.youtube.com/watch?v=ttMOJ
-oSSbQ.

4. Roberto Lovato, *Unforgetting: A Memoir of Family, Migration, Gangs,
and Revolution in the Americas* (New York: Harper, 2020), 53.

5. Inadmissible Aliens, 8 U.S.C §1182 (2020).

6. One of the ACLU-affiliated attorneys who visited Guatemala in 2018 in
an attempt to find parents who had been deported from the United States
without their children told reported to the *LA Times*, "We don't have tele-
phone numbers. We don't have exact addresses or email addresses. . . . There
is nothing we can do but move forward and keep fighting and searching for

these deported parents. Cindy Carcamo, "In Mountains of Guatemala, Searching for Parents Deported from U.S. Without Children," *Los Angeles Times*, August 31, 2018, https://www.latimes.com/world/la-fg-guatemala-separated-families-20180831-htmlstory.html.

7. United Nations High Commissioner for Human Rights, "The Principle of *Non-Refoulement* Under International Human Rights Law," https://www.ohchr.org/Documents/Issues/Migration/GlobalCompactMigration/ThePrincipleNon-RefoulementUnderInternationalHumanRightsLaw.pdf, 1.

8. Jeremy Slack, *Deported to Death: How Drug Violence Is Changing Migration on the US–Mexico Border* (Oakland: University of California Press, 2019).

9. Beth C. Caldwell, *Deported Americans: Life After Deportation to Mexico* (Durham, N.C.: Duke University Press, 2019).

10. Amnesty International, *Eritrea: 20 Years of Independence, But Still No Freedom* (London: Amnesty International, 2013).

11. Emily Bowerman, "Risks Encountered After Forced Removal: The Return Experiences of Young Afghans," *Forced Migration Review*, 2017, https://www.fmreview.org/sites/fmr/files/FMRdownloads/en/resettlement/bowerman.pdf.

12. The Rights in Exile program, a Guggenheim-funded project currently operating in thirty countries, has labored assiduously alongside partner organizations to publicize the reality that harm befalls denied asylum seekers after deportation. But their ambitious goal of systematically, globally monitoring individuals' progress through the deportation process and beyond has proved infeasible. "Most organisations in host countries do not have the capacity to do post deportation monitoring," the program's website explains. "Moreover, while organisations in receiving countries are willing to help, they simply do not know when someone is being deported." See https://www.refugeelegalaidinformation.org/.

13. Tia Palermo, Jennifer Bleck, and Amber Peterman, "Tip of the Iceberg: Reporting and Gender-Based Violence in Developing Countries," *American Journal of Epidemiology* 179, no. 5 (2014): 602–612, http://dx.doi.org/.

14. "Deported to Danger: United States Deportation Policies Expose Salvadorans to Death and Abuse," *Human Rights Watch*, February 5, 2020, https://www.hrw.org/report/2020/02/05/deported-danger/united-states-deportation-policies-expose-salvadorans-death-and.

15. The authors of the HRW report clearly acknowledge that the instances of post-deportation harm in El Salvador are likely underrepresented in their report because of the pragmatic difficulty of proving the harms took place.

16. Lovato, *Unforgetting*, 55.

17. A notable exception is in Mexico, where migrants are released on the southern side of the border on foot or via ground transport without traveling through an airport. Although less specific travel data is available in some of these cases, limited access still exists. We know, for instance, that such deportees are likely to be preyed on by extortionists who, in one ploy, wait at popular exit points from the United States, offering their phones on the seemingly humanitarian premise of giving deportees a chance to call their family members, then using the contact to extort the family for money. Margaret Regan, *Detained and Deported: Stories of Immigrant Families Under Fire* (Boston: Beacon, 2015), 134.

18. Patricia Sulbarán Lovera, "The Migrant Girl, 9, Detained by US for 531 Days and Counting," *BBC*, February 3, 2021, https://www.bbc.com/news /world-us-canada-55913216.

19. U.S. Department of Homeland Security, "Table 40. Aliens Returned by Region and Country of Nationality: Fiscal Years 2017 to 2019," September 17, 2020, https://www.dhs.gov/immigration-statistics/yearbook/2019/table40.

20. Entering the United States without permission is a civil, not criminal, offense. See Laura Jarrett, "Are Undocumented Immigrants Committing a Crime? Not Necessarily," *CNN*, February 25, 2017, https://edition.cnn.com /2017/02/24/politics/undocumented-immigrants-not-necessarily-criminal /index.html.

21. Sonia Wolf, *La migración forzada desde el Triángulo Norte de Centroamérica: Impulsores y experiencias* (Ciudad de México: Centro de Investigación y Docencia Económicas, 2020), http://www.politicadedrogas.org/PPD /documentos/20201028_104418_informe_analiticoespcorregidomerged.pdf.

22. Wolf, *La migración forzada desde el Triángulo Norte de Centroamérica*, 71.

23. Wolf, *La migración forzada desde el Triángulo Norte de Centroamérica*, 71. Interpretation my own.

24. César Cuauhtémoc García Hernández, *Migrating to Prison: America's Obsession with Locking up Immigrants* (Old Saybrook: Tantor Media, 2019), audio ed.

25. This is not to suggest that the current antideportation movement is not a formidable effort but rather that the effort is carried on the shoulders of a relatively few committed activists rather than borne as the shared responsibility of the nation as a whole.

26. Ryan Gunderson, *Making the Familiar Strange: Sociology Contra Reification* (Abingdon, N.Y.: Routledge, 2021), 13.

27. The Trump administration infamously established a practice of deporting detained children alone by waking them up in the middle of the night to put them on planes without even notifying their families—a practice so vicious

that it is met with disbelief despite firsthand accounts from the victims appearing in the *New York Times* and other major news outlets. Caitlin Dickerson, "10 Years Old, Tearful and Confused After a Sudden Deportation," *New York Times*, May 20, 2020, https://www.nytimes.com/2020/05/20/us/coronavirus -migrant-children-unaccompanied-minors.html.

28. Clara Long, "US Deporting More Long-Term Residents," *Human Rights Watch*, April 21, 2018, https://www.hrw.org/news/2018/04/21/us -deporting-more-long-term-residents; and TRAC Immigration, "About the Data," n.d., https://trac.syr.edu/phptools/immigration/nta/about_data.html.

29. U.S. Citizenship and Immigration Services, "USCIS to Take Action to Address Asylum Backlog," January 31, 2018, https://www.uscis.gov/archive /uscis-to-take-action-to-address-asylum-backlog.

30. Alberto Pradilla, *Caravana: Como el Exodo Centroamericano Salio de la Clandestinidad* (Mexico City: Penguin Random House Grupo Editorial, 2019), 20.

31. "'No Me Dieron La Oportunidad': Esta Madre Guatemalteca Fue Deportada de EE.UU. Sin Su Hijo," *Noticias Telemundo*, October 23, 2020, https://www.telemundo.com/noticias/edicion-noticias-telemundo/inmigrac ion/video/no-me-dieron-la-oportunidad-esta-madre-guatemalteca-fue-deport ada-de-eeuu-sin-su-hijo-tmvo9607973.

32. The suit charged that "immigration officers regularly tell individuals that: (1) if they do not agree to voluntary departure they will be incarcerated for months; and (2) if they take voluntary departure they can quickly and easily 'fix' their papers in Mexico so that they can thereafter reside legally in the United States. Such statements are patently false and fail to convey the consequences of taking voluntary departure." *Isidora Lopez-Venegas et al. v. Rand Beers et al.*, 13-cv-03972 JAK (PLA) (2013), https://www.aclu.org/sites/default /files/field_document/2013-10-02-first-amended-complaint-conformed_2.pdf.

33. *Perez-Funez v. District Director, INS*, 619 F. Supp. 656 (C.D. Cal. 1985), https://law.justia.com/cases/federal/district-courts/FSupp/619/656/1797928/.

34. Adam Goodman, *The Deportation Machine: America's Long History of Expelling Immigrants* (Princeton, N.J.: Princeton University Press, 2020), 208.

35. The link between suicide and deportation is not specific to Central America. See, for example Diane Taylor, Peter Walker, and Jamie Grierson, "Revealed: Two Suicide Attempts Every Day in UK Deportation Centres," *Guardian*, October 11, 2018, https://www.theguardian.com/uk-news/2018 /oct/11/revealed-two-suicide-attempts-every-day-uk-deportation-detention -centres; and Elizabeth Schumacher, "Austria: Six Men Attempt Suicide in Face of Deportation," *DW*, September 15, 2018, https://www.dw.com/en/austria-six -men-attempt-suicide-in-face-of-deportation/a-45503042.

36. Transactional Records Access Clearinghouse, "Asylum Representation Rates Have Fallen amid Rising Denial Rates," *TRAC Immigration*, November 28, 2017, https://trac.syr.edu/immigration/reports/491/.

37. Posted in Spanish on Bartolo Fuentes's Facebook page, September 26, 2018. Translation my own.

38. Kevin Sieff, "'It's time for me to go back': Deportees Join Migrant Caravan to Return to U.S.," *Washington Post*, October 21, 2018, https://www .washingtonpost.com/world/the_americas/migrant-caravan-swells-to-more -than-5000-as-group-marches-toward-us/2018/10/21/2c864bec-d546-11e8 -8384-bcc5492fef49_story.html.

39. Pradilla, *Caravana*, 47–48. My own interpretation from Spanish.

40. Warsan Shire, "Home," *Facing History*, n.d., https://www.facinghistory .org/standing-up-hatred-intolerance/warsan-shire-home.

41. María Martin, "'Nothing for Us Here': Deported Guatemalans Plan to Return to U.S.," *NBC News*, March 29, 2018, https://www.nbcnews.com /news/latino/nothing-us-here-deported-guatemalans-plan-return-u-s-n858231.

Postscript

1. Sarah Bishop, "Model Citizens: The Making of an American Throughout the Naturalization Process," *Communication, Culture & Critique* 10, no. 3 (2017): 479–498.

2. Linda Alcoff, "The Problem of Speaking for Others," *Cultural Critique* 20 (1991): 5–32, http://dx.doi.org/10.2307/1354221.

3. Tsedale M. Melaku, Angie Beeman, David G. Smith, and W. Brad Johnson, "Be a Better Ally," *Harvard Business Review*, November–December 2020, https://hbr.org/2020/11/be-a-better-ally.

4. Việt Thanh Nguyễn, Introduction to *The Displaced: Refugee Writers on Refugee Lives*, ed. Việt Thanh Nguyễn (New York: Abrams, 2018), 15–16.

5. Alcoff, "The Problem of Speaking for Others," 23.

6. Nguyễn, Introduction, 19–20.

7. Aleksandar Hemon, "Second Country," in *The Displaced: Refugee Writers on Refugee Lives*, ed. Việt Thanh Nguyễn, 91–104 (New York: Abrams, 2018), 92–93.

8. Uma Narayan, "The Project of Feminist Epistemology: Perspectives from a Non-Western Feminist," in *Gender/Body/Knowledge: Feminist Reconstructions of Being and Knowing*, ed. Alison M. Jagger and Susan Bordo, 256–269 (New Brunswick, N.J.: Rutgers University Press, 1989).

9. Liz Stanley and Sue Wise, *Breaking Out: Feminist Consciousness and Feminist Research* (London: Routledge & Kegan Paul, 1983).

10. United Nations High Commissioner for Refugees, "Global Trends: Forced Displacement in 2019," June 18, 2020, https://www.unhcr.org/global trends2019/.

11. U.S. Department of Homeland Security, "Table 16. Individuals Granted Asylum Affirmatively or Defensively: Fiscal Years 1990 to 2016," January 8, 2018, https://www.dhs.gov/immigration-statistics/yearbook/2016/table16; Adrian Edwards, "Forced Displacement at Record 68.5 Million," *Office of the United Nations High Commissioner for Refugees*, June 19, 2018, https://www.unhcr.org/en-us/news/stories/2018/6/5b222c494/forced-displacement -record-685-million.html; and Nadwa Mossad, "Annual Flow Report, Refugees and Asylees: 2018," *U.S. Department of Homeland Security Office of Immigration Statistics*, March 2019, https://www.dhs.gov/sites/default/files /publications/immigration-statistics/yearbook/2018/refugees_asylees_2018 .pdf.

12. Jasmine L. Tyler, "Human Rights Watch Urges Members of Congress to Reject the White House's Request for Increased Immigration Funding," *Human Rights Watch*, May 10, 2019, https://www.hrw.org/news/2019/05/10 /human-rights-watch-urges-members-congress-reject-white-houses-request -increased.

13. Reade Levinson, Kristina Cooke, and Mica Rosenberg, "Special Report: How Trump Administration Left Indelible Mark on U.S. Immigration Courts, Reuters, March 8, 2021, https://www.reuters.com/article/us-usa-immigration -trump-court-special-r/special-report-how-trump-administration-left -indelible-mark-on-u-s-immigration-courts-idUSKBN2B0179.

14. Levinson et al., "Special Report."

15. Alina Das, *No Justice in the Shadows: How America Criminalizes Immigrants* (New York: Bold Type, 2020); Sean Rahaag, "Judicial Review of Refugee Determinations: The Luck of the Draw?" *Queen's Law Journal* 38, no. 1 (2012): 1–58, http://dx.doi.org/10.2139/ssrn.2027517; and Jaya Ramiji-Nogales, Andrew Schoenholtz, and Philip Schrag, eds., *Refugee Roulette: Disparities in Asylum Adjudication and Proposals for Reform* (New York: New York University Press, 2011).

16. Gregory Boyle, *Barking to the Choir: The Power of Radical Kinship* (New York: Simon & Schuster, 2017), 56.

17. Hemon, "Second Country," 92.

18. Nguyễn, Introduction, 20.

19. See Shannon A. Moore, "Radical Listening: Transdisciplinarity, Restorative Justice and Change," *World Futures: The Journal of New Paradigm Research* 27, no. 7–8 (2018): 471–489, http://dx.doi.org/10.1080/02604027 .2018.1485436; and Nicki Pombier, "A Different Story: Narrative Allyship Across Ability," *Disability Alliances and Allies* 12 (2020): 225–257, http://dx.doi

.org/10.1108/S1479-354720200000012014. For more on critical approaches to listening, see Hannah Lee Johnson, *Rhetorics of Trans Allyship, Toward and Ethic of Responsible Listening and Ally Labor*, doctoral dissertation, University of Iowa, Ames, Iowa, 2019, http://dx.doi.org/10.17077/etd.ej69-ovz5; and Sam Osborne, "*Kulini*: Framing Ethical Listening and Power-Sensitive Dialogue in Remote Aboriginal Education and Research," *Learning Communities* 22 (2017): 26–37.

20. Novuyo Rosa Tshuma, "New Lands, New Selves," in *The Displaced: Refugee Writers on Refugee Lives*, ed. Việt Thanh Nguyễn, 159–174 (New York: Abrams, 2018), 167.

21. Dina Nayeri, "The Ungrateful Refugee: 'We Have No Debt to Repay,'" *Guardian*, April 4, 2017, https://www.theguardian.com/world/2017/apr/04/dina-nayeri-ungrateful-refugee. Nayeri has published a book by the same name: *The Ungrateful Refugee: What Immigrants Never Tell You* (Edinburgh: Canongate, 2020).

22. In my written correspondence with some detained asylum seekers sent via the U.S. Postal Service, I sometimes receive returned letters a month or more after I have sent them, stamped with a notice from the detention center that reads only: "RETURN TO SENDER: NOT IN THIS FACILITY."

23. Das, *No Justice in the Shadows*, 18.

24. Ingrid Eagly and Steven Shafer, "Access to Council in Immigration Court," *American Immigration Council*, September 2016, https://www.americanimmigrationcouncil.org/sites/default/files/research/access_to_counsel_in_immigration_court.pdf, pp. 2, 19.

25. Transactional Records Access Clearinghouse, "Record Number of Asylum Cases in FY 2019," *TRAC Immigration*, January 8, 2020, https://trac.syr.edu/immigration/reports/588/.

26. Transactional Records Access Clearinghouse, "Contrasting Experiences: MPP vs. Non-MPP Immigration Court Cases," *TRAC Immigration*, December 19, 2019, https://trac.syr.edu/immigration/reports/587/.

27. Bruce Einhorn, "Consistency, Credibility, and Culture," in *Refugee Roulette: Disparities in Asylum Adjudication and Proposals for Reform*. Ed. Philip G. Schrag, Andrew I. Schoenholtz, and Jaya Ramji-Nogales, 187–201 (New York: New York University Press, 2009), 197.

Appendix: Methods and Trauma-Informed Research Design

1. Michelle Rodino-Colocino, "Participant Activism: Exploring a Methodology for Scholar-Activists Through Lessons Learned as a Precarious Labor

Organizer," *Communication, Culture & Critique* 5 (2012): 544, http://dx.doi .org/10.1111/j.1753-9137.2012.01140.x.

2. Rodino-Colocino, "Participant Activism," 546.

3. See Rosario Undurraga, "Interviewing Women in Latin America: Some Reflections on Feminist Research Practice," *Equality, Diversity and Inclusion: An International Journal* 31 (2012): 418–434, http://dx.doi.org/10.1108 /02610151211235442.

4. "Best Practices," Oral History Association, n.d., https://www.oralhistory .org/best-practices/.

5. Patrick Risan, Per-Einar Binder, and Rebecca Jane Milne, "Establishing and Maintaining Rapport in Investigative Interviews of Traumatized Victims: A Qualitative Study," *Policing: A Journal of Policy and Practice* 12, no. 4 (2018): 372–387, http://dx.doi.org/10.1093/police/pax031.

6. Sonja K. Foss, *Rhetorical Criticism: Exploration & Practice* (Long Grove, Ill.: Wavelend, 2009).

7. While the Sixth Amendment to the U.S. Constitution provides every criminal defendant the right to an attorney, deportation is a civil sanction rather than a criminal one, so asylum seekers are not eligible for this right.

8. Chris R. Brewin, "Cognitive and Emotional Reactions to Traumatic Events: Implications for Short-Term Interventions," *Advances in Mind-Body Medicine* 17, no. 3 (2001): 163–168, https://psycnet.apa.org/record/2001 -18075-001.

9. Patrick Risan, Rebecca Milne, and Per-Einar Binder, "Trauma Narratives: Recommendations for Investigative Interviewing," *Psychiatry, Psychology and Law* 4 (2020): 678–694, http://dx.doi.org/10.1080/13218719.2020.1742237.

10. Åse Langballe and Jon-Håkon Schultz, "'I couldn't tell such things to others': Trauma-Exposed Youth and the Investigative Interview," *Police Practice & Research* 18, no. 1 (2017): 62–74, http://dx.doi.org/10.1080/15614 263.2016.1229185.

11. On the open-endedness of interview questions and the potential effect on interviewee emotions, see Khiet P. Truong, Gerben J. Westerhof, Sanne M. A. Lamers, and Franciska de Jong, "Towards Modeling Expressed Emotions in Oral History Interviews: Using Verbal and Nonverbal Signals to Track Personal Narratives," *Literary and Linguistic Computing* 29, no. 4 (2014): 621– 636, https://doi.org/10.1093/llc/fqu041.

12. See Emma Head, "The Ethics and Implications of Paying Participants in Qualitative Research," *International Journal of Social Research Methodology* 12, no. 4 (2009): 335–344.

13. See Clara Greed, "The Professional and the Personal: A Study of Women Quantity Surveyors," in *Feminist Praxis: Research, Theory and Epistemology in Feminist Sociology*, ed. Liz Stanley, 145–155 (London: Routledge, 1990).

14. Philip Lapote, *To Show and to Tell: The Craft of Literary Nonfiction* (New York: Simon and Schuster, 2013).

15. See Annie S. Lemoine, "Good Storytelling: A Trauma-Informed Approach to the Preparation of Domestic Violence-Related Asylum Claims," *Loyola Journal of Public Interest Law* 19, no. 27 (2017), https://heinonline.org/HOL/LandingPage?handle=hein.journals/loyjpubil19&div=6&id=&page=, especially the section "Instilling Self-Care Practices to Alleviate Vicarious Trauma."

Bibliography

Aakhus, Mark, Dawna Ballard, Andrew J. Flanagin, Timothy Kuhn, Paul Leonardi, Jennifer Mease, and Katherine Miller. "Communication and Materiality: A Conversation in the CM Café." *Communication Monographs* 78 (2011): 557–568. http://dx.doi.org/10.1080/03637751.2011.618358.

Acevedo, Martina J. "Battered Immigrant Mexican Women's Perspectives Regarding Abuse and Help-Seeking." *Journal of Multicultural Social Work* 8, no. 3–4 (2000): 243–282. http://dx.doi.org/10.1300/J285v08n03_04.

Akehurst, Lucy, Günter Köhnken, Aldert Vrij, and Ray Bull. "Lay Persons' and Police Officers' Beliefs Regarding Deceptive Behaviour." *Applied Cognitive Psychology* 10, no. 6 (1996): 461–471.

Akin, Deniz. "Queer Asylum Seekers: Translating Sexuality in Norway." *Journal of Ethnic and Migration Studies* 43, no. 3 (2017): 458–474. http://dx.doi.org/10.1080/1369183X.2016.1243050.

Alcoff, Linda. "The Problem of Speaking for Others." *Cultural Critique* 20 (1991): 5–32. http://dx.doi.org/10.2307/1354221.

Alvarez, Priscilla. "I don't want to be deported": Inside the Tent Courts on the US-Mexico Border." *CNN*, January 28, 2020. https://www.cnn.com/2020/01/28/politics/tent-courts-remain-in-mexico/index.html.

American Immigration Lawyers Association. "Call for Examples: USCIS Rejection of Forms I-589 Due to Claimed Incompleteness." December 23, 2019.

Amnesty International. "Amnesty International Statement for Hearing on 'Examining the Human Rights and Legal Implications of DHS's "Remain in Mexico" Policy.'" November 18, 2019. https://www.amnestyusa.org/our -work/government-relations/advocacy/amnesty-international-statement -for-hearing-on-examining-the-human-rights-and-legal-implications-of -dhss-remain-in-mexico-policy/.

——. *Eritrea: 20 Years of Independence, But Still No Freedom*. London: Amnesty International, 2013.

Appadurai, Arjun. *Modernity at Large: Cultural Dimensions of Globaliza- tion*. Minneapolis: University of Minnesota Press, 1996.

Arendt, Hannah. *Eichmann in Jerusalem: A Report on the Banality of Evil*. New York: Viking, 1963.

Argyle, Michael. "Non-Verbal Communication in Human Social Interaction." *Non-Verbal Communication* 2 (1972).

Ashcraft, Karen Lee, Timothy R. Kuhn, and François Cooren. "Constitutional Amendments: 'Materializing' Organizational Communication." *Academy of Management Annals* 3, no. 1 (2009): 1–64. http://dx.doi.org/10.1080 /19416520903047186.

Baugh, Ryan. "Annual Flow Report, Refugees and Asylees: 2019." US Depart- ment of Homeland Security Office of Immigration Statistics, Septem- ber 2020. https://www.dhs.gov/sites/default/files/publications/immigration -statistics/yearbook/2019/refugee_and_asylee_2019.pdf.

Berry, Mike, Inaki Garcia-Blanco, and Kerry Moore. "Press Coverage of the Refugee and Migrant Crisis in the EU: A Content Analysis of Five Euro- pean Countries." United Nations High Commission for Refugees. 2016. http://www.unhcr.org/56bb369c9.pdf.

Beyer, Audun, Jan-Paul Brekke, and Kjerstl Thorbjørnsrud. "Communicating Borders: Informing Migrants and Potential Asylum Seekers Through Social Media." *Institutt for Samfunnsforskning*. 2017. http://hdl.handle.net/11250 /2452544.

Bhabha, Jacqueline. "Independent Children, Inconsistent Adults: Child Migra- tion and the Legal Framework." *UNICEF Innocenti Research Centre*, May 2008. https://www.unicef-irc.org/publications/503-independent-children -inconsistent-adults-international-child-migration-and-the-legal.html.

Bishop, Sarah C. "Model Citizens: The Making of an American Throughout the Naturalization Process." *Communication, Culture & Critique* 10, no. 3 (2017): 479–498.

——. *U.S. Media and Migration: Refugee Oral Histories*. London: Routledge, 2016.

Blinken, Antony J. "Suspending and Terminating the Asylum Cooperative Agreements with the Governments El Salvador, Guatemala, and Honduras."

February 6, 2021. https://www.state.gov/suspending-and-terminating-the
-asylum-cooperative-agreements-with-the-governments-el-salvador-guate
mala-and-honduras/.

Blommaert, Jan. "Investigating Narrative Inequality: African Asylum Seekers'
Stories in Belgium." *Discourse & Society* 12, no. 4 (2001): 413–449.
http://dx.doi.org/10.1177/0957926501012004002.

Bødker, Henrik. "Stuart Hall's Encoding/Decoding Model and the Circulation
of Journalism in the Digital Landscape." *Critical Studies in Media Communication* 33, no. 5 (2016): 409–423. http://dx.doi.org/10.1080/15295036
.2016.1227862.

Bögner, Diana, Jane Herlihy, and Chris R. Brewing. "Impact of Sexual Violence on Disclosure During Home Office Interviews." *British Journal of
Psychiatry* 191, no. 1 (2007): 75–81. http://dx.doi.org/10.1192/bjp.bp.106
.030262.

Bohmer, Carol, and Amy Shuman. "Producing Epistemologies of Ignorance
in the Political Asylum Application Process." *Identities* 14, no. 5 (2007):
603–629. http://dx.doi.org/10.1080/10702890701662607.

Bond, Charles F., Jr., and Adnan Omar Atoum. "International Deception." *Personality and Social Psychology Bulletin* 26, no. 3 (2000): 385–395. http://dx
.doi.org/10.1177/0146167200265010.

Bond, Charles F., Jr., Adnan Omar, Adnan Mahmoud, and Richard Neal Bonser. "Lie Detection Across Cultures." *Journal of Nonverbal Behavior* 14
(1990): 189–204.

Bowerman, Emily. "Risks Encountered After Forced Removal: The Return
Experiences of Young Afghans." *Forced Migration Review*, 2017. https://
www.fmreview.org/sites/fmr/files/FMRdownloads/en/resettlement
/bowerman.pdf.

Boyle, Gregory. *Barking to the Choir: The Power of Radical Kinship*. New
York: Simon & Schuster, 2017.

Brainerd, C. J., Lilian M. Stein, Ronie A. Silveira, Gustavo Rohenkohl, and
Valerie F. Reyna. "How Does Negative Emotion Cause False Memories?"
Psychological Science 19, no. 9 (2008): 919–925. http://dx.doi.org/10.1111
/j.1467-9280.2008.02177.x.

Bremner, J. Douglas, and Charles R. Marmar, eds. *Trauma, Memory, and Dissociation*. Washington, D.C.: American Psychiatric Press, 1998.

Brewin, Chris R. "Cognitive and Emotional Reactions to Traumatic Events:
Implications for Short-Term Interventions." *Advances in Mind-Body
Medicine* 17, no. 3 (2001): 163–168. https://psycnet.apa.org/record/2001
-18075-001.

Caldwell, Beth C. *Deported Americans: Life After Deportation to Mexico*.
Durham, N.C.: Duke University Press, 2019.

Carey, James. *Communication as Culture: Essays on Media and Society*. New York: Routledge, 1992.

Carrillo, Héctor. "Immigration and LGBT Rights in the USA: Ironies and Constraints in U.S. Asylum Cases." In *Routledge Handbook of Sexuality, Health and Rights*, ed. Peter Aggleton and Richard Parker, 466–474. New York: Routledge, 2010.

Catholic Legal Immigration Network. "Motions for Telephonic/VTC Appearance FOIA Request." October 2, 2019. https://cliniclegal.org/resources/free dom-information-act/motions-telephonicvtc-appearance-foia-request.

Chodkowski, William M. "The United States Information Agency Fact Sheet." *American Security Project*, November 2012. https://www.americansecu rityproject.org/ASP%20Reports/Ref%200097%20-%20The%20United %20States%20Information%20Agency.pdf.

Cisneros, J. David. "Contaminated Communities: The Metaphor of 'Immigrant as Pollutant' in Media Representations of Immigration." *Rhetoric and Public Affairs* 11, no. 4 (2008): 569–601.

Crespo, María, and Violeta Fernández-Lansac. "Memory and Narrative of Traumatic Events: A Literature Review." *Psychological Trauma: Theory, Research, Practice and Policy* 8, no. 2 (2016): 149–56. http://dx.doi.org/10 .1037/tra0000041.

Dalal-Dheini, Sharvari, and Michael Turansick. "AILA Policy Brief: USCIS's 'No Blank Space' Policy Leads to Capricious Rejections of Benefits Requests." *American Immigration Lawyers Association*, October 22, 2020. AILA Doc. No. 20101990. https://www.aila.org/File/DownloadEmbedded File/86619.

Danticat, Edwidge. Foreword to *We Are All Suspects Now: Untold Stories from Immigration After 9/11*, ed. Tram Nguyen, vii–xii. Boston: Beacon, 2005.

Das, Alina. *No Justice in the Shadows: How America Criminalizes Immigrants*. New York: Bold Type, 2020.

De Jong, Gordon F. "Expectations, Gender, and Norms in Migration Decision-Making." *Population Studies* 54, no. 3 (2000): 307–319. http://dx.doi.org /10.1080/713779089.

Dekel, Sharon, and George A. Bonanno. "Changes in Trauma Memory and Patterns of Posttraumatic Stress." *Psychological Trauma: Theory, Research, Practice and Policy* 5, no. 1 (2013): 26–34. http://dx.doi.org/10.1037/a00 22750.

"Deported to Danger: United States Deportation Policies Expose Salvadorans to Death and Abuse." *Human Rights Watch*, February 5, 2020. https:// www.hrw.org/report/2020/02/05/deported-danger/united-states-deporta tion-policies-expose-salvadorans-death-and.

Eagly, Ingrid, and Steven Shafer. "Access to Council in Immigration Court." *American Immigration Council*, September 2016. https://www.american immigrationcouncil.org/sites/default/files/research/access_to_counsel_in _immigration_court.pdf.

Edwards, Adrian. "Forced Displacement at Record 68.5 Million." *Office of the United Nations High Commissioner for Refugees*, June 19, 2018. https://www.unhcr.org/en-us/news/stories/2018/6/5b222c494/forced -displacement-record-685-million.html.

Einhorn, Bruce. "Consistency, Credibility, and Culture." In *Refugee Roulette: Disparities in Asylum Adjudication and Proposals for Reform*, ed. Philip G. Schrag, Andrew I. Schoenholtz, and Jaya Ramji-Nogales, 187–201. New York: New York University Press, 2009.

Engelhard, Iris M., Marcel A. van den Hout, and Richard J. McNally. "Memory Consistency for Traumatic Events in Dutch Soldiers Deployed to Iraq." *Memory* 16, no. 1 (2008): 3–9. https://dx.doi.org/10.1080/09658210701334022.

Eskritt, Michelle, and Kang Lee. "Do Actions Speak Louder Than Words? Preschool Children's Use of the Verbal-Nonverbal Consistency Principle During Inconsistent Communications." *Journal of Nonverbal Behavior* 27, no. 1 (2003): 25–41.

"Fact Sheet: Immigration Detention in the United States by Agency." *American Immigration Council*. January 2, 2020. https://www.americanimmi grationcouncil.org/research/immigration-detention-united-states-agency.

Fassin, Didier. "Policing Borders, Producing Boundaries: The Governmentality of Immigration in Dark Times." *Annual Review of Anthropology* 40, no. 1 (2011): 213–226. http://dx.doi.org/10.1146/annurev-anthro-081309 -145847.

Fassin, Didier, and Estelle d'Halluin. "The Truth from the Body: Medical Certificates as Ultimate Evidence for Asylum Seekers." *American Anthropologist* 107 (2005): 597–608. http://dx.doi.org/10.1525/aa.2005.107.4.597.

Flores, Lisa. "Constructing Rhetorical Borders: Peons, Illegal Aliens, and Competing Narratives of Immigration." *Critical Studies in Media Communication* 20, no. 4 (2003): 362–387. http://dx.doi.org/10.1080/07393180320 00142025.

Fobear, Katherine. "I Thought We Had No Rights": Challenges in Listening, Storytelling, and Representation of LGBT Refugees." *Studies in Social Justice* 9, no. 1 (2015): 102–117. http://dx.doi.org/10.26522/ssj.v9i1.1137.

Foss, Sonja K. *Rhetorical Criticism: Exploration & Practice*. Long Grove, Ill.: Wavelend, 2009.

Foucault, Michel. *Security, Territory, Population: Lectures at the Collège de France, 1977–78*. Ed. Arnold I. Davidson. Trans. Graham Burchell. Basingstoke: Palgrave Macmillan, 2007.

García Hernández, César Cuauhtémoc. *Migrating to Prison: America's Obsession with Locking Up Immigrants.* Old Saybrook, Conn.: Tantor Media, 2019. Audio ed.

Gibb, Robert, and Anthony Good. "Interpretation, Translation and Intercultural Communication in Refugee Status Determination Procedures in the UK and France." *Language and Intercultural Communication* 14, no. 3 (2014): 385–399. http://dx.doi.org/10.1080/14708477.2014.918314.

Global Deception Research Team. "A World of Lies." *Journal of Cross-Cultural Psychology* 37, no. 1 (2006): 60–74. http://dx.doi.org/10.1177/002202210 5282295.

Golinkin, Lev. "Guests of the Holy Roman Empress Maria Theresa." In *The Displaced: Refugee Writers on Refugee Lives*, ed. Việt Thanh Nguyễn, 67–72. New York: Abrams, 2018.

Goodman, Adam. *The Deportation Machine: America's Long History of Expelling Immigrants.* Princeton, N.J.: Princeton University Press, 2020.

Graham, Belinda, Jane Herlihy, and Chris R. Brewin. "Overgeneral Memory in Asylum Seekers and Refugees." *Journal of Behavior Therapy and Experimental Psychiatry* 45, no. 3 (2014): 375–80. http://dx.doi.org/10.1016/j.jbtep.2014.03.001.

Gramer, Robbie. "Human Rights Groups Bristling at State Department Report: What's Not in the Report Is as Important as What's in It." *Foreign Policy*, April 21, 2018. https://foreignpolicy.com/2018/04/21/human-rights-groups-bristling-at-state-human-rights-report/.

Grande, Reyna. "The Parent Who Stays." In *The Displaced: Refugee Writers on Refugee Lives*, ed. Việt Thanh Nguyễn, 73–82. New York: Abrams, 2018.

Greed, Clara. "The Professional and the Personal: A Study of Women Quantity Surveyors." In *Feminist Praxis: Research, Theory and Epistemology in Feminist Sociology*, ed. Liz Stanley, 145–155. London: Routledge, 1990.

Gudykunst, William B., Stella Ting-Toomey, and Elizabeth Chua. *Culture and Interpersonal Communication.* Newbury Park, Calif.: Sage, 1988.

Gunderson, Ryan. *Making the Familiar Strange: Sociology Contra Reification.* Abingdon, N.Y.: Routledge, 2021.

Gupta, Anjum. "Dead Silent: Heuristics, Silent Motives, and Asylum." *Columbia Human Rights Law Review* 48, no. 1 (2016): 1–52.

Haas, Bridget M. "Citizens-in-Waiting, Deportees-in-Waiting: Power, Temporality, and Suffering in the US Asylum System." *Ethos* 45, no. 1 (2017): 75–97. http://dx.doi.org/10.1111/etho.12150.

Hall, Stuart. "Encoding/Decoding." In *Media Texts: Authors and Readers*, ed. David Graddol and Oliver Boyd-Barrett, 200–211. Clevedon, UK: Open University.

Head, Emma. "The Ethics and Implications of Paying Participants in Qualitative Research." *International Journal of Social Research Methodology* 12, no. 4 (2009): 335–344.

Hellawell, Steph J., and Chris R. Brewin. "A Comparison of Flashbacks and Ordinary Autobiographical Memories of Trauma: Content and Language." *Behaviour Research and Therapy* 42, no. 1 (2004): 1–12. http://dx.doi.org /10.1016/s0005-7967(03)00088-3.

Heller, Pamela. "Challenges Facing LGBT Asylum-Seekers: The Role of Social Work in Correcting Oppressive Immigration Processes." *Journal of Gay & Lesbian Social Services* 21, no. 2–3 (2009): 294–308. http://dx.doi.org/10 .1080/10538720902772246.

Hemon, Alexander. "Second Country." In *The Displaced: Refugee Writers on Refugee Lives*, ed. Việt Thanh Nguyễn, 91–104. New York: Abrams, 2018.

Herlihy, Jane, and Stuart W. Turner. "Asylum Claims and Memory of Trauma: Sharing Our Knowledge." *British Journal of Psychiatry* 191 (2007): 3–4. http://dx.doi.org/10.1192/bjp.bp.106.034439.

Hlavka, Heather R. "Normalizing Sexual Violence: Young Women Account for Harassment and Abuse." *Gender & Society* 28, no. 3 (2014): 337–358. http://dx.doi.org/10.1177/0891243214526468.

Ho, Elaine Lynn-Ee, and Madeleine E. Hatfield (née Dobson). "Migration and Everyday Matters: Sociality and Materiality." *Population, Space, and Place* 17 (2011): 707–713. http://dx.doi.org/10.1002/psp.636.

Hodge, Paul. "A Grievable Life? The Criminalisation and Securing of Asylum Seeker Bodies in the 'Violent Frames' of Australia's Operation Sovereign Borders." *Geoforum* 58 (2015): 122–131. http://dx.doi.org/10.1016/j.geo forum.2014.11.006.

Human Rights Watch. "Q&A: Trump Administration's 'Remain in Mexico' Program." January 29, 2020. https://www.hrw.org/news/2020/01/29/qa -trump-administrations-remain-mexico-program.

Jack, Rachael E., Roberto Caldara, and Philippe G. Schyns. "Internal Representations Reveal Cultural Diversity in Expectations of Facial Expressions of Emotion." *Journal of Experimental Psychology: General* 141, no. 1 (2012): 19–25. http://dx.doi.org/10.1037/a0023463.

Jacquemet, Mario. "Asylum and Superdiversity: The Search for Denotational Accuracy During Asylum Hearings." *Language & Communication* 44 (2015): 72–81.

——. "Transcribing Refugees: The Entextualization of Asylum Seekers' Hearings in a Transidiomatic Environment." *Text & Talk* 29, no. 5 (2009): 525–546. http://dx.doi.org/10.1515/TEXT.2009.028.

Jarrett, Laura. "Are Undocumented Immigrants Committing a Crime? Not Necessarily." *CNN*. February 25, 2017. https://edition.cnn.com/2017/02/24 /politics/undocumented-immigrants-not-necessarily-criminal/index.html.

Jennewein, Chris. "Report: Few Migrants Granted Asylum Under 'Remain in Mexico' Program." *Times of San Diego*, December 16, 2019. https:// timesofsandiego.com/politics/2019/12/16/report-few-migrants-granted -asylum-under-remain-in-mexico-program/.

Johnsen, Grethe E., and Arve E. Asbjørnsen. "Verbal Learning and Memory Impairments in Posttraumatic Stress Disorder: The Role of Encoding Strategies." *Psychiatry Research* 165, no. 1–2 (2009): 68–77. http://dx.doi.org /10.1016/j.psychres.2008.01.001.

Johnson, Hannah Lee. "Rhetorics of Trans Allyship, Toward and Ethic of Responsible Listening and Ally Labor." Doctoral dissertation, University of Iowa, Ames, Iowa, 2019. http://dx.doi.org/10.17077/etd.ej69-ovz5.

Johnson, Toni A. M. "On Silence, Sexuality and Skeletons: Reconceptualizing Narrative in Asylum Hearings." *Social & Legal Studies* 20, no. 1 (2011): 57–78. http://dx.doi.org/10.1177/0964663910391205.

Kagan, Michael. "Is Truth in the Eye of the Beholder? Objective Credibility Assessment in Refugee Status Determination." *Scholarly Works* 633 (2003): 367–413.

Kälin, Walter. "Troubled Communication: Cross-Cultural Misunderstandings in the Asylum-Hearing." *International Migration Review* 20 (1986): 230–241.

Kennan, John, and James R. Walker. "Modeling Individual Migration Decisions." In *International Handbook on the Economics of Migration*, ed. Amelie F. Constant and Klaus F. Zimmermann, 39–54. Cheltenham, England: Edward Elgar, 2013.

Langballe, Åse, and Jon-Håkon Schultz. "'I couldn't tell such things to others': Trauma-Exposed Youth and the Investigative Interview." *Police Practice & Research* 18, no. 1 (2017): 62–74. http://dx.doi.org/10.1080/15614 263.2016.1229185.

Lapote, Philip. *To Show and to Tell: The Craft of Literary Nonfiction*. New York: Simon and Schuster, 2013.

Leeds-Hurwitz, Wendy. *Semiotics and Communication: Signs, Codes, Cultures*. New York: Erlbaum, 1993.

Lemoine, Annie S. "Good Storytelling: A Trauma-Informed Approach to the Preparation of Domestic Violence-Related Asylum Claims." *Loyola Journal of Public Interest Law* 19, no. 27 (2017). https://heinonline.org/HOL /LandingPage?handle=hein.journals/loyjpubil19&div=6&id=&page=.

Levine, Timothy R., Kelli Jean K. Asada, and Hee Sun Park. "The Lying Chicken and the Gaze Avoidant Egg: Eye Contact, Deception, and Causal

Order." *Southern Communication Journal* 71, no. 4 (2006): 401–411. http://dx.doi.org/10.1080/10417940601000576.

Lovato, Roberto. *Unforgetting: A Memoir of Family, Migration, Gangs, and Revolution in the Americas*. New York: Harper, 2020.

Mandal, Fatik Baran. "Nonverbal Communication in Humans." *Journal of Human Behavior in the Social Environment* 24, no. 4 (2014): 417–421. http://dx.doi.org/10.1080/10911359.2013.831288.

Mann, Samantha, Sarah Ewens, Dominic Shaw, Aldert Vrij, Sharon Leal, and Jackie Hillman. "Lying Eyes: Why Liars Seek Deliberate Eye Contact." *Psychiatry, Psychology and Law* 20, no. 3 (2013): 452–461. http://dx.doi.org /10.1080/13218719.2013.791218.

Mann, Samantha, Aldert Vrij, Sharon Leal, Pär Anders Granhag, Lara Warmelink, and Dave Forrester. "Windows to the Soul? Deliberate Eye Contact As a Cue to Deceit." *Journal of Nonverbal Behavior* 36, no. 3 (2012): 205–215. http://dx.doi.org/10.1007/s10919-012-0132-y.

Marsh, Abigail A., Hillary Anger Elfenbein, and Nalini Ambady. "Nonverbal 'Accents': Cultural Differences in Facial Expressions of Emotion." *Psychological Science* 14, no. 4 (2003): 373–376. http://dx.doi.org/10.1111/1467 -9280.24461.

Maryns, Katrijn. "Disclosure and (Re)Performance of Gender-Based Evidence in an Interpreter-Mediated Asylum Interview." *Journal of Sociolinguistics* 17, no. 5 (2013): 661–686. http://dx.doi.org/10.1111/josl.12056.

Maryns, Katrijn, and Jan Blommaert. "Stylistic and Thematic Shifting as a Narrative Resource: Assessing Asylum Seekers' Repertoires." *Multilingua* 20, no. 1 (2001): 61–84. http://dx.doi.org/10.1515/MULTI.2001.003.

Matsumoto, David. "Cultural Influences on the Perception of Emotion." *Journal of Cross-Cultural Psychology* 20 (1989): 92–105.

McFadyen, Gillian. "Memory, Language and Silence: Barriers to Refuge Within the British Asylum System." *Journal of Immigrant & Refugee Studies* 17, no. 2 (2019): 168–184. http://dx.doi.org/10.1080/15562948.2018 .1429697.

Médecins Sans Frontières. "Forced to Flee Central America's Northern Triangle: A Neglected Humanitarian Crisis." May 2017. https://www.doctors withoutborders.org/sites/default/files/2018-06/msf_forced-to-flee-central -americas-northern-triangle.pdf.

Melaku, Tsedale M., Angie Beeman, David G. Smith, and W. Brad Johnson. "Be a Better Ally." *Harvard Business Review*, November–December 2020. https://hbr.org/2020/11/be-a-better-ally.

Mengiste, Maaza. "This Is What the Journey Does." In *The Displaced: Refugee Writers on Refugee Lives*, ed. Việt Thanh Nguyễn, 129–136. New York: Abrams, 2018.

Millbank, Jenni. "From Discretion to Disbelief: Recent Trends in Refugee Determinations on the Basis of Sexual Orientation in Australia and the United Kingdom." *International Journal of Human Rights* 13, no. 2–3 (2009): 391–414. http://dx.doi.org/10.1080/13642980902758218.

Mishori, Ranit, Alisse Hannaford, Imran Mujawar, Hope Ferdowsian, and Sarah Kureshi. "'Their Stories Have Changed My Life': Clinicians' Reflections on Their Experience with and Their Motivation to Conduct Asylum Evaluations." *Journal of Immigrant and Minority Health* 18 (2016): 210–218. http://dx.doi.org/10.1007/s10903-014-0144-2.

Moore, Shannon A. "Radical Listening: Transdisciplinarity, Restorative Justice and Change." *World Futures: The Journal of New Paradigm Research* 27, no. 7–8 (2018): 471–489. http://dx.doi.org/10.1080/02604027.2018.1485436.

Mossad, Nadwa. "Annual Flow Report, Refugees and Asylees: 2018." U.S. Department of Homeland Security Office of Immigration Statistics, March 2019. https://www.dhs.gov/sites/default/files/publications/immigration-statistics/yearbook/2018/refugees_asylees_2018.pdf.

Narayan, Uma. "The Project of Feminist Epistemology: Perspectives from a Non-Western Feminist." In *Gender/Body/Knowledge: Feminist Reconstructions of Being and Knowing*, ed. Alison M. Jagger and Susan Bordo, 256–269. New Brunswick, N.J.: Rutgers University Press, 1989.

Narbutas, Nicholas. "The Ring of Truth: Demeanor and Due Process in U.S. Asylum Law." *Columbia Human Rights Law Review* 50, no. 1 (2018): 349–394.

Nayeri, Dina. *The Ungrateful Refugee: What Immigrants Never Tell You.* Edinburgh: Canongate, 2020.

Nelson, Katherine. "Self and Social Functions: Individual Autobiographical Memory and Collective Narrative." *Memory* 11, no. 2 (2003): 125–136. http://dx.doi.org/10.1080/741938203.

Nguyễn, Việt Thanh. Introduction to *The Displaced: Refugee Writers on Refugee Lives*, ed. Việt Thanh Nguyễn, 11–22. New York: Abrams, 2018.

O'Donnell, Angel-Luke. "Audience." *Early American Studies: An Interdisciplinary Journal* 16, no. 4 (2018): 591–598. http://dx.doi.org/10.1353/eam.2018.0022.

Ono, Kent A., and John M. Sloop. *Shifting Borders: Rhetoric, Immigration, and California's Proposition 187.* Philadelphia: Temple University Press, 2002.

Osborne, Sam. "*Kulini*: Framing Ethical Listening and Power-Sensitive Dialogue in Remote Aboriginal Education and Research." *Learning Communities* 22 (2017): 26–37.

"The Out Crowd." *This American Life.* November 15, 2019. https://www.thisamericanlife.org/688/the-out-crowd.

Pablo Cruz, Rosayra, and Julie Schwietert Collazo. *Book of Rosy: A Mother's Story of Separation at the Border.* New York: HarperCollins, 2020.

Palermo, Tia, Jennifer Bleck, and Amber Peterman. "Tip of the Iceberg: Reporting and Gender-Based Violence in Developing Countries." *American Journal of Epidemiology* 179, no. 5 (2014): 602–612. http://dx.doi.org/10.1093/aje/kwt295.

Phifer, Donica. "Donald Trump Calls Asylum Claims a 'Big Fat Con Job,' Says Mexico Should Stop Migrant Caravans from Traveling to US Border." *Newsweek*, March 29, 2019. https://www.newsweek.com/donald-trump-calls-asylum-claims-big-fat-con-job-says-mexico-should-stop-1379453.

Pombier, Nicki. "A Different Story: Narrative Allyship Across Ability." *Disability Alliances and Allies* 12 (2020): 225–257. http://dx.doi.org/10.1108/S1479-354720200000012014.

Pradilla, Alberto. *Caravana: Como el Exodo Centroamericano Salio de la Clandestinidad.* Mexico City: Penguin Random House Grupo Editorial, 2019.

Public Papers of the Presidents of the United States, Lyndon B. Johnson: Containing the Public Messages, Speeches, and Statements of the President, November 22, 1963 to January 20, 1969. Washington, D.C.: US Government Printing Office, 1965–1970.

Puumala, Eeva, Tarja Väyrynen, Anitta Kynsilehto, and Samu Pehkonen. "Events of the Body Politic: A Nancian Reading of Asylum-Seekers' Bodily Choreographies and Resistance." *Body & Society* 17, no. 4 (2011): 83–104. http://dx.doi.org/10.1177/1357034X11410453.

Puumala, Eeva, Riitta Ylikomi, and Hanna-leena Ristimäki. "Giving an Account of Persecution: The Dynamic Formation of Asylum Narratives." *Journal of Refugee Studies* 31, no. 2 (2018): 197–215. http://dx.doi.org/10.1093/jrs/fex024.

Ramiji-Nogales, Jaya, Andrew Schoenholtz, and Philip Schrag, eds. *Refugee Roulette: Disparities in Asylum Adjudication and Proposals for Reform.* New York: New York University Press, 2011.

Rasoulpour, Amir. "Writing Your Asylum Story." *RIF*, N.d. https://static1.squarespace.com/static/55e65ac9e4b028016a8e7b2b/t/5e276e58775bac40e4c6afbe/1579642462314/Asylum+Story_English.pdf.

Regan, Margaret. *Detained and Deported: Stories of Immigrant Families Under Fire.* Boston: Beacon, 2015.

Rahaag, Sean. "Judicial Review of Refugee Determinations: The Luck of the Draw?" *Queen's Law Journal* 38, no. 1 (2012): 1–58. http://dx.doi.org/10.2139/ssrn.2027517.

Risan, Patrick, Per-Einar Binder, and Rebecca Jane Milne. "Establishing and Maintaining Rapport in Investigative Interviews of Traumatized Victims:

A Qualitative Study." *Policing: A Journal of Policy and Practice* 12, no. 4 (2018): 372–387. http://dx.doi.org/10.1093/police/pax031.

Risan, Patrick, Rebecca Milne, and Per-Einar Binder. "Trauma Narratives: Recommendations for Investigative Interviewing." *Psychiatry, Psychology and Law* 4 (2020): 678–694. http://dx.doi.org/10.1080/13218719.2020 .1742237.

Rodino-Colocino, Michelle. "Participant Activism: Exploring a Methodology for Scholar-Activists Through Lessons Learned as a Precarious Labor Organizer." *Communication, Culture & Critique* 5 (2012): 541–562. http://dx .doi.org/10.1111/j.1753-9137.2012.01140.x.

Ruby, Charles L., and John C. Brigham, "Can Criteria-Based Content Analysis Distinguish Between True and False Statements of African-American Speakers?" *Law and Human Behavior* 22 (1998): 369–388. http://dx.doi .org/10.1023/A:1025766825429.

Samuelson, Kristin W. "Post-Traumatic Stress Disorder and Declarative Memory Functioning: A Review." *Dialogues in Clinical Neuroscience* 13, no. 3 (2011): 346–351. http://dx.doi.org/10.31887/DCNS.2011.13.2/ksamuelson.

Schock, Katrin, Rita Rosner, and Christine Knaevelsrud. "Impact of Asylum Interviews on the Mental Health of Traumatized Asylum Seekers." *European Journal of Psychotraumatology* 6 (2015): 1–9. http://dx.doi.org/10 .3402/ejpt.v6.26286.

Shuman, Amy, and Carol Bohmer. "Representing Trauma: Political Asylum Narrative." *Journal of American Folklore* 117, no. 466 (2004): 394–414.

Slack, Jeremy. *Deported to Death: How Drug Violence Is Changing Migration on the US–Mexico Border.* Oakland: University of California Press, 2019.

Smith-Khan, Laura. "Contesting Credibility in Australian Refugee Visa Decision Making and Public Discourse." Doctoral dissertation, Macquarie University, North Ryde, New South Wales, Australia, 2018. https://www .languageonthemove.com/wp-content/uploads/2019/02/Smith-Khan -2018-Contesting-Credibility-Final-PhD-Thesis.pdf.

——. "Migration Practitioners' Roles in Communicating Credible Refugee Claims," *Alternative Law Journal* 45, no. 2 (2020): 119–124. http://dx.doi .org/10.1177/1037969X19884205.

——. "Telling Stories: Credibility and the Representation of Social Actors in Australian Asylum Appeals." *Discourse & Society* 28, no. 5 (2017): 512–534. http://dx.doi.org/10.1177/0957926517710989.

Southwick, Steven M., C. Andrew Morgan, Andreas L. Nicolaou, and Dennis S. Charney. "Consistency of Memory for Combat-Related Traumatic Events in Veterans of Operation Desert Storm." *American Journal of Psychiatry* 154, no. 2 (1997): 173–177.

Spotti, Massimiliano. "'It's all about naming things right': The Paradox of Web Truths in the Belgian Asylum-Seeking Procedure." In *Asylum Determination in Europe: Ethnographic Perspectives*, ed. N. Gill and A. Good, 69–90. Cham, Switz.: Palgrave MacMillan, 2018. http://dx.doi.org/10.1007/978-3-319-94749-5.

Stanley, Liz, and Sue Wise. *Breaking Out: Feminist Consciousness and Feminist Research*. London: Routledge & Kegan Paul, 1983.

Stewart, Liam. "Storytelling and the Lives of Asylum Seekers." *West Coast Line* 44, no. 4 (2011): 16–22.

Stillman, Sarah. "When Deportation Is a Death Sentence." *New Yorker*, January 8, 2018. https://www.newyorker.com/magazine/2018/01/15/when-deportation-is-a-death-sentence.

Strange, Deryn, and Melanie K. T. Takarangi. "Memory Distortion for Traumatic Events: The Role of Mental Imagery." *Frontiers in Psychiatry* 6, no. 27 (2015). http://dx.doi.org/10.3389/fpsyt.2015.00027.

Stromwall, Leif A. "To Act Truthfully: Nonverbal Behaviour and Strategies During a Police Interrogation." *Psychology, Crime & Law* 12, no. 2 (2006): 207–219. http://dx.doi.org/10.1080/10683160512331331328.

Sullivan, Shannon. "White Ignorance and Colonial Oppression: Or, Why I Know So Little About Puerto Rico." In *Race and Epistemologies of Ignorance*, ed. Shannon Sullivan and Nancy Tuana. Albany: State University of New York Press, 2007.

Ting-Toomey, Stella, and Leeva C. Chung. *Understanding Intercultural Communication*. New York: Oxford University Press, 2012.

Transactional Records Access Clearinghouse. "Asylum Decisions Vary Widely Across Judges and Courts—Latest Results." *TRAC Immigration*, January 13, 2020. https://trac.syr.edu/immigration/reports/590/.

——. "Asylum Representation Rates Have Fallen amid Rising Denial Rates," *TRAC Immigration*, November 28, 2017. https://trac.syr.edu/immigration/reports/491/.

——. "Contrasting Experiences: MPP vs. non-MPP Immigration Court Cases." *TRAC Immigration*. December 19, 2019. https://trac.syr.edu/immigration/reports/587/.

——. "Record Number of Asylum Cases in FY 2019." *TRAC Immigration*. January 8, 2020. https://trac.syr.edu/immigration/reports/588/.

Truong, Khiet P., Gerben J. Westerhof, Sanne M. A. Lamers, and Franciska de Jong. "Towards Modeling Expressed Emotions in Oral History Interviews: Using Verbal and Nonverbal Signals to Track Personal Narratives." *Literary and Linguistic Computing* 29, no. 4 (2014): 621–636. https://doi.org/10.1093/llc/fqu041.

Tshuma, Novuyo Rosa. "New Lands, New Selves." In *The Displaced: Refugee Writers on Refugee Lives*, ed. Việt Thanh Nguyễn, 159–174. New York: Abrams, 2018.

Turner, Stuart. "Torture, Refuge, and Trust." In *Mistrusting Refugees*, ed. E. Valentine Daniel and John Chr. Knudsen, 56–73. Berkeley: University of California Press, 1995.

Tyler, Jasmine L. "Human Rights Watch Urges Members of Congress to Reject the White House's Request For Increased Immigration Funding." *Human Rights Watch*, May 10, 2019. https://www.hrw.org/news/2019/05/10/human-rights-watch-urges-members-congress-reject-white-houses-request-increased.

Tyson, Judy A., and Shavaun M. Wall. "Effect of Inconsistency Between Counselor Verbal and Nonverbal Behavior on Perceptions of Counselor Attributes." *Journal of Counseling Psychology* 30, no. 3 (1983): 433–437.

Undurraga, Rosario. "Interviewing Women in Latin America: Some Reflections on Feminist Research Practice." *Equality, Diversity and Inclusion: An International Journal* 31 (2012): 418–434. http://dx.doi.org/10.1108/02610151211235442.

United Nations High Commissioner for Human Rights. "Committee on the Elimination of Racial Discrimination Examines Report of Norway." December 6, 2018. https://www.ohchr.org/EN/NewsEvents/Pages/DisplayNews.aspx?NewsID=23986&LangID=E.

——. "Global Trends: Forced Displacement in 2017." June 25, 2018. https://www.unhcr.org/globaltrends2017/.

——. "Global Trends: Forced Displacement in 2019." June 18, 2020. https://www.unhcr.org/globaltrends2019/.

——. "The Principle of *Non-Refoulement* Under International Human Rights Law." N.d. https://www.ohchr.org/Documents/Issues/Migration/GlobalCompactMigration/ThePrincipleNon-RefoulementUnderInternationalHumanRightsLaw.pdf.

U.S. Citizenship and Immigration Services. "I-589, Application for Asylum and for Withholding of Removal, 09/10/19 Edition." September 10, 2019. https://www.uscis.gov/i-589.

——. "USCIS to Take Action to Address Asylum Backlog," January 31, 2018, https://www.uscis.gov/archive/uscis-to-take-action-to-address-asylum-backlog.

U.S. Customs and Border Protection. "CBP Commissioner Discusses Dangers of Crossing U.S. Border, Awareness Campaign." July 2, 2014. https://www.cbp.gov/newsroom/national-media-release/cbp-commissioner-discusses-dangers-crossing-us-border-awareness.

———. "Southwest Border Unaccompanied Alien Children." June 4, 2014. https://web.archive.org/web/20140604084428/http://www.cbp.gov/news room/stats/southwest-border-unaccompanied-children.

———. "U.S. Border Patrol Nationwide Apprehensions by Citizenship and Sector FY 2007–FY 2018." March 2019. https://www.cbp.gov/sites/default /files/assets/documents/2019-Mar/BP%20Apps%20by%20Sector%20 and%20Citizenship%20FY07-FY18.pdf.

U.S. Department of Homeland Security. "Table 16. Individuals Granted Asylum Affirmatively Or Defensively: Fiscal Years 1990 to 2016." January 8, 2018. https://www.dhs.gov/immigration-statistics/yearbook/2016/table16.

———. "Table 40. Aliens Returned by Region and Country of Nationality: Fiscal Years 2017 to 2019." September 17, 2020. https://www.dhs.gov/immigra tion-statistics/yearbook/2019/table40.

U.S. Department of Justice. "Asylum Decision Rates by Nationality." Workload and Adjudication Statistics. 2020. https://www.justice.gov/eoir/page /file/1107366/download.

U.S. Department of State. "Migration and Refugees: Agreement Between the United States and Guatemala." Signed at Washington, July 26, 2019, entered into force November 15, 2019. Treaties and Other International Acts series, 19-1115. https://www.state.gov/wp-content/uploads/2020/01 /19-1115-Migration-and-Refugees-Guatemala-ACA.pdf.

———. "2020 Country Reports on Human Rights Practices." Bureau of Democracy, Human Rights, and Labor, 2021, https://www.state.gov/reports /2020-country-reports-on-human-rights-practices/.

U.S. Embassy Havana. "Decreasing B2 Visa Validity for Cuban Nationals." *U.S. Embassy in Cuba*, March 15, 2019. https://cu.usembassy.gov/decr easing-b2-visa-validity-for-cuban-nationals/.

U.S. Government Accountability Office. "Immigration Courts: Actions Needed to Reduce Case Backlog and Address Long-Standing Management and Operational Challenges." June 2017. https://www.gao.gov/assets/690 /685022.pdf.

Wang, Qi. "Culture Effects on Adults' Earliest Childhood Recollection and Self-Description: Implications for the Relation Between Memory and the Self." *Journal of Personality and Social Psychology* 81, no. 2 (2001): 220–233. http://dx.doi.org/10.1037/0022-3514.81.2.220.

———. "Remembering the Self in Cultural Contexts: A Cultural Dynamic Theory of Autobiographical Memory." *Memory Studies* 9, no. 3 (2016): 295–304. http://dx.doi.org/10.1177/1750698016645238.

Watson, Julie, and Matthew Lee. "Trump Plans to Slash Refugee Admissions to US to Record Low." *U.S. News & World Report*, October 1, 2020.

https://www.usnews.com/news/us/articles/2020-09-30/trump-set-to-miss-required-deadline-for-2021-refugee-quota.

Weathers, Monica D., Elaine M. Frank, and Leigh Ann Spell. "Differences in the Communication of Affect: Members of the Same Race Versus Members of a Different Race." *Journal of Black Psychology* 28, no. 1 (2002): 66–77. http://dx.doi.org/10.1177/0095798402028001005.

Weiss, Jeff. "INS Guidelines for Children's Asylum Claims." *American Immigration Lawyers Association*, December 10, 1998. https://www.aila.org/infonet/ins-guidelines-for-childrens-asylum-claims.

Wernesjö, Ulrika. "Across the Threshold: Negotiations of Deservingness Among Unaccompanied Young Refugees in Sweden." *Journal of Ethnic and Migration Studies* 46, no. 2 (2020): 389–404. http://dx.doi.org/10.1080/1369183X.2019.1584701.

Wheeler, William. *State of War: MS-13 and El Salvador's World of Violence.* New York: Columbia Global Reports, 2020.

Whelan, Clea Wright, Graham F. Wagstaff, and Jacqueline M. Wheatcroft. "High-Stakes Lies: Verbal and Nonverbal Cues to Deception in Public Appeals for Help with Missing or Murdered Relatives." *Psychiatry, Psychology, and Law* 21, no. 4 (2014): 523–537. http://dx.doi.org/10.1080/13218719.2013.839931.

Wolf, Sonia. *La migración forzada desde el Triángulo Norte de Centroamérica: Impulsores y experiencias.* Ciudad de México: Centro de Investigación y Docencia Económicas. 2020. http://www.politicadedrogas.org/PPD/documentos/20201028_104418_informe_analiticoespcorregidomerged.pdf.

Wood, Julia T. "The Normalization of Violence in Heterosexual Romantic Relationships: Women's Narratives of Love and Violence." *Journal of Social and Personal Relationships* 18, no. 2 (2001): 239–261. http://dx.doi.org/10.1177/0265407501182005.

Woolley, Agnes. "Narrating the 'Asylum Story:' Between Literary and Legal Storytelling." *International Journal of Postcolonial Studies* 19, no. 3 (2016): 376–394. http://dx.doi.org/10.1080/1369801X.2016.1231585.

Wyshak, Grace. "The Relation Between Change in Reports of Traumatic Events and Symptoms of Psychiatric Distress." *General Hospital Psychiatry* 16, no. 4 (1994): 290–297. http://dx.doi.org/10.1016/0163-8343(94)90009-4.

Zazueta-Castro, Lorenzo. "VIDEO: CBP Head Touts Campaign to Deter Immigrants from Illegally Crossing into US." *Monitor*, August 26, 2015.

Index

GPSR Authorized Representative: Easy Access System Europe, Mustamäe tee 50, 10621 Tallinn, Estonia, gpsr.requests@easproject.com